ADVANCED DESIGN TECHNIQUES IN
ADOBE® PHOTOSHOP® CS2
REVEALED
DELUXE EDUCATION EDITION

Chapter 1
Page 1–2: Image 100/Getty Images
Page 1–2: Image 100/Getty Images
Page 1–14: top left, Comstock Images/Getty Images
Page 1–18: Comstock Images/Getty Images
Page 1–30: Comstock Images/Getty Images
Page 1–30: Digital Vision/Getty Images
Page 1–33: Digital Vision/Getty Images
Page 1–34: Photodisc Red/Getty Images

Chapter 3
Page 3–2: Getty Images
Page 3–3: Digital Vision/Getty Images
Page 3–31: Stockdisc/Getty Images
Page 3–48: Photodisc/Getty Images

Chapter 4
Page 4–2: Rubberball/Getty Images

Chapter 5
Page 5–1: Burke/Triolo/Getty Images
Page 5–1: Chip Simons/Taxi/Getty Images
Page 5–1: Erik Von Weber/Getty Images

Page 5–1: Erik Von Weber/Stone/Getty Images
Page 5–1: Pete Turner/Imagebank/Getty Images
Page 5–1: Photodisc/Getty Images
Page 5–1: Willie Maldonado/Stone/Getty Images
Page 5–15: Photodisc/Getty Images

Chapter 6
Page 6–2: Ken Weingart/Getty Images
Page 6–40: Steve McAlister/Getty Images
Page 6–67: Barbara Mauer/Getty Images

Chapter 7
Page 7–60: Comstock/Getty Images

Chapter 8
Page 8–2: BaMonica Lau/Getty Images
Page 8–14: Barbara Maurer/Getty Images
Page 8–46: Stockbyte/Getty Images

Chapter 9
Page 9–2: Ken Weingart/Getty Images
Page 9–8: Rubberball Productions/Getty Images

Chapter 10
Page 10–2: Eryan McVay/Getty Images
Page 10–2: Eddie Hironaka/Getty Images
Page 10–2: Erin Patrice O'Brien/Getty Images
Page 10–2: I Vanderharst/Getty Images
Page 10–25: Michael Sharkey/Getty Images
Page 10–28: Neil Emmerson/Getty Images
Page 10–42: Robert Warren/Getty Images
Page 10–42: Shannon Fagan/Getty Images

ADVANCED DESIGN TECHNIQUES IN
ADOBE® PHOTOSHOP® CS2
REVEALED
DELUXE EDUCATION EDITION

Chris Botello

THOMSON

COURSE TECHNOLOGY

Advanced Design Techniques in Adobe Photoshop CS2—Revealed, Deluxe Education Edition

Chris Botello

Managing Editor:
Marjorie Hunt

Product Manager:
Jane Hosie-Bounar

Associate Product Manager:
Shana Rosenthal

Editorial Assistant:
Janine Tangney

Production Editor:
Catherine G. DiMassa

Developmental Editor:
Ann Fisher

Marketing Manager:
Joy Stark

Composition House:
GEX Publishing Services

QA Manuscript Reviewers:
Danielle Shaw, Ashlee Welz,
Jeff Schwartz, Susan Whelan

Text Designer:
Ann Small

Cover Design:
Deborah Van Rooyen,
Steve Deschene

Copyeditor:
Mark Goodin

Proofreader:
Susan Forsyth

Indexer:
Alexandra Nickerson

Revealed Series Vision

The Revealed Series is your guide to today's hottest multimedia applications. These comprehensive books teach the skills behind the application, showing you how to apply smart design principles to multimedia products such as dynamic graphics, animation, Web sites, software authoring tools, and digital video.

A team of design professionals including multimedia instructors, students, authors, and editors worked together to create this series. We recognized the unique learning environment of the multimedia classroom and created a series that:

- Gives you comprehensive step-by-step instructions
- Offers in-depth explanation of the "Why" behind a skill
- Includes creative projects for additional practice
- Explains concepts clearly using full-color visuals

It was our goal to create a book that speaks directly to the multimedia and design community—one of the most rapidly growing computer fields today. We think we've done just that, with a sophisticated and instructive book design.

—The Revealed Series

Author's Vision

Many thanks go out to all the great people who contributed to the making of this book. First and foremost, as always, thank you to Ann Fisher, my longtime friend and editor, not only for her skill and dedication, but also for her excitement and enthusiasm for the content. Thank you to Nicole Pinard and Marjorie Hunt for their vision, for being open to the concept of an advanced Photoshop book, and for rocking and rolling with my suggestions for a new format. Thank you to Jane Hosie-Bounar for keeping us on course, and to Deborah Van Rooyen and Steve Deschene for their guidance in adapting the art for the cover, and to Christina Micek for procuring permissions. Thank you to Danielle Shaw, Ashlee Welz, Jeff Schwartz, and Susan Whelan for all the testing and quality control, and to Cathie DiMassa for all her help with production. Finally, thank you to the reviewers for their time, their insights, and their feedback, which was so important to me as I developed the exercises. These reviewers include Betty Vickrey at Estrella Mountain Community College; Rebecca Gallagher at Touro College; Lynn Bowen at Valdosta Technical College; and Luis Hernandez at Mesa Community College.

—Chris Botello

SERIES & AUTHOR VISION

Introduction to Advanced Design Techniques in Adobe Photoshop CS2

Welcome to *Advanced Design Techniques in Adobe Photoshop CS2—Revealed, Deluxe Education Edition.* This book offers creative projects, concise instructions, and extensive coverage of advanced design and Photoshop skills, helping you to create polished, professional-looking graphics. Use this book both in the classroom and as your own reference guide.

This book is organized into ten chapters. In these chapters, you will explore many aspects of advanced design using Photoshop CS2. In fact, this book is sure to take your design skills to the next level with its sophisticated projects. You'll work with curves, levels, blending modes, special effects, and painting and drawing tools. You'll not only be challenged as a Photoshop CS2 user, but as a designer working with real-world projects.

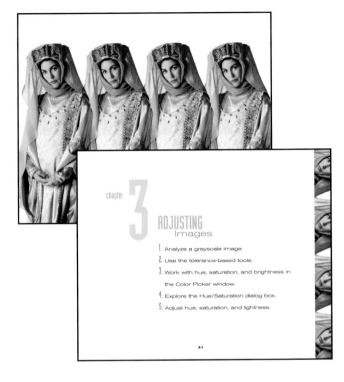

chapter 3

ADJUSTING
Images

1. Analyze a grayscale image.

2. Use the tolerance-based tools.

3. Work with hue, saturation, and brightness in the Color Picker window.

4. Explore the Hue/Saturation dialog box.

5. Adjust hue, saturation, and lightness.

3-1

LESSON 6

MERGE TWO
Images

What You'll Do

Merging two images to create a third image is perhaps the most delicate surgery you can do in Photoshop, especially when it involves somebody's face. It's one thing to paste a tree into a field; it's a whole different thing to take the eyes from one photo and paste them onto the face in another photo—with nobody catching on. You might be surprised at how often it's done. I do a lot of work with movie posters, and in most cases, the actor's head and the actor's body are from two different original photos. This happens because, when choosing from originals, the face in one photo might be perfect for the concept, but the body might be in the wrong position. But in another photo, the body is in a great position, but the actor won't approve the face shot. So a merge is necessary—put this head on that body.

Sometimes, as you'll see in this lesson, it's not even the actor's body. This happens all the time at the agency where I work. We have an in-house photo studio and a professional photographer on staff. When we come up with a concept, we get the studio to send over costumes, then we hire models to pose in the position that we need to work with. Sometimes,

ADVANCED PHOTOSHOP 5-48

Designing with Multiple Images Chapter 5

What You'll Do

A What You'll Do figure begins every lesson. This figure gives you an at-a-glance look at what you'll do in the chapter, thereby providing context and a specific goal as you work.

Lesson Narrative

In this book, you jump right into each project with a detailed explanation of its scope and challenges. Also included in the text are tips and Design Notes to help you work more efficiently and creatively, or to teach you a bit about the history or design philosophy behind the skill you are using.

Step-by-Step Instructions

This book provides concise steps in which you create an image in Photoshop CS2. Each set of steps guides you through a lesson where you will create, modify, or enhance the image. The step-by-step instructions refer to large, colorful figures that provide a visual representation of the project as it is being built. The Data Files for the steps are on the CDs included in the book.

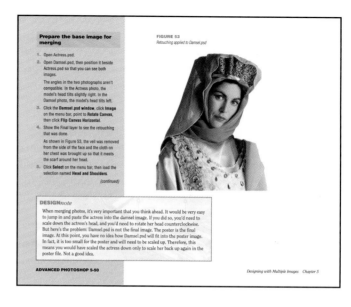

Projects

This book contains end-of-chapter materials for additional practice and reinforcement. The Project Builders require you to apply the skills you've learned in the chapter and take them in a new direction. When you have finished the chapters in this book, you should have an impressive portfolio of the advanced design work you have created using Adobe Photoshop CS2.

What Instructor Resources Are Available with This Book?

The Instructor Resources CD-ROM is Course Technology's way of putting the resources and information needed to teach and learn effectively into your hands. All the resources are available for both Macintosh and Windows operating systems, and many of the resources can be downloaded from www.course.com.

Instructor's Manual

Available as an electronic file, the Instructor's Manual is quality-assurance tested and includes chapter overviews and detailed lecture topics for each chapter, with teaching tips. The Instructor's Manual is available on the Instructor Resources CD-ROM, or you can download it from www.course.com.

Syllabus

Prepare and customize your course easily using this sample course outline (available on the Instructor Resources CD-ROM).

PowerPoint Presentations

Each chapter has a corresponding PowerPoint presentation that you can use in lectures, distribute to your students, or customize to suit your course.

Figure Files

Figure Files contain all the figures from the book in bitmap format. Use the figure files to create transparency masters or use them in a PowerPoint presentation.

Data Files for Students

To complete most of the chapters in this book, your students will need Data Files. The Data Files are available on the CDs included in this book. Instruct students to use the Data Files List at the end of this book. This list gives instructions on organizing files.

Solutions to Exercises

Solution Files are Data Files completed with comprehensive sample answers. Use these files to evaluate your students' work. Or distribute them electronically so students can verify their work. Sample solutions to all lessons and end-of-chapter material are provided.

Test Bank and Test Engine

ExamView is a powerful testing software package that allows instructors to create and administer printed, computer (LAN-based), and Internet exams. ExamView includes hundreds of questions that correspond to the topics covered in this text, enabling students to generate detailed study guides that include page references for further review. The computer-based and Internet testing components allow students to take exams at their computers, and also save the instructor time by grading each exam automatically.

x

CHAPTER 3   ADJUSTING IMAGES

CHAPTER 4   TACKLING LEVELS AND CURVES

CHAPTER 7   WORKING WITH TYPE, SHAPE LAYERS, AND FILTERS

CHAPTER 8   INVESTIGATING PRODUCTION TRICKS AND TECHNIQUES

Intended Audience

This book is designed for the experienced Photoshop user who wants to learn advanced design techniques using Photoshop CS2. The book presents real world assignments and takes you through the design decisions you might be faced with as you tackle an assignment. By the end of the book, you'll not only understand the how behind certain design decisions, but the why.

Approach

The book allows you to work at your own pace through step-by-step tutorials. A concept is presented and the process is explained, followed by the actual steps. To learn the most from the book, you should adopt the following habits:

- Make sure you understand the design technique and the Photoshop skill being taught in each step before you move on to the next step.

- After finishing a set of steps, ask yourself if you could do it on your own, without referring to the steps. If the answer is no, review the steps.

Icons, Buttons, and Pointers

Symbols for icons, buttons, and pointers are shown in the step each time they are used.

Windows and Macintosh

Photoshop CS2 works virtually the same on Windows and Macintosh operating systems. In those cases where there is a significant difference, the abbreviations (Win) and (Mac) are used.

The nature of working with graphics requires detailed work. In Photoshop, this means that you will need to magnify areas of an image.

Because monitor sizes and resolution preferences vary, be sure to set the magnification to the setting that allows you to work comfortably. The figures shown in this book are displayed at a monitor resolution of 1024×768.

Data Files

To complete the lessons in this book, you need to obtain the Data Files provided on the CDs included in this book. You can store these files on a hard drive, a network server, or a USB storage device. The instructions in the lessons will refer to "the drive and folder where your Data Files are stored" when referring to the Data Files for the book.

land of aloha

chapter

1

WORKING WITH
Layers

1. Lock transparent pixels.
2. Apply a Hue/Saturation adjustment layer.
3. Work with a layer mask.
4. Use one layer to mask another layer.
5. Mask a layer with the Paste Into command.
6. Scale an image.
7. Use the Free Transform command.
8. Use a single layer to mask multiple layers.
9. Paint in a layer mask.
10. Add a stroke layer style.
11. Add a drop shadow layer style.
12. Apply an adjustment layer to multiple layers.
13. Edit layer styles.
14. Copy layer styles between layers.

LOCK TRANSPARENT
Pixels

What You'll Do

Photoshop is an application that you use to create art, and all art ultimately comes from the heart. So it's fair to say that Photoshop is an application that you use with your heart. But make no mistake: Photoshop is also an application that you use with your head. That's because Photoshop is a smart, well-designed, and powerful graphic arts application, and over the years, with each successive version, it's become a very intricate and complex application as well.

When you're designing in Photoshop, you need to keep your wits about you; you have to keep that brain active, even if you feel that you know the application through and through. There's always something new that you can learn, so you must take the time to notice.

Notice what, you ask? Everything. Not all at once, but along the way. Notice how the application works. Notice how its interface

has been designed. The interface is the language that the application uses to communicate with you, and only by staying alert will you hear what it's saying to you.

So yes, of course, work with your heart—wholeheartedly, as they say. But always keep awake and alert to the Photoshop interface and everything it's telling you about itself.

FIGURE 1
Land of Aloha layer

Lock transparent pixels

1. Open AP 1-1.psd, click **File** on the menu bar, then click **Save As**.

2. Type **HAWAII** in the File name text box (Win) or the Save As text box (Mac), click the **Format list arrow**, click **Photoshop (*.PSD; *.PDD)** (Win) or **Photoshop** (Mac), then click **Save**.

   TIP The Photoshop Format Options dialog box may open, asking if you want to maximize compatibility. You can program Photoshop to always maximize compatibility in the File Handling preferences dialog box. Click Edit (Win) or Photoshop (Mac) on the menu bar, point to Preferences, click File Handling, click the Maximize PSD and PSB File Compatibility list arrow, click Always, then click OK.

3. Click the **Land of Aloha layer** in the Layers palette.

   TIP Clicking a layer is called **targeting** a layer.

4. Press and hold **[Alt]** (Win) or **[option]** (Mac), click the **Indicates layer visibility button** 👁 beside the targeted layer, then compare your screen to Figure 1.

   Pressing [Alt] (Win) or [option] (Mac) while clicking the targeted layer hides all other layers. This is a quick method for viewing only that which is on a single layer. Note that the text is the only artwork on this layer. All of the other pixels on this layer are transparent, represented by the gray and white checkerboard pattern.

   (continued)

DESIGN*note*

The Photoshop (*.PSD) file format is the "native" format for Photoshop—in other words, the document is simply a Photoshop document. It's not a Tiff or an EPS or a PICT or any of the common formats. All Adobe products, such as InDesign, GoLive or Illustrator, can interface with Photoshop documents.

5. Press **[D]** to revert to default foreground and background colors.

6. Press **[X]** to switch foreground and background colors.

7. Press and hold **[Alt]** (Win) or **[option]** (Mac), then press **[Delete]** (Win) or **[delete]** (Mac).

   Pressing [Alt][Delete] (Win) or [option][delete] (Mac) fills the entire layer with the foreground color—white in this case. Applying fills in this manner is much faster than using the Fill command on the Edit menu.

   TIP If you use the Fill command on the Edit menu to fill an object, you'll be able to choose other fill settings, including blending modes and transparency, in the Fill dialog box.

8. Click **Edit** on the menu bar, then click **Undo Fill Layer**.

9. Click the **Lock transparent pixels button**, as shown in Figure 2.

   When the Lock transparent pixels button is activated for a targeted layer, the transparent pixels on the layer—the gray and white checkerboard—cannot be modified.

   (continued)

FIGURE 2
Layers palette

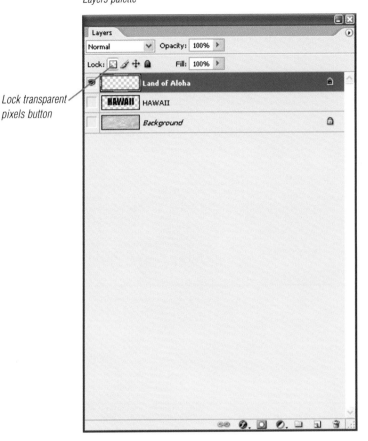

Lock transparent pixels button

DESIGN*note*

This is an opportunity to take the time to investigate how the application and the interface have been designed. At Adobe, you can be sure that much thought went into the decision to use that gray and white checkerboard to represent transparent pixels. Stay alert to these choices—that awareness will help you to build a strong, intuitive relationship with the application.

Only the black pixels are filled with the foreground color. The transparent pixels are unaffected by the white fill.

11.Press and hold **[Alt]** (Win) **[option]** (Mac), then click the **Indicates layer visibility button**  on the Land of Aloha layer.

The two hidden layers become visible.

12.Compare your screen to Figure 3, then save your work.

FIGURE 3

Filling only the black pixels with white on the Land of Aloha layer

DESIGN*note*

Make a note of the lock icon on the right side of the targeted layer. If you position your cursor over it, a tool tip will appear to explain its function—Indicates layer is partially locked. If you didn't take the time to do this—if you didn't know the name of that icon—you might reasonably think the whole layer is locked. It's not—just the transparent pixels are locked. Thus the layer is partially locked.

APPLY A HUE/SATURATION
Adjustment Layer

What You'll Do

If you're relatively new to Photoshop, you might not fully appreciate how revolutionary the introduction of adjustment layers was to the application.

Before adjustment layers, when you made an adjustment—like a color correction with curves, levels, or hue saturation, for example—once you made it, you couldn't go back and modify it. You were stuck with it. There were ways to work around the issue, but that's all they were—work-arounds.

Adjustment layers offer you the ability to make an adjustment and then go back at any time to the same dialog box and modify the adjustment. From the designer's perspective, it's the difference between being trapped with your choices and being free to experiment.

And that's not all—adjustment layers are also a record of the adjustments you've made. For example, if you're working on a new layer and want to know what color correction you made to a previous layer, all you need to do is check the adjustment layer. In the old days, you used an old-fashioned method to keep track of this information—a pencil and paper!

FIGURE 4
New Layer dialog box

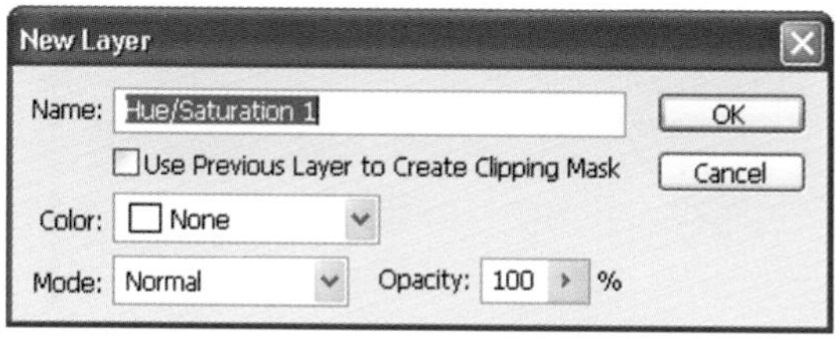

New Layer

Name: Hue/Saturation 1   OK

☐ Use Previous Layer to Create Clipping Mask   Cancel

Color: ☐ None ▾

Mode: Normal ▾   Opacity: 100 ▸ %

FIGURE 5
Modifying the hue of the water image

Apply a Hue/Saturation Adjustment Layer

1. Target the **Background layer**.
2. Drag the **Background layer** to the Create a new layer button 🔲 on the Layers palette, then release.
3. Rename the Background copy layer **Deep Blue Sea**.
4. Click **Layer** on the menu bar, point to **New Adjustment Layer**, then click **Hue/Saturation**.

   The New Layer dialog box opens, as shown in Figure 4.
5. Type **Deep Blue Sea** in the Name text box.
6. Click the **Use Previous Layer to Create Clipping Mask check box** to add a check mark.
7. Click **OK**.

   The Hue/Saturation dialog box opens.
8. Drag the **Hue slider** all the way to the left, then click **OK** so that your canvas resembles Figure 5.

(continued)

Note that the Layer thumbnail on the Deep Blue Sea layer hasn't changed—it's still blue even though the image on the canvas is red. That's because it is the adjustment layer that is creating the red effect—the Deep Blue Sea layer itself has not been modified.

9. Target the **Background layer** so that you can see the adjustment layer clearly.

As shown in Figure 6, the half-black/half-white circle is the icon for an adjustment layer. The bent arrow is the icon for Use Previous Layer to Create Clipping Mask—make a note of that.

> **TIP** By default, adjustment layers are created with a layer mask, which is transparent by default.

10. Double-click the **adjustment layer icon** on the Deep Blue Sea adjustment layer.

The Hue/Saturation dialog box opens showing the last settings chosen.

(continued)

FIGURE 6
Identifying an adjustment layer

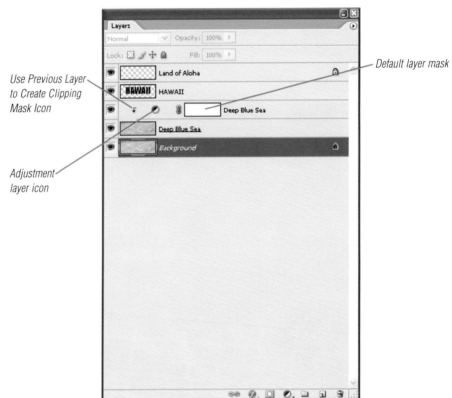

Use Previous Layer to Create Clipping Mask Icon

Adjustment layer icon

Default layer mask

DESIGN*note*

This terminology—Use Previous Layer to Create Clipping Mask—is new to Photoshop CS2. It's a new name, but not a new function. It used to be called Group with Previous Layer. Clicking Use Previous Layer to Create Clipping Mask means that the adjustments made in this adjustment layer will affect only the "previous" layer—the layer that was targeted when you created the adjustment layer. If this choice is not activated, the adjustment layer will affect *all* the layers below it in the Layers palette.

11. Drag the **Hue slider** to the right so that the Hue text box value is +155.
12. Drag the **Saturation slider** to the right so that the Saturation text box value is +28.
13. Click **OK**, then compare your screen to Figure 7.
14. Save your work.

FIGURE 7

Viewing a different hue adjustment

WORK WITH A
Layer Mask

What You'll Do

Think about this for a moment: In the early versions of Photoshop, layers didn't exist. That's right—no layers. You had one flat canvas to work with, and if you layered one image over another, when you deselected, the two images became one.

The introduction of layers opened up a whole new realm of possibilities of what you could create with Photoshop. And with layers came layer masks. Layer masks are essential to working with layers; they allow you to choose which areas of the layer are visible and which areas are not visible.

The layer mask interface is very straightforward: Paint black over the areas that you do not want to show.

Another great thing about layer masks is that they are always available to be modified. In other words, you can paint white over the areas that you painted black, and those areas will show again.

But layer masks are not just black and white. Gray is neither white nor black; it's somewhere in between. Areas that you paint with gray in a layer mask are neither visible nor invisible—they're somewhere in between. Therein lies the power of gray in conjunction with layer masks: the ability to create semi-transparency for images on layers.

FIGURE 8

Layer mask thumbnail on the Deep Blue Sea adjustment layer

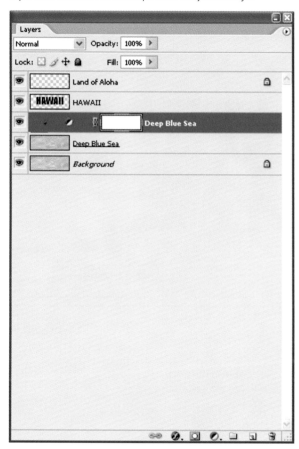

1. Click the **Layers palette list arrow**, click **Palette Options**, click the **second largest thumbnail icon** in the Thumbnail Size section, then click **OK**.

2. Click the **Layer mask thumbnail** on the Deep Blue Sea adjustment layer to activate the layer mask, then compare your Layers palette to Figure 8.

3. Press **[D]**, press **[X]**, then fill the layer mask with the black foreground color.

   The effect of the adjustment layer—the red water—disappears on the canvas. Black areas of a layer mask are completely opaque—wherever black appears in the layer mask, the adjustment layer is no longer visible.

4. Press **[X]**, then fill the layer mask with the white foreground color.

   The adjustment layer effect is restored. White areas of a layer mask are completely transparent—wherever white appears in the layer mask, the adjustment layer is visible.

5. Click the **Gradient Tool** , then click the **Linear Gradient button** on the Options bar at the top of the window, if necessary.

(continued)

6. Position your cursor at the top center of the image, click and drag straight down, then release at the bottom of the image.

   You did not apply the gradient to the artwork on the layer—you applied the gradient to the adjustment layer's layer mask, which was activated. A gradient now appears in the layer mask and the adjustment layer effect fades down the artwork as shown in Figure 9.

   (continued)

FIGURE 9

Using a layer mask to gradate the effect of an adjustment layer

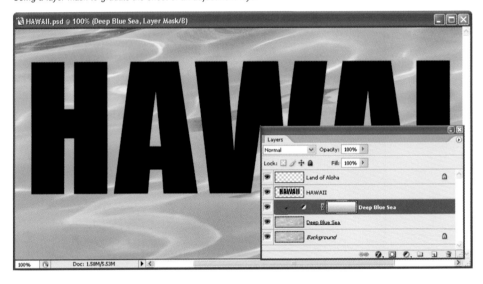

DESIGN*note*

Take some time to examine this effect. Where the layer mask is white, the adjustment layer effect is visible. Where the mask is black, the effect is not visible. And because the layer mask gradates from white to black, the adjustment layer effect gradates too—from visible to not visible.

7. Double-click the **adjustment layer icon** in the Deep Blue Sea adjustment layer. Drag the **Hue slider** so that its setting reads +24.

8. Click **OK**, then compare your canvas to Figure 10.

   This is the real power of adjustment layers: you can always go back and tweak the adjustment.

9. Save your work.

FIGURE 10
Modifying an adjustment layer

Lesson 3   Work with a Layer Mask

USE ONE LAYER TO
Mask Another Layer

What You'll Do

Now, of course, they can be done in Photoshop. Actually, they can be done many different ways in Photoshop, and these next few lessons are going to examine those methods closely.

Masking is a great effect for you to have in your designer's bag of tricks. Working on a project that incorporates multiple masking techniques and complex interrelationships between artwork on layers is one of the best ways to investigate the many powerful options available in the Layers palette.

Masking effects have enjoyed a long and illustrious career in the graphic arts. Long before the advent of computer graphics, masking had staked its territory as a popular and beloved design effect: think of those 50's postcards that had great beach photos inside the word FLORIDA! Come to think of it, if you can get your hands on some of those old postcards, please do. They are a great example of classic effects that were done in the days before digital.

FIGURE 11

Preparing to clip the 2 Women layer

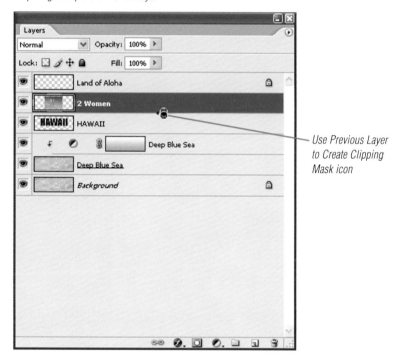

Use Previous Layer
to Create Clipping
Mask icon

1. Open Two Women.psd from your Data Files folder, select all, copy, then close the file.

   TIP Try doing Step 1 using four keyboard commands: [Ctrl][O], [Ctrl][A], [Ctrl][C], [Ctrl][W] (Win) or ⌘[O], ⌘[A], ⌘[C], ⌘[W] (Mac).

2. Zoom in or out so that you are viewing the canvas at 50%, if necessary.

   You should be able to see the entire canvas.

3. Target the **HAWAII layer**.

4. Click **Edit** on the menu bar, then click **Paste**.

   The Two Women.psd image is pasted on its own layer immediately above the targeted layer. When you paste in Photoshop, the contents are pasted on their own layer, always above the targeted layer.

5. Name the new layer **2 Women**.

6. Press and hold **[Alt]** (Win) or **[option]** (Mac), then position your cursor between the 2 Women and HAWAII layers in the Layers palette so that you see the pointer shown in Figure 11.

(continued)

DESIGN*note*

When you set the view percentage for a document so that you can see the entire canvas, anything you paste into the document will be centered on the canvas. Though this doesn't sound like such a big deal, knowing this can come in very handy, especially when you are aligning pasted images or trying to center images on the canvas.

7. Click the line between the two layers, then compare your work to Figure 12.

The 2 Women image is masked—or "clipped"—by the pixels on the layer below it—the HAWAII layer. The 2 Women image is visible only where there are pixels on the HAWAII layer. Where the HAWAII layer is transparent, the 2 Women image is not visible.

TIP Note that the 2 Women layer now has the bent arrow icon which represents the Use Previous Layer to Create Clipping Mask option.

(continued)

FIGURE 12
Clipped image

FIGURE 13

Positioning the 2 Women image

8. Click the **Move Tool** ⊹, then move the graphic so that the two women are positioned in the letter H, as shown in Figure 13.

    TIP Use the arrow keys to move the image in small increments. Each time you press an arrow, the image moves 1 pixel in that direction. Press and hold [Shift] when you press an arrow, and the image will move 10 pixels in that direction.

9. Save your work.

Lesson 4   Use One Layer to Mask Another Layer

MASH A LAYER WITH THE
Paste Into Command

What You'll Do

Paste is probably one of the first commands you learned when you sat down at a computer for the first time. First copy, then paste. Paste Into is not quite so popular. It's a bit obscure, a bit awkward, and how it fits into the big picture is not so obvious.

Paste Into is pretty cool and a very effective way of masking a graphic—in some ways, it's more effective than some of the more popular methods that you probably use.

Paste Into is inextricably linked to layer masks, and it's this important relationship that makes Paste Into a smart choice for complex masking effects.

FIGURE 14
All pixels on Hawaii layer are selected

Mask a layer with the Paste Into command

1. Open Family.psd, select all, copy, then close the file.

2. Target the **HAWAII layer**.

3. Press and hold **[Ctrl]** (Win) or ⌘ (Mac), then click the **HAWAII Layer thumbnail**.

   As shown in Figure 14, all of the pixels on the HAWAII layer are selected.

   TIP Pressing and holding [Ctrl] (Win) or ⌘ (Mac), then clicking a layer thumbnail loads a selection of all the pixels on the layer. If the layer has transparent areas, the transparent areas will not be selected.

4. Click the **Rectangular Marquee Tool** ⬚, verify that the Style choice in the Options bar reads Normal, press and hold **[Alt]** (Win) or **[option]** (Mac), then drag a box around the letter H only.

   The letter H is deselected.

   TIP Pressing and holding [Alt] (Win) or [option] (Mac) when creating a selection removes the selection from the currently selected area.

5. Click the **Polygonal Lasso Tool** ⟊, then verify that the feather value in the Options bar is set at 0 px.

   (continued)

6. Press and hold [**Alt**] (Win) or [**option**] (Mac), then draw a box around the letters WAII.

The letters are deselected. Only the letter A is selected.

7. Target the **2 Women layer**, click **Edit** on the menu bar, then click **Paste Into**.

As shown in Figure 15, the Family.psd image is pasted on a new layer above the 2 Women layer. The new layer is created automatically with a layer mask that represents the selection that was pasted into—a white A on a black background.

(continued)

FIGURE 15
Viewing the new layer and its layer mask

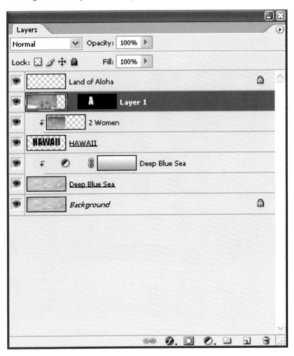

DESIGN*note*

You used the Polygonal Lasso Tool because it is able to make diagonal selections, which made it easy to navigate around the letter A. Using the Rectangular Marquee Tool would have made the task much more difficult—in fact, it wouldn't be possible to remove areas from the selection in just one step. This is a fine example of how knowing when to use the right tool for the right task saves you time and effort.

FIGURE 16
Positioning the Family graphic

8. Name the new layer **Family**, press and hold **[Alt]** (Win) or **[option]** (Mac), then click the **Layer mask thumbnail** to view the mask.

   TIP Pressing and holding [Alt] (Win) or [option] (Mac) when clicking a layer mask thumbnail displays the layer mask on the canvas.

9. Click the **Family thumbnail** to view the image again, click the **Move Tool**, then move the image so that the woman is positioned in the letter A as shown Figure 16.

   Regardless of how you move the image, it is visible only within the letter A, because of the layer mask.

10. Save your work.

SCALE AN
Image

What You'll Do

Chances are, you've scaled a graphic in Photoshop before. You use the same method to scale a graphic that is part of a mask, but the mask makes it more interesting.

Use this lesson to hone your skills for scaling and repositioning a graphic within a mask *before* executing the scale. It's an important skill to have. Here's why: Any time you scale a graphic, by definition, you change the pixel structure that creates the graphic.

If you reduce the graphic, you use less pixels; that means pixels are discarded. If you enlarge the graphic, you need more pixels. Where are you going to get them from? Any guesses? You're going to get the new pixels from the pixels you already have. Using a process called interpolation, Photoshop creates new pixels based on the data of the original pixels.

In either case—but especially when enlarging—the quality of the image will be reduced as the original pixel structure is modified. What this all means is—if you have to scale a graphic—you want to scale it just once whenever possible.

FIGURE 17
Identifying the bounding box

Scale an image

1. Target the **2 Women layer**, click **Edit** on the menu bar, point to **Transform**, then click **Scale**.

   As shown in Figure 17, a bounding box appears around the entire 2 Women image—even the parts that are not visible outside the letter H.

2. Press and hold **[Shift]**, position your cursor over the top-right corner point of the bounding box, click and drag in a northeast direction, then release when the W and H values in the Options bar are 110%.

   > **TIP** Pressing and holding [Shift] when scaling an image scales the image in proportion.

3. Still pressing and holding **[Shift]**, position your cursor over the bottom-left corner point of the bounding box, click and drag in a southwest direction, then release when the W and H values in the Options bar are 122%.

(continued)

Lesson 6   Scale an Image

ADVANCED PHOTOSHOP 1-23

4. Position your cursor over the bounding box so that a black arrow appears, then reposition the women within the letter H.

When moving a bounding box, do not click and drag the crosshair icon at the center of the bounding box—this would move the icon only, not the bounding box. The crosshair icon represents the point of origin for a transformation. If you move the crosshair, you move the point of origin.

For example, if you wanted to scale a graphic from a specific point other than its center, you would move the crosshair to that point.

5. Use the arrow keys to position the graphic as shown in Figure 18.

(continued)

FIGURE 18
Positioning the 2 Women graphic precisely using the arrow keys

Clicking the Move Tool offers you the choice to execute or to not execute the transformation. This is one of many ways to execute a transformation.

7. Undo and redo your last step to see the effects of scaling the image.

8. Compare your work to Figure 19, then save your work.

FIGURE 19
Scaled graphic

USE THE FREE
Transform Command

What You'll Do

Once upon a time, you could apply only one transformation at a time. If you wanted to scale and rotate and flip a graphic, you had to first scale it, click OK, then rotate it, click OK, then flip it.

Enter the Free Transform command. Simply put, Free Transform allows you to make all of your transformations at once. Scale, rotate, distort, flip—you can do it with one bounding box and one execution.

When you understand the quality benefits of applying multiple transformations with just one execution, that's when you appreciate the power and importance of the Free Transform command.

FIGURE 20
Positioning the graphic

1. Target the **Family layer**, click **Edit** on the menu bar, then click **Free Transform**.

   The object here is to fit the Family image in the letter A. The choice of the photo was a good one, since the four people are positioned roughly in a triangular shape. The image will need to be scaled and rotated to fit into the letter A with all four people showing.

2. Press and hold **[Shift]**, position your cursor over the top-right corner point of the bounding box, click and drag toward the center of the image, then release when the W and H values in the Options bar are 50%.

   The bounding box is now almost completely outside of the letter A.

   TIP The W and H text boxes in the Options bar are interactive—you could have entered 50% in each after choosing the Free Transform command.

3. Position your cursor over the bounding box so that a black arrow appears, then reposition the graphic as shown in Figure 20.

   TIP When transforming, you can move the bounding box any time you like. It is a good idea to reposition the bounding box as you test out different transformations. By repositioning the graphic, you can get a better sense of what you need to do to make it fit.

   (continued)

4. Position your cursor just outside of the bounding box.

   The Rotate icon appears.

5. Click and drag in a counterclockwise direction, then release when the Rotate value in the Options bar is −25.

6. Reposition the image, trying to fit all four faces into the letter A.

   Be sure that the bounding box covers the entire A. If it doesn't, that means that there will be no areas of the Family graphic in that area of the letter A. At this scale and rotation, the image does not fill the letter in a satisfactory way.

7. Type **44.2** in the W and H text boxes to scale the graphic to a smaller size.

   When transforming a graphic, you'll often want to zoom in and out as you work. But that poses a problem: If you click the Zoom Tool while the bounding box is still active, it's the same as clicking the Move Tool—Photoshop will ask if you want to execute the transformation. This is where you rely on your keyboard commands. Press and hold [Spacebar][Ctrl] (Win) or [Spacebar] ⌘ (Mac) and your cursor will change to the Zoom Plus Tool ⊕. Press and hold [Spacebar][Alt] (Win) or [Spacebar][option] (Mac) to access the Zoom Minus Tool ⊖. Make a note of these two important quick key combinations.

   (continued)

FIGURE 21

Repositioning the graphic

8. Rotate the graphic counterclockwise to
   −33.4%.

9. Reposition the bounding box so that the
   graphic fills the letter A as shown in
   Figure 21.

10. Press **[Enter]** (Win) or **[return]** (Mac) to
    execute the transformation, then compare
    your canvas to Figure 22.

11. Save your work.

FIGURE 22

Results of the free transformation—both a scale and a rotation

land of aloha

DESIGN*note*

Take a moment to remind yourself of the two methods that you've used so far to
place these two images. Note that the right areas in the 2 Women graphic are
visible in the W, whereas the Family image is visible only in the letter A. Each of
the two images is being masked, but in different ways. Which is better? In this
exercise, neither. But be sure to remember the Paste Into method we used for the
Family graphic—it can be useful when you want the image to appear only in a
specific area and not show anywhere else.

USE A SINGLE LAYER TO
Mask Multiple Layers

What You'll Do

Things get really interesting in the Layers palette when multiple layers all "clip" themselves into a single layer that plays the role of the mask. That single layer can be used to mask multiple images placed on multiple layers; you don't need to use multiple masks to achieve the effect.

As you work through this lesson, keep in mind the complex tasks that the Layers palette handles with such ease.

FIGURE 23

Viewing the new and automatically clipped layer

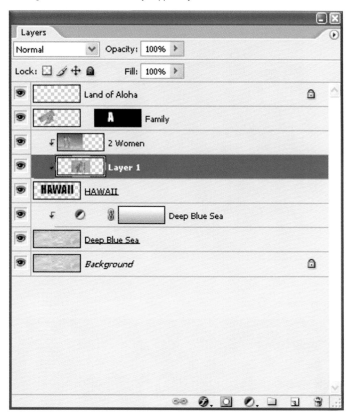

Use a single layer to mask multiple layers

1. Open Beach Girls.psd, select all, copy, then close the file.

2. Target the **HAWAII layer**.

3. Click **Edit** on the menu bar, then click **Paste**.

   As shown in Figure 23, the new layer is automatically "clipped" by the HAWAII layer because it was pasted *beneath* the 2 Women layer, which was already being "clipped." Note the bent arrow icon on the new layer.

4. Name the layer **Beach Girls**.

   The Beach Girls image is obscured by the right areas of the 2 Women image, which is on the layer above it. However, no part of the Family graphic obscures the Beach Girls image. This is a great example of how the different choices you make along the way when building an illustration can yield different results and different issues you need to address.

   (continued)

5. Drag the **Beach Girls layer** above the 2 Women layer.

   As shown in Figure 24, the Beach Girls image is no longer obscured by the 2 Women image in the letter W. Despite the move, the Beach Girls layer continues to be masked by the HAWAII layer.

6. Reposition the Beach Girls image so that your canvas resembles Figure 25.

7. Open Stretch.psd, select all, copy, then close the file.

8. Target the **Beach Girls layer**, apply the Paste command, then name the layer **Stretch**.

   The Stretch image is not masked.

   (continued)

FIGURE 24
Reordering clipped layers in the Layers palette

FIGURE 25
Repositioning the Beach Girls graphic

FIGURE 26
Preparing to clip a layer

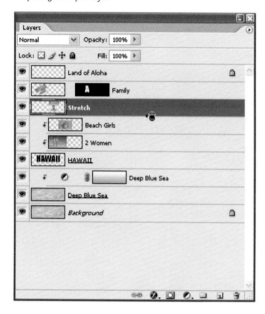

FIGURE 27
Clipped Stretch image

9. Click the **Move Tool** ⊹, then move the Stretch image over the second letter A in HAWAII.

10. Press and hold **[Alt]** (Win) or **[option]** (Mac), then position your cursor in the Layers palette over the line between the Stretch and Beach Girls layers so that you see the icon shown in Figure 26.

11. Click between the two layers.

The Stretch image is clipped into the mask, as shown in Figure 27. There's an important distinction that you need to make here: The Stretch image is being masked by the HAWAII layer, *not* the Beach Girls layer. When you have a series of clipped layers—as you do here—it is the bottommost layer that clips the layers above it.

(continued)

Lesson 8   Use a Single Layer to Mask Multiple Layers

12. Open Oar.psd, then using the same steps that you used for the Stretch image, clip it into the first letter I and position it as shown in Figure 28.

(continued)

FIGURE 28
Oar graphic, clipped and positioned

Working with Layers   Chapter 1

FIGURE 29

Snorkelers graphic, clipped and positioned

13. Open Snorkelers.psd, clip it into the second letter I, then position it as shown in Figure 29.
14. Save your work.

PAINT IN A
Layer Mask

What You'll Do

When you finish this lesson, take a moment to stop and examine the status of the Layers palette. Take a look at all the components being used to create the artwork on your canvas: transparent layers. An adjustment layer. Multiple layer masks—one with a gradient that fades the adjustment layer. Multiple layers clipped into one layer, all of them using layer masks.

The power of the Layers palette is on display when the various features are all being used and are working together in harmony.

This illustration's Layers palette is complex—and the amazing thing is, we've just scratched the surface of what layers can do.

FIGURE 30

Positioning the Stretch image

1. Name the new layers **Oar** and **Snorkelers**, respectively.

2. Hide the Oar and Snorkelers layers.

3. Target the **Stretch layer**, scale the image 85%, then position it as shown in Figure 30.

   Note that part of the Stretch image still overlaps the Beach Girls image to the left.

4. Click **Layer** on the menu bar, point to **Layer Mask**, then click **Reveal All**.

   A white-filled layer mask is added to the Stretch layer.

5. Press **[D]**, then press **[X]** so that your foreground color is black, click the **Brush Tool** , then choose Hard Round 19 pixels from the Brush pull-down menu on the Options bar.

(continued)

DESIGN*note*

From a designer's perspective, the placement of the Stretch graphic is rather interesting. Note that the triangle in the letter A cuts into her face. It would probably be your first instinct to avoid that triangle—to try to position the graphic so that the face is on either side of the triangle, as with the Family image. However, the triangle cutting into the woman's face actually yields a more interesting effect—a playful interaction with the mask. Rather than detract from the image, it makes it more intriguing.

6. With the layer mask still activated in the Layers palette, paint *on the canvas* everywhere that the Stretch image overlaps the Beach Girls image.

The Stretch image disappears where you paint. Your canvas should resemble Figure 31.

TIP Note that black appears in the layer mask representing where you painted in the canvas.

7. Make the Oar layer visible, target it, then click the **Add layer mask button**  on the Layers palette.

A transparent (white) layer mask is added to the layer.

8. Paint in the layer mask to remove the areas of Oar that overlap Stretch.

Your canvas should resemble Figure 32.

(continued)

FIGURE 31
Beach Girls image no longer obscured by the Stretch image

FIGURE 32
Stretch image no longer obscured by the Oar image

9. Make the Snorkelers layer visible, then scale it and position it as shown in Figure 33.

10. Apply a layer mask, then mask the areas of Snorkelers that overlap Oar.

11. Save your work, then compare it to Figure 34.

FIGURE 33

Repositioning the Snorkelers image

FIGURE 34

Six images positioned in six letter forms

Lesson 9   Paint in a Layer Mask

ADD A STROKE
Layer Style

What You'll Do

At this point, we've hit a landmark point in the construction of this illustration. All six images have been placed into the mask and have been masked so that none interferes with any other. As a designer, this is the point where you'd want to take a moment to assess the art as it appears at this stage and decide how it can be improved to achieve a finished look.

The first thing to note is that the letter forms seem a bit bare. They simply butt up against the water image in the background. To remedy this, in this lesson you will apply a stroke to the letter forms.

As a designer, it is worth your time to think about and experiment with strokes. They can be very effective, or they can be trite and predictable. What makes the difference? It's hard to say. Sometimes the color makes it or breaks it. A stroke works when the art calls for it—it's that simple.

The art in this chapter is a good example. The effect is of six different images placed into six different letter forms. The key here is the word *different*—each picture and letter form should be distinct from the others. As you go through this lesson, give some thought to how a stroke makes each letterform more distinct and how the stroke lends impact to the image within the letterforms and to the illustration as a whole.

FIGURE 35

Layer Style dialog box

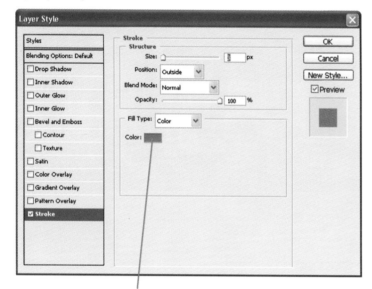

Set color of stroke box

Add a stroke layer style

1. Target the **HAWAII layer**, click **Layer** on the menu bar, point to **Layer Style**, then click **Stroke**.

   The Layer Style dialog box opens, and the Stroke check box is checked, as shown in Figure 35.

2. Verify that the Preview check box is checked, then click the **Set color of stroke box** to open the Color Picker.

3. Type **255** in the R, G, and B text boxes, then click **OK**.

4. Click the **Position list arrow**, then click **Inside**.

   (continued)

5. Drag the **Size slider** to 8 px, then compare your canvas to Figure 36.

> **TIP** If you do not see the stroke applied to the artwork, click directly to the left of Effects in the layer below the Hawaii layer. You will see the Toggle all layer effects visibilities button appear. This button allows you to hide or show the layer effects for a particular layer.

(continued)

FIGURE 36
Stroke positioned inside the mask

DESIGNnote

It is important that you understand that you are applying the stroke to the HAWAII layer. The stroke appears *over* the five images that have been "clipped" into the HAWAII layer, even though they are above the HAWAII layer. When an image is clipped into a given layer, the image takes on the layer styles applied to that given layer. However, the stroke does *not* appear in the letter A because the Family layer is above the HAWAII layer and is not clipped. Again, this is another good example of how the choices you make when building an illustration will affect choices you make later on down the line.

FIGURE 37

Stroke positioned outside the mask

6. Click the **Position list arrow**, then click **Outside**.

   The stroke on HAWAII is no longer obscured by the Family graphic because the stroke is positioned outside of the Family graphic.

7. Drag the **Size slider** to 3 px, click **OK**, then compare your canvas to Figure 37.

   Note that an Effects layer and a Stroke layer now appear in sublayers beneath the HAWAII layer.

   TIP Layer styles are listed in sublayers within the layer to which they are applied.

8. Save your work.

ADD A DROP SHADOW
Layer Style

What You'll Do

As a designer, you should keep the word "flat" in the back of your mind whenever you assess your work at a given stage. Flat is usually not a good thing—not an objective you are trying to achieve.

The HAWAII art at this stage is flat. Note that even with the multiple images, the masking and the stroke, the overall effect remains stubbornly two dimensional. We want the HAWAII art to "pop"—to jump off the page.

A drop shadow is a tried and true solution for adding the illusion of depth to an illustration. In this lesson, you are going to add a drop shadow to create the effect that the word HAWAII is floating above the water in the background.

FIGURE 38

Drop Shadow settings in the Layer Style dialog box

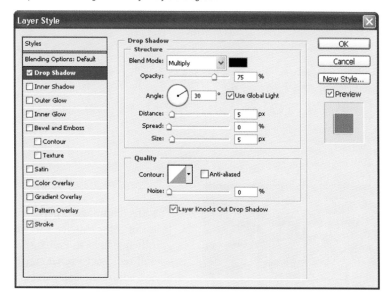

FIGURE 39

Viewing the drop shadow

Add a drop shadow layer style

1. With the HAWAII layer still targeted, click the **Add a Layer Style button** 🔵 on the Layers palette, then click **Drop Shadow**.

   As shown in Figure 38, the Drop Shadow check box is automatically checked because you chose Drop Shadow from the list. The Stroke check box is also checked because you previously added a stroke style, and it is still active.

2. Drag the **Distance slider** to 16 px.

   The Distance slider determines the offset of the shadow—how far it is positioned from the object.

3. Drag the **Angle slider** counterclockwise so that the text box reads 45.

4. Drag the **Size slider** to 5 px.

   Along with the size of the shadow, the Size slider determines the softness of the shadow.

5. Click the **Set color of shadow button** to open the Color Picker.

6. Type **13R/8G/57B** to choose a dark blue color, then click **OK**.

7. Drag the **Opacity slider** to 85, click **OK**, then compare your work to Figure 39.

   Take some time to note how the drop shadow adds a sense of depth to the illustration. Note how the 16-pixel distance that you chose for the offset defines the degree of depth. Note too how the images in the letter forms appear more vibrant in contrast to the dark shadow behind them.

8. Save your work.

APPLY AN ADJUSTMENT
Layer to Multiple Layers

What You'll Do

The Stretch image is perhaps the best in terms of color balance and vibrancy. The Family image lacks contrast and has an overall red cast to it. Of course, you could always adjust the color in each image. In this lesson, however, you will use an adjustment layer to modify the color in all the layers, with the goal of adding some degree of color consistency across all six letter forms.

Whenever you work with multiple images in a single piece of art, color consistency is something you need to consider.

The images that you are working with in this chapter are from a photo service and were taken in different settings, under different lighting conditions and by different photographers.

If you looked at them separately, you might not notice any distinct differences, but side by side, the inconsistency is apparent.

FIGURE 40
Color effect of the adjustment layer

Apply an adjustment layer to multiple layers

1. Click the **Layer thumbnail** on the Family layer.

   When a layer has a layer mask, you can target either the image or the layer mask.

   A white frame appears around the targeted thumbnail in the Layers palette.

2. Press **[Tab]** to hide all palettes.

3. Click **Layer** on the menu bar, point to **New Adjustment Layer**, then click **Color Balance**.

4. Type **Add Red** in the Name text box, then, if necessary, remove the check mark in the Use Previous Layer to Create Clipping Mask check box.

   You would activate the Use Previous Layer to Create Clipping Mask check box if you wanted to apply the adjustment only to the Family layer. In this case, you want to apply the adjustment to all layers beneath the adjustment layer.

5. Click **OK**.

6. Drag the **top slider** to the right—toward Red—until the value in the first Color Levels text box reads +50, then compare your canvas to Figure 40.

(continued)

7. Drag the **slider** left until the value reads +20, click OK, then compare your canvas to Figure 41.

8. Press **[Tab]**, then hide and show the adjustment layer in the Layers palette to note the color change and which layers were affected.

   All of the layers are affected by the adjustment layer except Land of Aloha, which is on a layer above the adjustment layer. Note how the addition of red across all the images adds a sense of consistency and continuity. However, note too that the water in the background looks a bit purple, which is not what we want.

9. Press and hold **[Alt]** (Win) or **[option]** (Mac), position your cursor in the Layers palette between the adjustment layer and the Family layer, then click.

   The adjustment layer is clipped into the Family layer. If you hide and show the adjustment layer, you will see that the Family layer is now the only layer being affected by the adjustment layer.

   (continued)

FIGURE 41
Changing the Red value to +20

FIGURE 42

Color effect of the adjustment layer clipped into the mask

10. Press and hold **[Alt]** (Win) or **[option]** (Mac), position your cursor in the Layers palette between the Family layer and the Snorkelers layer, then click.

11. Compare your artwork to Figure 42.

Hide and show the adjustment layer, then take a moment to study the Layers palette. Because the Family layer is now part of the group that is clipped into the HAWAII layer, the adjustment layer now affects all of the clipped images. However, it does not affect the water in the background, because those two layers are not part of the clipped group.

12. Save your work.

Lesson 12   Apply an Adjustment Layer to Multiple Layers

EDIT LAYER
Styles

What You'll Do

As with adjustment layers, layer styles can be modified at any time. This is yet another example of how Photoshop has evolved to allow you the freedom to execute design choices knowing that you can modify them at a later time. For example, you applied a stroke as a layer style even though you could have applied it using the Stroke command. The big difference, of course, is that the stroke created with the layer style can be edited.

FIGURE 43
Three layer styles applied to the artwork

DESIGN*note*

From a design perspective there's a lot to look at as the result of these three simple changes. First, note how the black stroke is so much better for the illustration than the white stroke. The black stroke delineates the letter forms, but it does so without calling attention to itself. Compare that to the white stroke, which practically screamed, "Hey, look at me! I'm a white stroke!" Note too how the black stroke is a segue to the dark drop shadow behind it. The reduction of the opacity of the shadow from 85% to 70% creates a more consistent transparency effect with the 50% opacity of the inner shadow.

Earlier, we discussed goals of adding depth to the image. Note how the drop shadow and the innershadow conflict in such an interesting way. The drop shadow moves the masked images up off the page, as though they are floating and casting a shadow on the water. But the inner shadow pushes them back, as though they are beneath something that is casting a shadow. This is especially apparent on the first letter A. On the left edge, note how the drop shadow creates the effect that the A is above the water. On the right edge, note how the inner shadow creates the effect that the water is casting a shadow on the A—as though the letter forms are "cut out" of the water and the water is casting the shadow. Interesting, yes? What's even more interesting is that the eye does not register the conflict between these effects as a problem. Instead, the varying depth effects created by the shadow layer styles serve to make the overall effect more intriguing.

Edit layer styles

1. Target the **HAWAII layer**, then double-click the **Stroke effect** listed beneath the HAWAII layer in the Layers palette.

   The Layer Style dialog box opens showing the stroke settings you applied earlier.

2. Click the **Set color of stroke box** to open the Color Picker, type **0** in the R, G, and B text boxes, then click **OK**.

3. Click **Drop Shadow** in the list on the left side of the dialog box.

   TIP Be sure to click the Drop Shadow name itself, not the check box beside it.

   The Layer Style dialog box changes to show the drop shadow settings you applied earlier, and a check mark appears automatically beside Drop Shadow in the list.

4. Drag the **Opacity slider** to 70%.

5. Click **Inner Shadow** in the list on the left side of the dialog box.

6. Drag the **Distance slider** to 8 px, drag the **Opacity slider** to 50%, click **OK**, then compare your canvas to Figure 43.

   An Inner Shadow effects layer now appears in the Layers palette between Drop Shadow and Stroke.

   TIP Layer styles are listed in alphabetical order, regardless of the order in which they are applied.

7. Save your work.

COPY LAYER STYLES
Between Layers

What You'll Do

We've spent much time up to this point discussing how adjustment layers and layer styles are so powerful because they can be modified at any time. We also have discussed how they remain in the Layers palette as a record of the adjustments and styles that you've applied to the image.

This lesson brings these two great features together. Layer styles can be copied between layers. This allows you to create a specific style only once and then use it multiple times in the document.

The ability to modify layer styles becomes very important when duplicating layer styles. Duplicating a later style is a quick and effective method for applying the same style to multiple layers. However, the specific style settings for one layer may or may not work for the artwork on other layers. No problem. With layer styles, you can simply adjust the style to fit the new artwork.

FIGURE 44

Dragging the Effects layer to the Land of Aloha layer

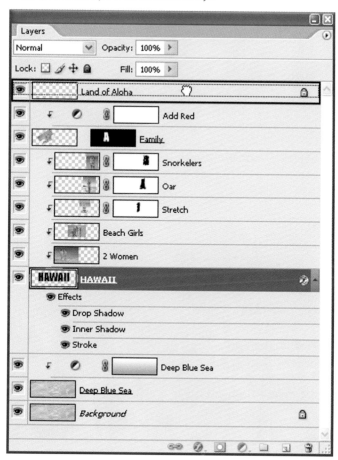

Copy styles between layers

1. Note the three layer styles listed beneath the HAWAII layer, then note the Effects layer listed above all three.

   TIP The Effects layer represents all the styles applied to the layer.

2. Verify that you can see all the layers in the Layers palette.

3. Press and hold the **Effects layer** beneath HAWAII, then drag it up to the Land of Aloha layer, releasing when you see a black rectangle around the layer, as shown in Figure 44.

   (continued)

4. Compare your artwork to Figure 45.

   The three layer styles are moved—not copied—from the HAWAII layer to the Land of Aloha layer.

5. Undo the move.

6. Press and hold [Alt] (Win) or [option] (Mac), then drag only the Drop Shadow layer style up to the Land of Aloha layer.

   As shown in Figure 46, the Drop Shadow layer style is copied to the Land of Aloha layer.

   TIP Pressing and holding [Alt] (Win) or [option] (Mac), then dragging a single layer style or the Effects layer creates a copy of the effect(s) on the destination layer.

7. If you do not see the drop shadow, click to the left of Effects to show the Toggle all layer effect visibilities button.

8. Double-click the Drop Shadow layer style in the Land of Aloha layer.

9. Drag the Distance slider to 6 px, change the Opacity to 95%, then click OK.

9. Press [Tab] to hide the palettes, hide the rulers if they are visible, then press the [F] twice.

   Your canvas should appear alone against a black screen.

   TIP Pressing [F] toggles three views of the canvas. Those views correspond with the three screen mode buttons on the toolbox.

10. Compare your canvas to Figure 47.

11. Press [F], save your work, then close HAWAII.psd.

FIGURE 45
Results of moving the layer style

FIGURE 46
Copied layer style

FIGURE 47
Finished artwork

Use layered artwork as masks

1. Open AP 1-2.psd, then save it as **On the Beach**.
2. Fill the artwork on the Outer Beach layer with white.
3. Fill the artwork on the Inner Beach layer with black.
4. Open the file named Beach Scene.psd, select all, copy, then close the file.
5. Target the Inner Beach layer, then paste.
6. Name the new layer **Beach Scene**.
7. Duplicate the Beach Scene layer, then rename the duplicate **Outer Scene**.
8. Drag the Outer Scene layer down so that it is above the Outer Beach layer.
9. Hide the Outer Scene and Outer Beach layers.
10. Clip the Beach Scene layer into the Inner Beach layer.
11. Hide the Beach Scene and the Inner Beach layers, then show the Outer Scene and Outer Beach layers.
12. Clip the Outer Scene layer into the Outer Beach layer.
13. Save your work.

Use adjustment layers and layer masks

1. Target the Outer Scene layer, then create a Hue/Saturation adjustment layer. (*Hint:* Accept the default name; Be sure to click the Use Previous Layer to Create Clipping Mask check box.)
2. Drag the Saturation to -100, then click OK.
3. Target the Outer Beach layer, then change its blending mode to Luminosity. (*Hint:* To change a blending mode, click the Normal list arrow at the top of the Layers palette, then choose a blending mode from the list.)

4. Reduce the opacity to 75%.
5. Target the Outer Scene layer, click Layer on the menu bar, point to New Adjustment Layer, then click Brightness/Contrast. (*Hint:* The top third of the Outer Scene artwork is too dark for the illustration. We will brighten all of the artwork, then use a layer mask to affect just the top third.)
6. Type **Brighten Top Third Only** in the Name dialog box, verify that the Use Previous Layer to Create Clipping Mask check box is checked, then click OK.
7. Drag the Brightness slider to +35, then click OK.
8. Add a layer mask to the Brighten Top Third Only layer.
9. Set your foreground color to white, then set your background color to black.
10. Click the Gradient Tool, then click the Linear Gradient button on the Options bar, if necessary. (*Hint:* You may want to verify that the Foreground to Background gradient is the active gradient in the Gradient Picker.)
11. Position your cursor at the top center of the Outer Beach artwork, click and drag straight down, then release at the bottom of the Outer Beach artwork.
12. Toggle the Brightness/Contrast adjustment layer on and off to see the change.
13. Open the Brightness/Contrast adjustment layer, then increase the Brightness value to +50.
14. Show the Beach Scene and Inner Beach layers, then compare your artwork to Figure 48.
15. Save your work, then close On the Beach.

FIGURE 48
Completed Project Builder 1

1. Open AP 1-3.psd, then save it as **On the Beach Styles**.
2. Target the Inner Beach layer.
3. Click Layer on the menu bar, point to Layer Style, then click Drop Shadow.
4. Verify that shadow color is set to black.
5. Verify that the blend mode is set to Multiply and the Opacity is set to 50%.
6. Check the Use Global Light check box, then set the angle to 144.
7. Verify that the Distance, Spread and Size values are set to 9, 0, and 5 respectively.
8. On the left side of the dialog box, click the words Outer Glow.
9. Verify that the blend mode is set to Multiply and the Opacity is set to 75%.
10. Set the color of the glow to black.
11. Verify that the Technique is set to Softer, the Spread is set to 5 and the Size is set to 9.
12. On the left side of the dialog box, click the word Stroke.
13. Set the size to 2 pixels, then set the Position to Outside.
14. Set the stroke color to black, then click OK to close the Layer Style dialog box.
15. Target the Outer Beach layer.
16. Click Layer on the menu bar, point to Layer Style, then click Inner Shadow.
17. Verify that the blend mode is set to Multiply and the Opacity is set to 75%.
18. Check the Use Global Light check box, then set the angle to 144.
19. Set the Distance, Choke and Size values to 6, 0, and 5 respectively.
20. Click OK, then compare your results to Figure 49.
21. Save your work, then close On the Beach Styles.

FIGURE 49
Completed Project Builder 2

chapter

2

WORKING WITH
Layer Styles

1. Copy and paste from Illustrator to Photoshop.
2. Import layers from Adobe Illustrator.
3. Create a Chisel Hard Emboss layer style.
4. Select specific areas of layer-styled artwork.
5. Create a Smooth Emboss layer style.
6. Create and apply a Gradient Overlay to a layer style.
7. Create a Pillow Emboss layer style.
8. Copy layer styles between layers.
9. Create a chrome effect without using layer styles.
10. Duplicate a chrome effect without using layer styles.

COPY AND PASTE FROM
Illustrator to Photoshop

What You'll Do

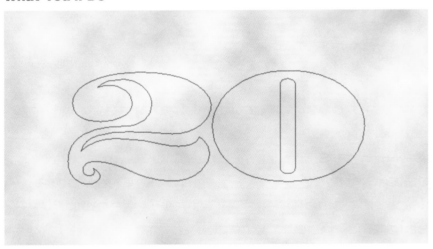

Adobe Photoshop and Adobe Illustrator have always been closely related—so much so that many designers refer to them as "sister" applications. With the upgrade to the Creative Suite and now with CS2, that relationship has been highlighted. With Photoshop and Illustrator now bundled together with InDesign, the relationship between the Adobe Trinity is seamless—and powerful.

Photoshop and Illustrator overlap each other in their abilities. Of the two, Photoshop is the dominant package. Photoshop can do a lot of things that Illustrator can do; the Pen Tool offers the ability to draw vector graphics, and Photoshop's text-handling capabilities have been upgraded dramatically from recent versions. Illustrator, on the other hand, is exclusively a vector-based application; the bitmap world belongs to Photoshop.

Nevertheless, Illustrator is an articulate and powerful software package. In many ways, it's also more challenging than Photoshop. Illustrator graphics and typography are easier to create and manipulate and often more interesting and sophisticated than what most designers come up with in Photoshop. That's a sweet edge to have in the competitive field of graphic design.

The key, of course, is moving graphics from Illustrator into Photoshop—into the photographic artwork. With CS2, that transition is as seamless as Copy/Paste.

FIGURE 1
Pasting art from Illustrator into Photoshop

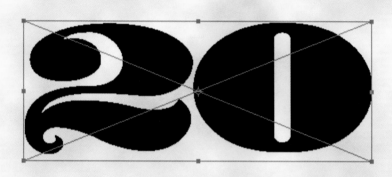

DESIGN*note*

The PDF option allows you to paste Illustrator artwork into applications that prefer the pasted data in PDF format. To copy and paste Illustrator artwork into InDesign, for example, you need to copy as a PDF. The PDF format will also preserve transparency settings. For Photoshop, you usually want to copy Illustrator artwork as paths. AICB is the format native to Illustrator; it offers you two options, depending on the type of artwork. In most cases, that artwork will be relatively simple paths and text. For this type of art, choose AICB and check the Preserve Paths option. If you have complex Illustrator artwork and it is important that you maintain every aspect of its appearance (patterns, mesh objects, effects, etc.), you need to choose the Preserve Appearance option before you paste.

Copy and paste from Illustrator to Photoshop

1. Open AP 2-1.ai in Illustrator, click **Edit** (Win) or **Illustrator** (Mac) on the menu bar, point to **Preferences**, then click **File Handling & Clipboard**.

2. In the Clipboard on Quit section, verify that only the PDF check box is checked, then click **OK**.

3. Click the **Selection Tool** , select the two numbers, then copy them.

4. Switch to Photoshop, open AP 2-2.psd in Photoshop, then save it as **Paste From Illustrator**.

5. Display the Layers palette, if necessary.

6. Click **Edit** on the menu bar, then click **Paste**.

   As shown in Figure 1, the artwork is pasted in a bounding box, which can be resized, rotated, and so on.

7. Click the **Move Tool** , then click **Place**.

   The artwork is pasted onto its own layer.

8. Delete the new layer, then switch back to Illustrator.

9. Return to the File Handling & Clipboard Preferences dialog box.

10. In the Clipboard on Quit section, remove the PDF check mark, click the **AICB (no transparency support) check box**, click the **Preserve Paths option button**, then click **OK**.

(continued)

11. Click **Edit** on the menu bar, click **Copy**, then switch back to Photoshop.

12. Click the **Default Foreground and Background Colors button** 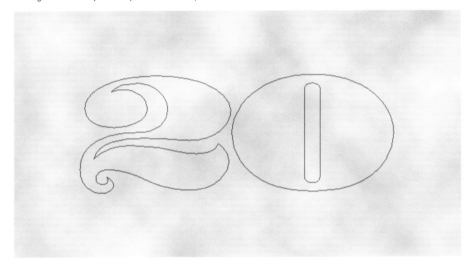 in the toolbox.

13. Click **Edit** on the menu bar, then click **Paste**.

    The Paste dialog box appears, offering you four paste choices.

14. Click the **Pixels option button**, then click **OK**.

    The paste is identical to the paste you executed earlier in this lesson.

15. Click the **Move Tool**, then click **Place**.

    When you paste as pixels, the result of the paste is a bitmap graphic, which is pasted as a new layer. No vector information is pasted with the graphic.

16. Delete the new layer.

17. Click **Edit** on the menu bar, click **Paste**, click the **Path option button**, then click **OK**.

    As shown in Figure 2, the path from Illustrator is pasted; a new layer is *not* created.

18. Click **Window** on the menu bar, click **Paths**, then note that the path was pasted as a new Work Path.

19. Click below the Work Path in the Paths palette to turn the Work Path off.

    The path disappears.

    (continued)

FIGURE 2
Pasting an Illustrator path as a path in Photoshop

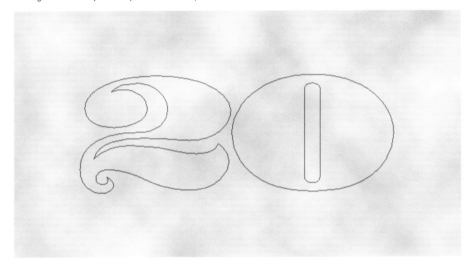

DESIGN*note*

If you want to copy Illustrator art into Photoshop as a shape layer or as a path, you must first choose AICB in the File Handling & Clipboard preferences dialog box. Sound simple? It is, but you would be amazed at how many professional designers don't know about or don't remember where to find this option. Why? Because this is such a common operation—copying artwork as a Shape layer or path—and because Adobe has buried its activation deep in the Preferences dialog box, under the seldom-used heading of File Handling & Clipboard, and with the unfriendly name of AICB (no transparency support). So yes, it's easy enough to do, but it's really difficult to remember where to do it. Make a note. It's a great bit of knowledge to have in your skills set. Then, when you're a junior art director and the creative director is frustrated because she doesn't know about this preference, you can quickly solve her problem and be the hero. One little click: that's how promotions happen.

FIGURE 3

Pasting an Illustrator path as a Shape layer in Photoshop

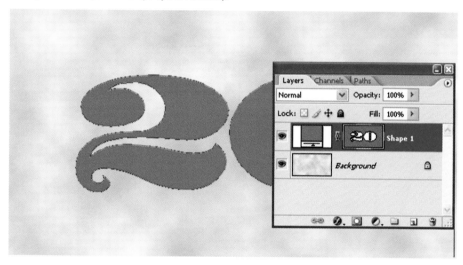

20. Change the foreground color to any red swatch in the Swatches palette.

21. Paste again, click the **Shape Layer option button**, then click **OK**.

As shown in Figure 3, the artwork is pasted as a shape layer and uses the foreground color as its fill.

A shape layer is a powerful and relatively new feature in Photoshop. Essentially, shape layers are vector graphics positioned on layers in a Photoshop document. As vectors, they can be scaled and otherwise transformed without any loss in quality. This makes shape layers ideal for handling type from Illustrator.

22. Save your work, close AP 2-1.ai, then close the Paste from Illustrator document.

IMPORT LAYERS FROM
Adobe Illustrator

What You'll Do

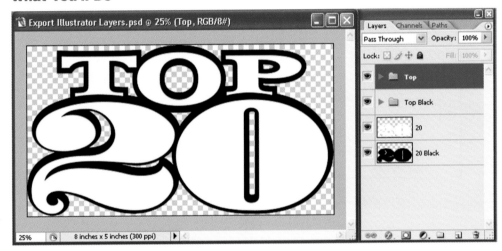

N ever forget that Photoshop and Illustrator are remarkably compatible. Incorporating the power of Illustrator into your Photoshop skills set expands your overall skills set as a designer exponentially. Indeed, when you are as fluent in Illustrator as you are in Photoshop, you'll find that much of the artwork you want to create in Photoshop is often best started in Illustrator, with all of its great drawing tools and precise typographical abilities.

With each upgrade, Adobe has strived to make Photoshop and Illustrator more and more compatible. One of the best features of that compatibility is the ability to export layered artwork from Illustrator to Photoshop while maintaining the layer structure created in Illustrator. This is an amazing feature and bravo! to Adobe for putting it in place. Once you've created layered artwork in Illustrator, this powerful option allows you to target those layers individually after the artwork has been exported to Photoshop. In other words, you maintain the same working relationship with the artwork from one application to the other.

FIGURE 4

Export dialog box

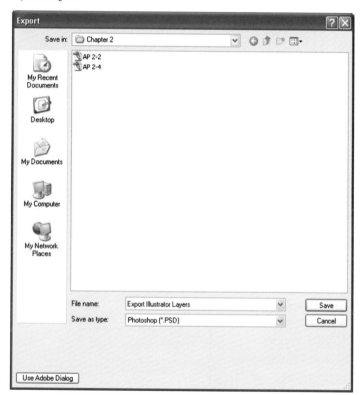

1. Open AP 2-3.ai in Adobe Illustrator, then save it as **Export Illustrator Layers**.

   TIP Click OK in the Illustrator Options dialog box.

2. Click the **Selection Tool** then pull the individual pieces of the illustration apart, keeping an eye on the Layers palette.

3. Click **File** on the menu bar, click **Revert,** then click **Revert** in the dialog box that follows.

4. Click **File** on the menu bar, then click **Export.**

5. Click the **Save as type list arrow** (Win) or the **Format list arrow** (Mac) in the Export dialog box, then click **Photoshop (*.PSD)** (Win) or Photoshop (psd) (Mac), as shown in Figure 4.

   TIP Note that the file to be exported is automatically named with the .psd extension: Export Illustrator Layers.psd.

6. Click **Save**.

   The Photoshop Export Options dialog box opens.

   (continued)

7. Click the **Color Model list arrow**, click **RGB**, if necessary, then click the **High (300 ppi) option button**.

It is important to understand that, with this export, you are creating a Photoshop file. The choices you made in this step determined the color model of the file—RGB—and the resolution of the file—300 ppi.

8. In the Options section, verify that the file is being exported as Photoshop CS2.

9. Click the **Write Layers option button**, click the **Maximum Editability check box**, then click the **Anti-alias check box** so that your dialog box resembles Figure 5.

With these choices, you have specified that you want to save or "write" the layers from the Illustrator file to the Photoshop file and that you want the artwork to be anti-aliased in the Photoshop file.

(continued)

FIGURE 5
Photoshop Export Options dialog box

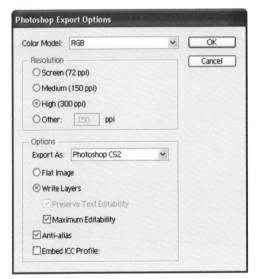

DESIGN*note*

It's a good idea to always choose the highest resolution for the exported file. In Photoshop, you can always reduce the resolution if you want to. Remember the first rule of changing resolution in Photoshop: It is always better, from an image quality standpoint, to reduce the resolution of a Photoshop file than it is to increase the resolution.

10. Click **OK**, then close the Illustrator document.

11. Open **Export Illustrator Layers.psd** in Photoshop.

12. Notice that the layers from Illustrator—including their layer names—were exported into the Photoshop Layers palette, as shown in Figure 6.

13. Close Export Illustrator Layers.

FIGURE 6

Illustrator artwork and layers exported to Photoshop

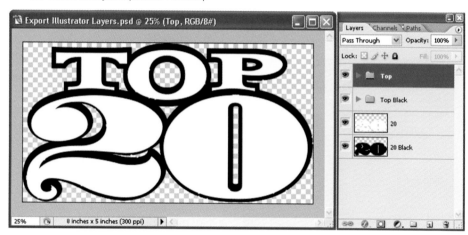

CREATE A CHISEL HARD
Emboss Layer Style

What You'll Do

Chisel Hard Emboss, the first of many layer styles you'll experiment and work with in this chapter, creates a dramatic, three-dimensional effect. A chisel is anything but a gentle tool, and this layer style delivers exactly what its name implies: A chiseled effect with a hard edge. Chisel Hard Emboss, a subset of the Bevel and Emboss layer style, is a very useful layer style, one that you will use often, especially when you want to create the effect of a hard metal edge.

DESIGN*note*

Take a few minutes here to examine the illustration—hide and show the layers to see how it was built. It's a fairly simple illustration—just four layers—a background layer, two foreground layers, and a text layer. The number 2 is a nicely designed path, and the 0 is charmingly fat. The way the word TOP interacts with the number 20 is a fine example of the nuanced path work that makes Illustrator such a great program. With all the layers showing, note that the background gray graphic plays the role of a stroke around all five shapes—as though each shape had a gray stroke of varying weight, and those strokes overlap. Clearly, this is artwork that you would want to create in Illustrator, not in Photoshop. Even though Photoshop does have a very sophisticated Pen Tool and vector capabilities, Illustrator is far and away the best application for creating line art. So consider this illustration as being sophisticated yet simple. Take a mental picture of it, because you are going to be amazed at what you can create in Photoshop from these sophisticated yet simple shapes imported from Illustrator.

Create a Chisel Hard Emboss layer style

1. Open AP 2-4.psd, then save it as **Top 20**.
2. Verify that you are viewing the document at 25%.
3. Hide the Text layer and the 20 layer, then target the **20 Back layer**.
4. Click **Layer** on the menu bar, point to **Layer Style**, then click **Bevel and Emboss**.
5. Verify that the Preview check box is checked, then move the dialog box so that you can see as much of the artwork as possible.

   TIP If you can't see much of the art, click Cancel, reduce the view of the art to 12.5%, then return to the Layer Style dialog box.

6. Verify that Style is set to Inner Bevel in the Structure section.
7. Click the **Technique list arrow**, then click **Chisel Hard**.
8. Drag the **Size slider** to 29, then experiment by dragging the slider to different values.

   When you choose Chisel Hard, the size has an enormous impact on the final effect. Note that the more you increase the value, the greater the edge becomes. Note too that the greater the edge becomes, the less "interior" you have to the artwork.

   (continued)

9. Return the **Size slider** to 29.

10. Type **42** in the Angle text box.

   The angle determines the angle that the light source strikes the artwork.

11. Experiment with various angle values, then return to **42**.

12. Click the **Gloss Contour list arrow**, then click **Ring** (the second thumbnail in the second row.

   Gloss contours are preset curves—just like the curves you use to color correct an image—that dramatically affect the contrast and the appearance of the layer effect. Explore the other contours, but be sure to return to Ring.

13. Click the **Anti-aliased check box**, and note the effect on the artwork.

14. For a dramatic effect, increase the contrast by dragging the **Highlight Mode Opacity slider** to 95%.

15. Click the **Contour check box** directly beneath the Bevel and Emboss check box in the Styles section on the left.

   Like a gloss contour, the Contour check box applies a preset curve.

16. Compare your Layer Style dialog box to Figure 7.

   (continued)

FIGURE 7
Bevel and Emboss settings in the Layer Style dialog box

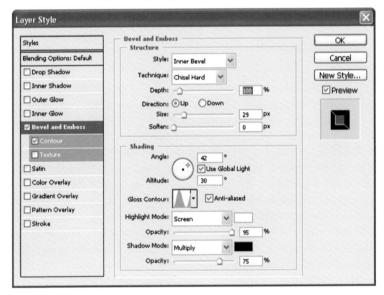

FIGURE 8

Effect of applying the Chisel Hard Inner Bevel layer style

*Aberration is a round
shiny circle which
should not be here*

17. Click **OK**, then compare your canvas to Figure 8.

    Note that an aberration has occurred between the *O* and the *P* in the word *TOP*. It's that round shiny circle, and it shouldn't be there.

18. Zoom in on the aberration, click the **Polygonal Lasso Tool** 🦋, draw a marquee around the circular aberration, then hide the Effects layer.

    A single pixel that is darker than the surrounding pixels caused the Bevel and Emboss layer style to create a Chisel Hard Emboss at this spot.

    | **TIP** You'll need to really zoom in to see the pixel.

19. Use the Eyedropper Tool 🖊 to sample the surrounding gray pixels, then fill the marquee with the sampled gray.

    (continued)

20. Return the view to 25%, then make the Effects layer visible again.

As shown in Figure 9, the aberration has disappeared because the dark pixel is no longer there. This is a fine example of how layer styles are dynamic. Changing the artwork changes the effect that the layer style has on the artwork.

21. Save your work.

FIGURE 9
The effect without the aberration

FIGURE 10
Identifying other aberrations

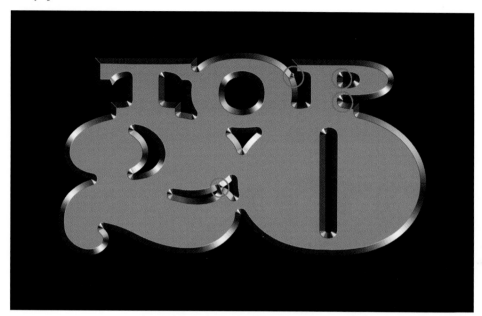

DESIGN*note*

Whenever you are working with layer styles, expect aberrations to occur. It's important that you understand that the dramatic effects that you create with layer styles are achieved by applying complex mathematical algorithms to the artwork. When artwork overlaps or when a stray pixel gets involved, strange results can occur. Figure 10 shows other, less obvious aberrations that resulted from using an Inner Bevel style with a Chisel Hard Emboss technique. Zoom in on them, and keep an eye on them as you progress through the chapter.

SELECT SPECIFIC AREAS OF
Layer-Styled Artwork

What You'll Do

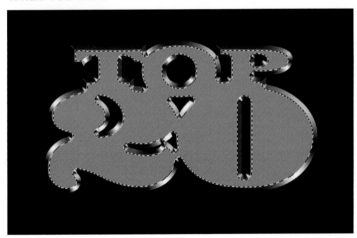

Fasten your seatbelts—we're going to hit the brakes! In this lesson we are going to select only the gray pixels that are inside the chiseled edge, as shown in the "What You'll Do" figure for Lesson 4. Sounds simple enough, right? As you will see, that simple goal is not so simple. This is going to be a tricky set of steps—a roadblock, if you will.

Roadblocks are part of the game, like it or not. Every designer encounters them, probably with every project. You're moving right along, everything's working, then boom! Something doesn't work the way you expect it to. The lesson of this lesson is to accept that roadblocks happen and that you just need to work your way around them by

trying different methods and experimenting. The bigger lesson of this lesson is that figuring your way around a roadblock often makes you a better designer: Not only do you learn new techniques, after a few successes, you find the confidence in yourself that somehow you'll always figure out a new way.

We are going to attempt to achieve the goal using various techniques, and many of them won't work. That's okay. The important thing is that, along the way, you will be exposed to a number of important concepts and useful techniques that involve menu commands, layer commands, quick keys, and channels. All of these will be great skills to learn and have in your arsenal, even though many of them won't work for this specific task.

FIGURE 11
Magic Wand Tool selection

FIGURE 12
Selected base art

Transform a selection marquee

1. Change the name of layer 20 Back to **Chisel Hard Emboss**.

2. Click the **Magic Wand Tool** ✎, set the **Tolerance value** to **0**, make sure that both the Anti-alias and the Contiguous check boxes are checked.

3. Verify that the Chisel Hard Emboss layer is targeted, click the **central gray area** on the artwork that is inside the chiseled edge.

   The selection that you get, shown in Figure 11, may not be what you expected. All of the artwork on the layer was selected, because all of the artwork on the layer is that same gray value.

4. Hide the Bevel and Emboss layer style in the Layers palette.

   All of the pixels were selected because they are all the same color, as shown in Figure 12. The Bevel and Emboss layer style makes it appear that there's a beveled edge, but that is just an illusion. The layer style changes the *appearance* of the base art, but it does not change the art itself. This is a very important concept for you to have in the back of your mind when you work with layer styles.

5. Show the Bevel and Emboss layer style in the Layers palette.

(continued)

6. Click **Select** on the menu bar, then click **Transform Selection**.

   A standard transform bounding box appears around the selection. Remember, the Transform Selection command allows you to transform the *selection marquee* itself. Usually, you transform the *pixels* that are selected by the selection marquee, but here you are transforming the marquee only.

7. Press and hold **[Shift]**, then drag any of the **corner handles** toward the center of the bounding box to reduce the size of the selection.

   As shown in Figure 13, you are able to reduce the selection, but no matter what you do, you won't be able to reduce it in a way that makes it select the gray areas only. Scaling the selection marquee won't work for an important reason: The outside edge of the beveled edge and the area you want to select are two different shapes.

8. Click the **Move Tool** 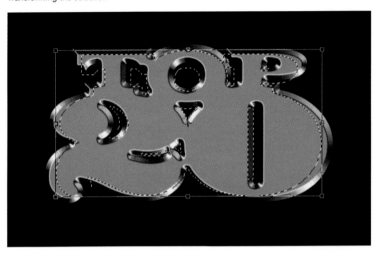, then click **Don't Apply**.

9. Keep the artwork selected.

Contract a selection marquee

1. Click **Select** on the menu bar, point to **Modify**, then click **Contract**.

2. Type **29**, then click **OK**.

   Because you specified the size of the chiseled edge as 29 pixels, you need to contract the selection by the same. As shown in Figure 14, this seems to have achieved the objective.

   (continued)

FIGURE 13
Transforming the selection

FIGURE 14
Contracted selection marquee

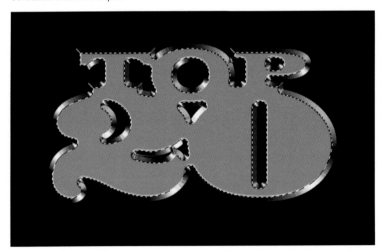

3. Change the foreground color to red, click the **Create a new layer button** 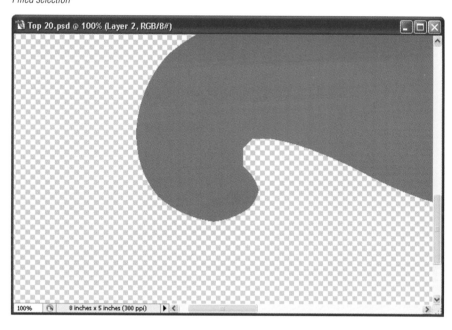 on the Layers palette, then fill the selection.

4. Deselect, hide the other layers, then zoom in to 100%.

On closer inspection, the edges are crudely drawn. This is especially visible on the curl at the base of the number 2, shown in Figure 15. This command was not able to contract the selection and also maintain the nuanced curves of the outer chiseled edge. The curves are poorly drawn—straight lines and pointy corners—and this will be noticeable in the final artwork.

(continued)

FIGURE 15
Filled selection

Top 20.psd @ 100% (Layer 2, RGB/8#)

100%   8 inches x 5 inches (300 ppi)

5. Show Layer 1, show the Chisel Hard Emboss layer, then examine how the red copy "sits" inside the gray area.

Figure 16 proves that the relationship is not satisfactory. The unsightly gaps and crude corners will be visible when the illustration is viewed or printed at 100%.

6. Zoom down to 25%, then delete the layer with the red graphic.

Create a channel to modify a selection

1. Target the **Chisel Hard Emboss layer**, click the **Magic Wand Tool** , then select the gray area again.

2. Click **Select** on the menu bar, then click **Save Selection**.

3. Name the selection **Stroke Trick**, then click **OK**.

(continued)

FIGURE 16
Examining the relationship between the filled selection and the background art

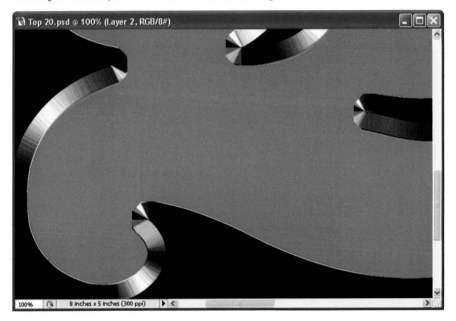

DESIGN*note*

Keep in mind, you are trying to create a powerful illustration here—one with a big WOW factor. As a designer, always remember that the bigger the WOW factor, the closer it will be examined by your audience. They're going to stop and look at it, appreciate it, critique it, and *look closely* to try to guess how you did it.

FIGURE 17
Saved selection in a channel

4. Click **Window** on the menu bar, click **Channels**, then click the **Stroke Trick channel**.

   When you save a selection, you create a channel. The channel *is* the selection. As shown in Figure 17, the selected areas are represented as white, and the unselected areas are represented by black. Note that the selection is still active.

5. Change the foreground color to Black.

6. Click **Edit** on the menu bar, then click **Stroke**.

   The default location setting for the stroke is Center, which means the stroke will be positioned equally on both sides of the selection marquee.

7. Type **58** in the Width text box.

   Your goal here is to reduce the selected areas (the white pixels in the channel) by making them black. You know that you want to reduce the selected area by 29 pixels. Since the stroke will be positioned equally on both sides of the marquee, you've doubled the width of the stroke to 58.

   TIP Though we could click Inside and set the Width value to 29, I hesitate to do so because I fear it would leave a slight white or gray line at the marquee line. In other words, it might not be perfect.

   (continued)

8. Click **OK**.

   With the black stroke, the white areas of channel are reduced by 29 pixels. Unfortunately, as shown in Figure 18, the result is similar if not identical to the result of contracting the selection marquee: unsightly rough corners.

9. Delete the Stroke Trick channel.

Duplicate a document

1. Verify that the Chisel Hard Emboss layer is targeted.

2. Click **Image** on the menu bar, then click **Duplicate**.

3. Type **Dupe** in the As text box, then click **OK**.

4. Click **Layer** on the menu bar, click **Flatten Image**, then click **OK** in the dialog box that follows to discard hidden layers.

5. Click the **Magic Wand Tool** , then click the **gray area**.

   Because the document is flattened, the Bevel and Emboss layer style is no longer on a layer. The Chisel Hard Emboss effect is no longer just an appearance. Thus, as shown in Figure 19, the Magic Wand Tool can make the selection that has been your goal all along.

6. Fill the selection with red.

7. Copy the selection, then close Dupe without saving changes.

   (continued)

FIGURE 18
Results of stroking the selection

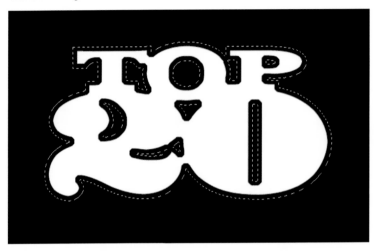

FIGURE 19
Selecting within the flattened artwork

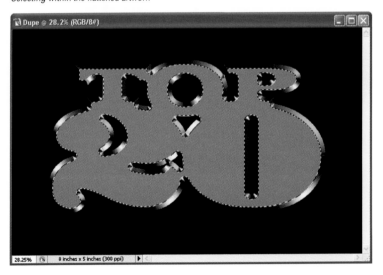

FIGURE 20
Filled selection

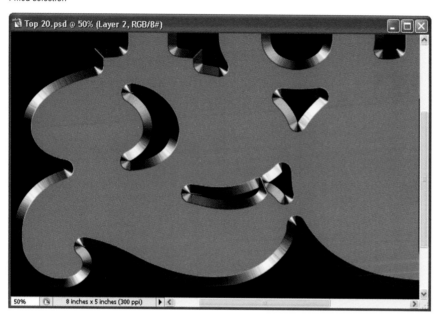

8. Paste the copied selection into the Top 20 document, then align it with the gray background area, if necessary.

   This method worked! As shown in Figure 20, the selection sits well against the embossed background without the poor edge quality that you saw with the previous methods that you tried.

9. Delete the new layer with the copied graphic.

   We will explore other methods of obtaining the selection, methods that do not require creating a duplicate file.

10. Save your work.

DESIGN*note*

It turns out that your first instinct—to use the Magic Wand Tool to make the selection—was indeed the correct choice. But you needed a flattened copy to do so. Creating a flattened duplicate is an old trick that designers use for getting around obstacles that occur when working with layers—get rid of the layers, get rid of the obstacles.

Create layers from layer styles

1. Hide Layer 1 so that only the Chisel Hard Emboss graphic is visible.

2. Target the **Chisel Hard Emboss layer**, if necessary.

3. Click **Layer** on the menu bar, point to **Layer Style**, then click **Create Layers**.

   The Create Layers command calculates the number of layer style(s) involved in the effect applied to the targeted layer, then creates layers that reproduce the effect—as many layers as necessary. In this case, two layers were created. As shown in Figure 21, both are clipped into the Chisel Hard Emboss layer.

4. Click **Window** on the menu bar, then click **History**, if necessary.

5. Click the **Create new snapshot button** 📷 on the History palette.

   As shown in Figure 22, a layer named Snapshot 1 appears at the top of the History palette.

(continued)

FIGURE 21
Results of applying the Create Layers command

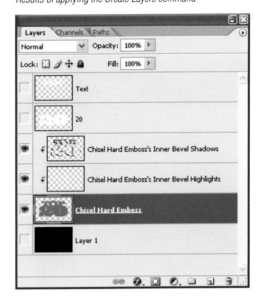

FIGURE 22
Creating a snapshot in the History palette

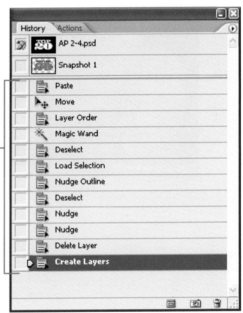

Your items may vary slightly

DESIGN*note*

You may find this hard to believe, but in the early days of Photoshop, there was only one Undo available. That's it. If you realized too late that you made a mistake, you had to use the Revert command. And heaven help you if you hadn't saved in a while. The History palette was truly a revolutionary addition to Photoshop. Make it a point to learn everything it has to offer. As you work, it logs your moves and, at any time you can click to return to that point. The palette lists only so many previous moves, however. This is why the Snapshot utility is so useful and important. At any stage of your work, take a snapshot and it's available in the palette for you to return to at any time.

FIGURE 23

Selection on merged art

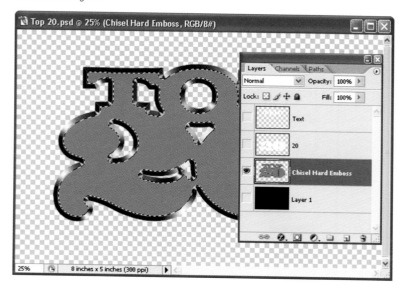

6. Examine the created layers, show the black background, then unclip the created layers to view them individually with or without the black background showing. Feel free to pull the document apart and move things around, hide show layers, and so on.

7. When you are done examining the new layers, click **Snapshot 1** in the History palette.

   The document is reverted to its status when you created Snapshot 1.

8. Click the **Layers palette list arrow**, then click **Merge Visible**.

   The visible layers are merged into a single layer.

9. Click the **Magic Wand Tool** on the gray area.

   As shown in Figure 23, the goal is achievable with this method.

10. Click **File** on the menu bar, then click **Revert**.

DESIGN*note*

The only problem with this method is that the Chisel Hard Emboss layer style can no longer be edited. When you work in Photoshop, you always want to leave yourself with as many options as possible. Yes, you could have first created a copy of the layer then applied the Create Layers command to the copy, but that would put you back to where you started in the last lesson—making dupes to achieve a goal. The Create Layers command can be very handy; however, for this task, it's not the best choice.

Use the Stamp Visible keyboard command

1. Verify that the Chisel Hard Emboss layer is targeted in the Layers palette and that the Bevel and Emboss layer style is showing.

2. Press **[Shift][Alt][Ctrl][N]** (Win) or **[Shift][option]** ⌘ **[N]** (Mac).

   As shown in Figure 24, this keyboard sequence creates a new empty layer above the layer that was targeted. The new layer is automatically targeted.

   (continued)

FIGURE 24
Creating a new layer

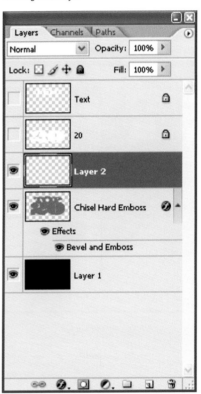

FIGURE 25

Using the Stamp Visible command

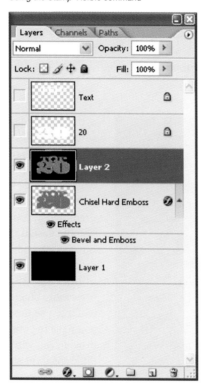

3. Press **[Shift][Alt][Ctrl][E]** (Win) or **[Shift][option]** ⌘ **[E]** (Mac).

   This keyboard sequence is called Stamp Visible. As shown in Figure 25, it takes a picture of the document in its current visible state, then replaces what's in the targeted layer with the picture. You have created a merged copy without merging the Chisel Hard Emboss layer style.

4. Click the **Magic Wand Tool** , then click the gray area in the new layer.

5. Click **Select** on the menu bar, then click **Inverse**.

6. Delete the selected pixels.

7. Save your work.

CREATE A SMOOTH
Emboss Layer Style

What You'll Do

In the early days of computer graphics, naysayers dismissed computer-generated art as automated and monotonous. Their idea was that you take some artwork, run a filter, and what you get is what you get. Of course, that is an extremely limited view of computer graphics. What it overlooks is that computer graphic design is not about "running a filter"—anybody can do that. Computer graphic design is about knowing all the utilities that you have at your disposal and, even more challenging, knowing how and when to use those tools to create an image that you have in your imagination. This lesson will provide you with a great example of using two different layer styles—each from the same dialog box—and making them work together in a way that they improve upon each other.

FIGURE 26

Settings for the Smooth Emboss

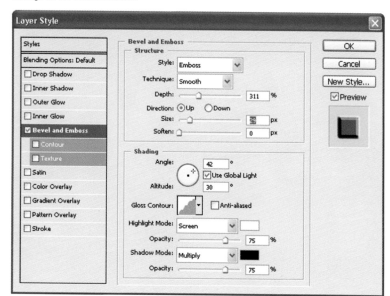

1. Rename Layer 2 **Smooth Emboss**, then verify that nothing is selected.

2. Click **Layer** on the menu bar, point to **Layer Style**, then click **Bevel and Emboss**.

3. Set the Style to **Emboss**, set the Technique to **Smooth**, then set the Depth to **311**.

4. Drag the **Size slider** to 29.

5. Click the **Gloss Contour list arrow**, then click **Rounded Steps**, the fifth icon in the second row.

6. Compare your Layer Style dialog box to Figure 26, then click **OK**.

(continued)

7. Hide the Chisel Hard Emboss layer so that you can see the Smooth Emboss layer on its own.

As shown in Figure 27, the Smooth Emboss effect is dramatically different than the Chisel Hard Emboss effect. Both feature a beveled edge, but where the Chisel Hard Emboss features a hard, shiny edge, the Smooth Emboss presents a much softer edge—thus the term Smooth Emboss. Note too the subtle "ghost" at the edges that adds nuance to the effect and also increases the sense of three-dimensionality.

(continued)

FIGURE 27
Smooth Emboss effect

8. Show the Chisel Hard Emboss layer, then hide and show the Smooth Emboss layer.

9. Show both embossed layers, then compare your canvas to Figure 28.

FIGURE 28

Viewing the relationship between the two layer styles

DESIGN*note*

Note how the interaction of the two Bevel and Emboss layer styles work so well together. Note how they complement each other, and how the Smooth Emboss sits neatly "inside" the Chisel Hard Emboss effect. Note that all you really see of the Chisel Hard Emboss layer is its hard shiny edge. Finally, with the Smooth Emboss layer visible, note how the two layer styles work together to create a visually complex and interesting graphic.

CREATE AND APPLY A
Gradient Overlay to a Layer Style

What You'll Do

In most illustrations in which gradients are utilized, the gradient is often an element that calls attention to itself. By its very nature, it has movement—the shift from one color to another—and that movement is often noticeable. In this lesson, you're going to use a Gradient Overlay for a very subtle effect: to enrich the Smooth Emboss you created in the previous lesson. You'll see how the Gradient Overlay adds complexity to the layer style effect and how it contributes to the metallic effects that are the key to this illustration. But there's a little twist. As you go through the later lessons in this chapter, you'll see that the Gradient Overlay will be covered mostly by other elements. In the final version of the illustration, it will be interesting for you to note the very subtle role that this Gradient Overlay ultimately plays.

FIGURE 29
Default gradient

1. Click the small triangle at the far right of the Smooth Emboss layer in the Layers palette.

   The layer expands to reveal the layer effects for the Smooth Emboss layer.

2. Double-click the **Effects sublayer** in the Smooth Emboss layer group.

3. Click **Gradient Overlay** in the Styles section to highlight it.

   As shown in Figure 29, a default black-and-white gradient is applied to the Smooth Emboss layer style. Note its effect on the Smooth Emboss.

4. Double-click the **black-and-white gradient** in the Gradient section.

5. Double-click the **far-left color stop** to open the Color Picker, type **41** in the R, G, and B text boxes, then click **OK**.

6. Double-click the **far-right color stop**, type **140** in the R, G, and B text boxes, then click **OK**.

7. Click the **gradient ramp** anywhere between the two color stops to add a third color stop.

8. Drag the **new color stop** left until the location text box value is 20.

(continued)

DESIGN*note*

In the RGB color space, a neutral gray color is created any time the three values are the same. The lower the value, the darker the gray, with 0, 0, and 0 being black. The higher the value, the lighter the gray, with 255, 255, and 255 being white.

9. Double-click the **new color stop**, type **150** in the R, G, and B text boxes, then click **OK**.

10. Click to the right of the new color stop to add a fourth, then drag it until the Location text box value is 43.

11. Double-click the **new color stop**, type **36** in the R, G, and B text boxes, then click **OK**.

12. Click to the right of the new color stop to add a fifth, then drag it until the Location text box value is 63.

13. Double-click the **new color stop**, type **176** in the R text box, **164** in the G and B text boxes, then click **OK**.

    This color stop has a slightly pink color cast.

14. Click to the right of the new color stop to add a sixth, then drag it until the Location text box value is 81.

    Your Gradient Editor dialog box should resemble Figure 30.

15. Double-click the **new color stop**, type **14** in the R, G, and B text boxes, then click **OK**.

16. Click **New**.

    The new gradient appears as a thumbnail in the Presets section, with the name Custom.

    (continued)

(continued)

FIGURE 30
Specifications for the gradient

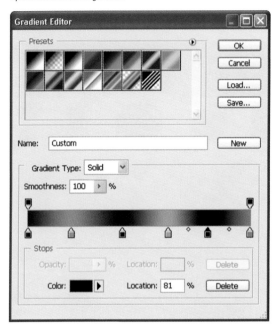

DESIGN*note*

Note how you avoided making the gradient too uniform. The color stops are not evenly spaced along the gradient ramp. The darker stops are not all the same color—none are pure black; they're various dark grays. The lighter stops are not uniform in color either, and one of them has a pink color cast.

FIGURE 31
New gradient layer style

FIGURE 32
Finished gradient layer style

17. Double-click the **Custom gradient**, type **Smooth Emboss Overlay** in the Name section, click **OK**, then click **OK** to close the Gradient Editor dialog box.

The new gradient appears in the Gradient section and is applied to the Smooth Emboss layer style.

18. Click **OK** to close the Layer Style dialog box, then compare your artwork to Figure 31.

A new sublayer named Gradient Overlay appears beneath Bevel and Emboss in the Smooth Emboss layer group. The colors of the gradient are good for the illustration, and the quick transitions from light to dark enhance the metallic feel, and the slightly pink highlight is unexpected and intriguing. Note, however, that the gradient is positioned at a 90° angle—from left to right—and that makes it obvious and a bit trite.

19. Double-click the **Gradient Overlay sublayer** to edit it in the Layer Style dialog box.

20. Type **51** in the Angle text box.

21. Experiment with the Scale slider.

22. Drag the **Scale slider** to **92**, click **OK,** then compare your artwork to Figure 32.

The often-overlooked Scale slider reduces or enlarges the Gradient Overlay within the layer style and can be useful for positioning the gradient in a way that is just right for the illustration.

CREATE A PILLOW EMBOSS
Layer Style

What You'll Do

This lesson demonstrates how exporting layers from Illustrator really pays off. You're going to apply yet another layer style, but this time, you are going to apply it to a new piece of artwork. You will apply a layer style to a foreground component created for this layered illustration—a different component to the background component that you've been working with so far. Keep an eye out for how the layer style adds an entirely new dimension to the illustration, and keep in mind that the basis for the effect was the foreground and background components from Illustrator.

FIGURE 33

Settings for the Pillow Emboss effect

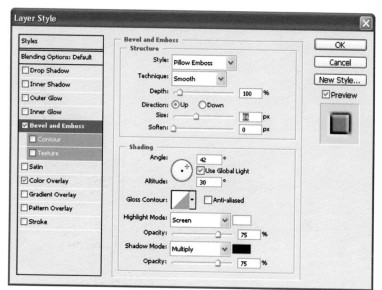

Create a Pillow Emboss layer style

1. Show the layer named **20**, then change its name to **Pillow Emboss**.

2. Click **Layer** on the menu bar, point to **Layer Style**, then click **Color Overlay**.

3. Click the **red swatch** to open the Color Picker, type **132** in the R, G, and B text boxes, then click **OK**.

4. Click **Bevel and Emboss** in the Styles section.

5. Click the **Style list arrow**, then click **Pillow Emboss**.

6. Verify that the Technique is set to Smooth and that the Depth is set to 100%.

7. Experiment with the Size slider to get a good sense of the Pillow Emboss effect.

8. Drag the **Size slider** to 84, then compare your dialog box to Figure 33.

(continued)

DESIGN*note*

When using bevel and emboss effects, create your basic artwork using a midrange tone—not too dark, not too light. Bevel and emboss effects are created by applying a dramatic highlight on one angle of the artwork and a dramatic shadow on the opposite angle. If the base art is very bright, the highlight is less apparent. If it is very dark, the shadow may get lost or lose its power. So if you can choose some base art that is largely middle tones, the highlight and shadow will be very noticeable.

Lesson 7   Create a Pillow Emboss Layer Style

9. Click **OK**, then compare your artwork to Figure 34.

10. Expand the Pillow Emboss layer to reveal the layer effects, then hide and show the Bevel and Emboss layer effect to see the effect.

Note that the Pillow Emboss layer style, in addition to embossing the basic artwork, also creates a soft highlight glow and a shadow glow. The highlight glow is immediately apparent—it is offset from the base artwork at a southwest angle. The shadow glow is more subtle; it is offset on a northeast direction, the opposite direction from the highlight glow.

(continued)

FIGURE 34
Results of the Pillow Emboss effect

DESIGN*note*

Note that the glows extend *beyond* the basic artwork. Give this a few second's thought because it's an important feature of this layer style: The layer style is creating an effect that *exceeds* the boundaries of the base art. This means that the layer style is not just stylizing base art, it is creating *new* art that adds nuance and complexity to the illustration.

11. Hide the Smooth Emboss and Chisel Hard Emboss layers to see the Pillow Emboss effect against the black background, then compare your canvas to Figure 35.

12. Show the Smooth Emboss and Chisel Hard Emboss layers, then save your work.

FIGURE 35
Viewing the Pillow Emboss layer style only

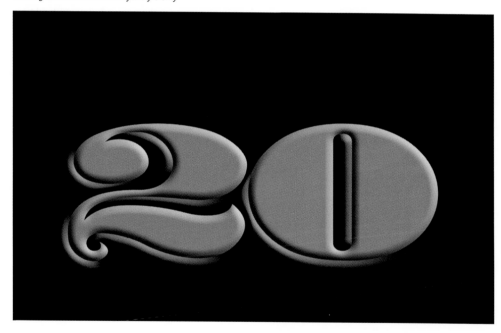

COPY LAYER STYLES
Between Layers

What You'll Do

Does this lesson title seem familiar? It should. It's the same name of a lesson from Chapter 1, the lesson when you moved the drop shadow from the HAWAII text to the Aloha text. Most of the steps in this lesson ask you to make similar moves. Why do it again, you ask? Because a fundamental part of working with layers involves duplicating layers and layer styles and duplicating layer styles and adjustment layers between layers. You are going to do it over and over and over again. In this lesson, the layer styles you're copying are more complex than a simple drop shadow. When you copy a layer style, you may need to click the black triangle next to the Indicates layer effects icon on a particular layer to view the applied layer styles. This triangle is called the Reveals layer effects in the palette button.

FIGURE 36

Illustration with the top text embossed

DESIGN*note*

Hiding and showing these two layers yields some interesting insights into the workings of this illustration. At this stage of construction, it is clear that the Chisel Hard and Smooth Emboss styles are the support structure for the illustration—they are in the background. The Chisel Hard Emboss remains a very important and visible element, but only at the edge of the illustration. The chiseled edge is obscured only by the white glow on the number 2. It's also interesting to note what gets hidden by the foreground art. Note how little of the Chisel Hard Emboss layer shows, yet notice how important what *does* show is to the effect. Same with the Smooth Emboss layer. Remarkably little of it shows. Turn it off and on, and note the role it plays. Note too the Gradient Overlay and its small but important effect.

Copy layer styles between layers

1. Show the Text layer, change its name to **Text Pillow**, then save your work.

2. Press and hold **[Alt]** (Win) or **[option]** (Mac), then drag the **Color Overlay layer style** in the Pillow Emboss layer group up until a black rectangle appears inside the Text Pillow layer.

   A copy of the Color Overlay layer style is applied to the Text Pillow layer.

3. Using the same method, copy the **Bevel and Emboss layer style** from the Pillow Emboss layer to the Text Pillow layer.

   The Bevel and Emboss layer style is copied and listed along with the Color Overlay layer style.

4. Revert the file.

5. Press and hold **[Alt]** (Win) or **[option]** (Mac) then drag the **Effects sublayer** in the Pillow Emboss layer group to the base of the Text Pillow layer.

   Dragging the Effects sublayer copies all the layer styles to the new destination.

6. Double-click the **Bevel and Emboss layer style** in the Text Pillow layer.

   TIP The Size setting on the Pillow Emboss layer style that you copied is too large for the Text Pillow artwork.

7. Drag the **Size slider** to 34, click **OK**, then compare your artwork to Figure 36.

8. Hide and show the Text Pillow and the Pillow Emboss layers, then save your work.

CREATE A CHROME EFFECT
Without Using Layer Styles

What You'll Do

They say that you can't teach an old dog new tricks. That may be true. But remember, it is often the case that the old dog remembers the old tricks that the new dog was never around to have seen in the first place. In so many ways, that is true of

Photoshop. With each upgrade, Photoshop has become so much more sophisticated. It has been designed to anticipate effects that designers want, like embosses, bevels, overlays and contour effects, and it provides settings and sliders that are preset to deliver

the goods. That makes for a great application, one in which you can create spectacular effects quickly and easily.

But if you've been around long enough, you remember the days when there were no layer styles. Heck, you remember when there were no layers! Back then, the effects that you wanted to create didn't come prepackaged with the software. You had to figure out how to create effects by combining such basic utilities as filters, selections, channels, and curves. The result is that you had to think harder and work longer. And some of the effects that you could create the old-fashioned way are so complex and unique that no dialog box could possibly duplicate them. That's the case with the chrome effect you will create in this lesson. It's an old recipe, handed down and traded around for years. So if you're a new dog, follow along while this old dog teaches you an old trick.

FIGURE 37

Preparing the artwork for the Emboss filter

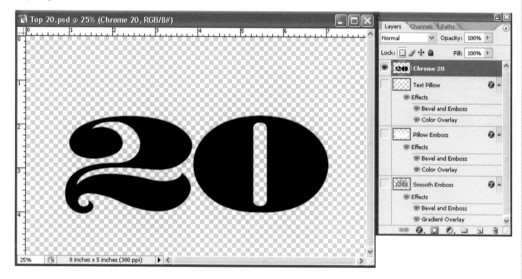

1. Target the **Pillow Emboss layer**, then drag it to the Create a new layer button on the Layers palette.

   The Pillow Emboss layer is duplicated.

2. Change the name of the duplicate layer to **Chrome 20**, then drag the **layer** to the top of the Layers palette.

3. Delete all the layer styles from the Chrome 20 layer, press **[D]** to access default colors in the toolbox, then click the **Lock transparent pixels button** on the Layers palette.

4. Fill the artwork with Black, then click the **Lock transparent pixels button** again to deactivate it.

5. Hide all the other layers, then compare your canvas to Figure 37.

6. Press and hold **[Ctrl]** (Win) or [⌘] (Mac), then click the **Layer thumbnail** on the Chrome 20 layer to load a selection of the artwork.

(continued)

DESIGNnote

Note that the white highlights have intensified at the bottom of the number 20. This is because the Bevel and Emboss layer style was doubled. Duplicating a layer duplicates its layer styles *and the visual effects* of its layer styles. Therefore, duplicating a layer is a simple and smart way to intensify or otherwise modify the effects of a given set of layer styles.

7. Click **Select** on the menu bar, click **Save Selection**, then type **Original 20** in the Name text box, as shown in Figure 38.

   Note that New is listed in the Channel text box.

8. Click **OK**, make the Channels palette visible, then compare your Channels palette to Figure 39.

   Saved selections are always saved in the Channels palette as new channels.

   (continued)

FIGURE 38

Naming the selection to be saved

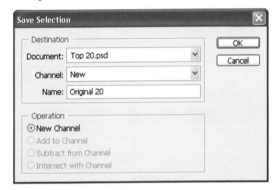

FIGURE 39

New channel in the Channels palette

FIGURE 40
Selection saved as a channel

FIGURE 41
Choosing a light gray swatch in the Color palette

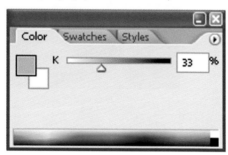

9. Click the **Original 20 channel** in the Channels palette, then compare your screen to Figure 40.

   The white areas of the channel represent the pixels that were selected when the selection was saved; conversely, the black areas represent those that were not selected.

10. Save your work.

Use the Emboss filter

1. Verify that the Chrome 20 layer is targeted and the artwork is still selected.

2. Click **Select** on the menu bar, then click **Feather**.

3. Type **18** in the Feather Radius text box, then click **OK**.

4. Display the Color palette, click the **Color palette list arrow**, then click **Grayscale Slider**.

5. Drag the **slider** to 33%, so that the foreground color is a light gray as shown in Figure 41.

6. Click **Edit** on the menu bar, then click **Stroke**.

(continued)

7. Click the **Inside option button**, type **24** in the Width text box, click **OK**, then compare your work to Figure 42.

8. Click **Select** on the menu bar, then click **Load Selection**.

9. In the Load Selection dialog box, click the **Channel list arrow**, click **Original 20**, then click **OK**.

   The original selection replaces the feathered selection.

10. Click **Filter** on the menu bar, point to **Stylize**, then click **Emboss**.

11. Type **135** in the Angle text box, type **13** in the Height text box, type **160** in the Amount text box, then click **OK**.

12. Deselect all, make **Layer 1** visible, then compare your artwork to Figure 43.

(continued)

FIGURE 42
Viewing the stroke

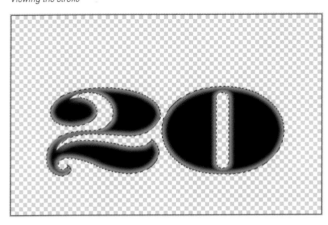

FIGURE 43
Result of the Emboss filter

DESIGN*note*

With this old-fashioned way of embossing, the stroke plays a major role in the final effect. Keep an eye on this gray stroke throughout this lesson.

FIGURE 44
Viewing the artwork

FIGURE 45
Curves dialog box

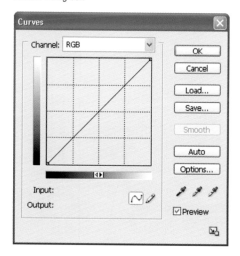

13. Show all the layers, then compare your artwork to Figure 44.

Apply a Curves adjustment layer

1. Verify that the **Chrome 20 layer** is targeted.

2. Click **Layer** on the menu bar, point to **New Adjustment Layer**, then click **Curves**.

3. Type **Emboss Curves** in the Name text box, click the **Use Previous Layer to Create Clipping Mask check box**, then click **OK**.

   The Curves dialog box opens. Compare your curves dialog box to Figure 45. Verify that the Channel menu at the top of the dialog box reads RGB.

   TIP Verify that the Preview check box is checked, and move your dialog box so that you can see as much of the artwork as possible.

(continued)

4. Drag the **black handle** at the lower-left corner straight up to the upper-left corner, so that your dialog box resembles Figure 46.

   Note the input/output values at the bottom of the dialog box. The value of the black handle that you moved was originally 0 (black). Now it is 255 (white). Every (imaginary) point on the horizontal line between the two points is at the top of the dialog box. This means that all the points on the line have a value of 255—they are all white.

5. Position your cursor over the horizontal line so that a + sign appears, then moving left to right, click to add three new points, as shown in Figure 47.

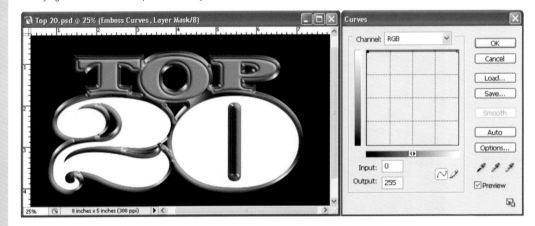

FIGURE 46
Modifying the curve to make all pixels on the layer white

FIGURE 47
Adding points to the curve

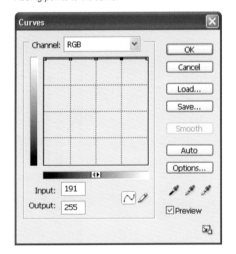

DESIGN*note*

As an introduction, the basic concept you need to understand about the Curves dialog box is that the black handle at the lower-left corner represents all the black (0) pixels in the targeted layer. The black handle at the upper-right corner represents all the white (255) pixels in the layer. The diagonal line represents all the other pixels in the layer that fall within the range of 0–255.

FIGURE 48

Changing the location of the second point on the curve

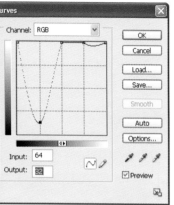

FIGURE 49

Changing the location of the fourth point

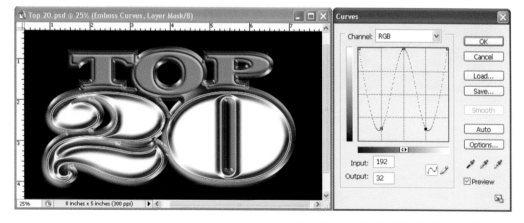

Modify curves to create a chrome effect

1. Drag the **second point** down to the position shown in Figure 48.

   TIP After you select a point, you can simply enter the input/output values shown in Figure 48 to reposition it.

2. Drag the **fourth point** down to the position shown in Figure 49.

3. Relocate the far-right point to different locations and note how the chrome effect becomes more intense.

   (continued)

DESIGN*note*

Using Curves after applying the Emboss filter, you create a chrome effect by twisting the curve roughly into the shape of the letter W. With this move, all of the pixels that had the value of 64 in the embossed artwork have been darkened to a value of 32.

4. Position the far-right point as shown in Figure 50.

5. Click **Save**.

6. Save the curves as **Chrome.acv**.

7. Click **OK**, then compare your work to Figure 51.

   Note that the Emboss Curves adjustment layer is the targeted layer in the Layers palette.

   | **TIP** When you apply an adjustment layer to a targeted layer, the adjustment layer is automatically targeted when you execute the adjustment.

8. Undo and redo the curves modification.

(continued)

FIGURE 50
Repositioning the rightmost point

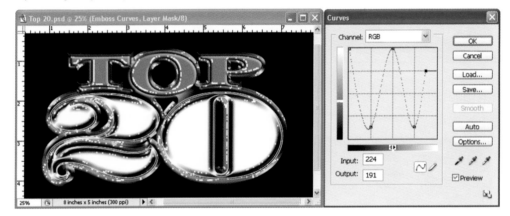

DESIGN*note*

All of the pixels that had the value of 192 in the embossed artwork—relatively very light pixels—have been darkened dramatically to a value of 32.

FIGURE 51
Result of the Curves modifications

9. Target the **Chrome 20 layer** in the Layers palette, then load the Original 20 selection that you saved.

10. Click **Select** on the menu bar, point to **Modify**, then click **Contract**.

11. Type **7** in the Contract By text box, then click **OK**.

12. Click **Select** on the menu bar, click **Feather**, type **3** in the Feather Radius text box, then click **OK**.

(continued)

DESIGNnote

The curves modification achieves a great effect. The only problem is that very harsh highlights can be seen at the edges of the artwork. Zoom in on them to get an idea of why they're creating an unappealing effect.

13. Click **Select** on the menu bar, then click **Inverse**.

14. Delete the selected pixels, then deselect all.

15. Compare your artwork to Figure 52.

16. Hide and show the Chrome 20 layer to see its relationship with the Pillow Emboss effect beneath it.

Because the Chrome 20 artwork is directly above the Pillow Emboss effect, it pretty much obscures the entire effect.

(continued)

FIGURE 52
Artwork after removing unwanted edge effects

17. Click the **Move Tool** , then move the Chrome 20 artwork straight up 11 pixels.

18. Compare your artwork to Figure 53, then save your work.

FIGURE 53
Offsetting the Chrome 20 layer

DESIGN*note*

Before moving on, take some time to analyze the role of the Pillow Emboss effect in the artwork. By moving the Chrome 20 artwork straight up, the Pillow Emboss artwork became visible. Turn the Pillow Emboss layer on and off to see its contribution to the illustration. Though only its edge shows, it nevertheless plays an important role in adding depth and complexity to the illustration.

DUPLICATE A CHROME EFFECT
Without Using Layer Styles

What You'll Do

In the last chapter, you created a chrome effect using a Curves adjustment layer rather than the Bevel and Emboss layer style. When you created that adjustment layer, you saved the curves data as a .crv file. In this lesson, you want to apply that same curve data to the text at the top of the illustration. As with layer styles, you can duplicate adjustment layers and apply the duplicate to a different layer. In this lesson, however, you're going to use a different method—an older method, one that has been available since the earliest versions of Photoshop. Rather than duplicate the adjustment layer, you will load the curve data that you saved in the previous lesson.

FIGURE 54

Applying a feathered stroke to the artwork

1. Duplicate the Text Pillow layer then change its name to **Chrome Text**.

2. Delete the effects, then fill the artwork with black.

   After filling the text with black, verify that the Lock transparent pixels button is not activated.

3. Press and hold **[Ctrl]** (Win) or ⌘ (Mac), then click the **Layer thumbnail** on the Chrome Text layer to load a selection of the artwork.

4. Save the selection as **Original Text**.

5. Click **Select** on the menu bar, then click **Feather**.

6. Type **9** in the Feather Radius text box, then click **OK**.

7. Click the **Color palette list arrow**, then verify that the Grayscale Slider is checked.

8. Drag the **slider** to 30%.

9. Click **Edit** on the menu bar, then click **Stroke**.

10. Choose the **Inside option button**, type **12** in the Width text box, then click **OK**.

11. Deselect, then compare your artwork to Figure 54.

12. Load the Original Text selection.

13. Click **Filter** on the menu bar, point to **Stylize**, then click **Emboss**.

(continued)

14. Type **135** in the Angle text box, type **6** in the Height text box, then type **160** in the Amount text box.

15. Click **OK**, then deselect all.

Your artwork should resemble Figure 55.

16. Save your work.

Load saved curves

1. Click **Layer** on the menu bar, point to **New Adjustment Layer**, then click **Curves**.

2. Type **Emboss Curves** in the Name text box, click the **Use Previous Layer to Create Clipping Mask check box**, then click **OK**.

The Curves dialog box opens.

3. Click **Load**, click **Chrome.acv**, then click **Load**.

4. Click **OK** to close the Curves dialog box.

5. Target the **Chrome Text layer** in the Layers palette, then load the Original Text selection.

6. Zoom in on the letter **T** so that you are viewing it at 100%.

7. Click **Select** on the menu bar, point to **Modify**, then click **Contract**.

8. Type **4** in the Contract By text box, then click **OK**.

9. Click **Select** on the menu bar, click **Feather**, type **3** in the Feather Radius text box, then click **OK**.

(continued)

FIGURE 55
Applying the Emboss filter to the artwork

FIGURE 56
Final artwork

10. Click **Select** on the menu bar, then click **Inverse**.

11. Press **[Delete]** (Win) or **[delete]** (Mac) two times.

12. Deselect, then zoom out so that you are viewing the artwork at 25%.

13. Click the **Move Tool** ⊹, then move the artwork straight up 10 pixels.

> **TIP** Pressing and holding [Shift] then pressing an arrow key moves a selection 10 pixels in the direction of the arrow you pressed.

14. Hide rulers, if necessary.

15. Click the **Full Screen Mode button** ⬚ on the toolbox.

    Your canvas is positioned within a black screen.

    > **TIP** Press [F] on your keypad to switch between the three screen modes.

16. Press **[Tab]** to hide all palettes

17. Compare your artwork to Figure 56.

18. Save your work, then close Top 20.psd.

DESIGN*note*

When you apply a feather to a selection then delete the selected pixels, remember that the pixels at the edge of the selection are not deleted entirely—because of the feather. Sometimes, as in this case, deleting twice is a good move. When working with a larger selection and a higher feather value, you might want to delete three times.

1. Open AP 2-5.psd, then save it as **Pink Lady**.
2. Create a new layer above the Background layer, then name it **Back Tray**.
3. Press and hold [Ctrl] (Win) or ⌘ (Mac), then click the Layer thumbnail to load the selection of the Lady layer.
4. Press and hold [Shift] [Ctrl] (Win) or [Shift] ⌘ (Mac), then click the Layer thumbnail to load and add the selection of the Luck layer so that you have a selection of both layers.
5. Target the Back Tray layer.
6. Click Select on the menu bar, point to Modify, then click Expand.
7. Type **18** in the Expand By dialog box, then click OK.
8. Click Edit on the menu bar, then click Fill.
9. Click the Use list arrow, choose 50% Gray, verify that the Opacity is set to 100%, then click OK.
10. Deselect all.
11. Click Layer on the menu bar, point to Layer Style, then click Bevel and Emboss.
12. Set the Style to Inner Bevel, set the Technique to Chisel Hard, set the Depth to 100, then set the Size to 10 pixels.

13. Click the Use Global Light check box, then set the Angle to 120.
14. Change the Gloss Contour to Gaussian, verify that the Anti-aliased check box is not checked, then click OK.
15. Target the Lady layer, then add a Bevel and Emboss layer style.
16. Set the Style to Pillow Emboss, set the Technique to Smooth, set the Depth to 100, then set the Size to 29 pixels.
17. Verify that the Use Global Light check box is checked, that the Angle is set to 120, then click OK.
18. Target the Luck layer, then add a Bevel and Emboss layer style.
19. Set the Style to Pillow Emboss, set the Technique to Chisel Hard, set the Depth to 100, then set the Size to 10 pixels.
20. Verify that the Use Global Light check box is checked and that the Angle is set to 120.
21. Set the Gloss Contour to Cove-Deep, then click OK.
22. Compare your artwork to Figure 57, save your work, then close Pink Lady.

FIGURE 57
Completed Project Builder 1

1. Open AP 2-6.psd, then save it as **Luck Be A Lady**. (*Hint*: The typeface is one of my favorites: Bellevue.)
2. Target the Pink layer, then add a Bevel and Emboss layer style.
3. Set the Style to Inner Bevel, set the Technique to Chisel Hard, set the Depth to 100, then set the Size to 32 pixels.
4. Verify that the Use Global Light check box is checked and that the Angle is set to 120.
5. Set the Gloss Contour to Ring.
6. Drag the Shadow Mode Opacity slider to 50%, then click OK.
7. Target the Black layer, then add a Bevel and Emboss layer style.
8. Set the Style to Outer Bevel, set the Technique to Chisel Hard, set the Depth to 161, then set the Size to 10 pixels.
9. Verify that the Use Global Light check box is checked and that the Angle is set to 120.
10. Click OK, then compare your artwork to Figure 58.
11. Save your work, then close Luck Be A Lady.

FIGURE 58
Completed Project Builder 2

3

ADJUSTING
Images

1. Analyze a grayscale image.

2. Use the tolerance-based tools.

3. Work with hue, saturation, and brightness in the Color Picker window.

4. Explore the Hue/Saturation dialog box.

5. Adjust hue, saturation, and lightness.

ANALYZE A
Grayscale Image

What You'll Do

Photoshop captures the imagination like no other application before or since. Even people who don't know what Photoshop is are thoroughly fascinated when it's demonstrated. Listen and you'll hear them say things like, "Did you see that? She took a picture of a man and gave him three eyes!"

As a graphic arts professional, you know that the man doesn't have three eyes. You know that it's just a bunch of pixels that are small enough and colored the right way to create the illusion of a man with three eyes. As a designer, its part of your job to demystify Photoshop, to get past the WOW factor and try to gain some intellectual understanding of what the program is and how it does what it does.

But face it, you are not programmers. In many areas, Photoshop is so wildly complex that you must accept the fact that you can't even imagine how it does some things that it does.

This chapter is about demystifying Photoshop at its most basic level: the pixel. In Photoshop, everything you do can be reduced to two basic actions: changing the color of pixels or changing the location of pixels. It's a rather stunning statement if you think about it for a few seconds. Everything that this powerful and vast and complex and magical piece of software does all comes down to these two actions.

In this chapter, you're going to focus on the color of pixels and how to adjust that color. You're also going to focus on what it means to adjust the color of a pixel, and how a pixel gets its color in the first place.

As a designer, you must never fully surrender your own personal WOW factor—it's what drew you to Photoshop in the first place. But you must see through the illusion to gain an understanding of the reality behind the illusion. It's not three eyes—it's just pixels.

So yes, when you emerge from this chapter, you may be a bit disillusioned. But guess what? Your WOW factor is going to

get bigger. Because when you begin to understand how Photoshop does what it does, only then do you begin to understand how amazing an application it truly is.

Sample the pixels in a grayscale image

1. Open AP 3-1.psd, click **File** on the menu bar, then click **Save As**.

2. Type **Levels of Gray** in the File name text box (Win) or Save As text box (Mac), verify that Photoshop (*.PSD; *.PDD) shows in the Format text box, then click **Save**.

3. Click **Image** on the menu bar, point to **Mode**, note that Grayscale is checked, then release.

   This image is in Grayscale mode.

4. Click **Window** on the menu bar, then click **Info** to show the Info palette.

5. Close other palettes that may be open so that you are only using the Info palette and the toolbox.

6. Click the **Info palette list arrow**, then click **Palette Options**.

7. Click the **Mode list arrow** for the First Color Readout, then click **RGB Color**.

8. Click the **Mode list arrow** for the Second Color Readout, click **HSB Color**, then click **OK** so that your Info palette resembles Figure 1.

   | **TIP**   Clicking the eyedroppers is another way to choose the desired color mode.

9. Zoom in the image to 1600%, then scroll around with the **Hand Tool** 🖐 .

   (continued)

FIGURE 1
Info palette

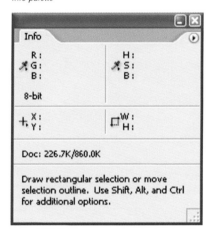

FIGURE 2
Sampling pixels

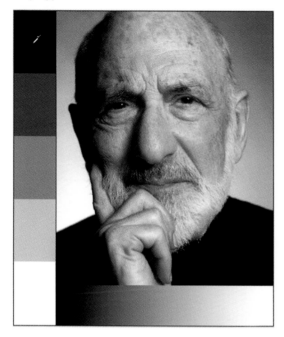

10. Click the **Eyedropper Tool** in the toolbox, then float it over the pixels.

    As you move the eyedropper, the Info palette displays the values of the pixels in the RGB and HSB modes simultaneously.

11. Position the pointer over a single pixel, then note its grayscale value in the Info palette.

    Terms such as grayscale and levels of gray have been bandied about for many years, and it seems that everyone uses them in a slightly different way. Here's what you need to know: In a grayscale image, a pixel can be one of 256 colors, from 0-255.

12. Zoom out so that you are viewing the image at 100%.

13. Float the eyedropper over the top black rectangle on the left, as shown in Figure 2, then note the grayscale values in the Info palette.

    TIP Designers and printing professionals refer to dark areas in an image—such as the top two squares in Figuure 2— as *shadows*.

14. Float the pointer over the bottom white rectangle.

    TIP Designers and printing professionals refer to light areas in an image—such as the bottom two squares in Figure 2—as *highlights*.

15. Float the pointer over the middle gray rectangle.

    128 is the middle value in the grayscale ramp.

    TIP Designers and printing professionals refer to middle values in an image as *midtones*.

(continued)

DESIGN*note*

A pixel is always one color, regardless of what color mode you are in. In the Info palette, the RGB Color mode identifies a pixel's grayscale value. In a grayscale image, a pixel can be one of 256 colors, from 0–255. Black pixels have a grayscale value of 0. White pixels have a grayscale value of 255. All other pixels fall somewhere in between.

15. Float the pointer over the light gray rectangle above the white rectangle.

   192 is the grayscale value between 128 and 255.

16. Float the pointer over the dark gray rectangle below the black rectangle.

   64 is the grayscale value between 0 and 128.

17. Position your pointer to the far left of the gradient below the image of the man, as shown in Figure 3, then note the grayscale value in the Info palette.

18. Try to find the black pixels in the gradient— the pixels with a value of 0.

19. Slowly move your pointer to the right, across the gradient, and note the grayscale values in the Info palette.

   The starting and ending colors for this gradient were black and white, respectively. If you move slowly, you should be able to identify every grayscale value from 0 to 255.

20. Explore the image to identify various grayscale values. Can you find pixels with a value of 0 in the dark sweater? Can you find pixels with a value of 255 in the man's beard? How about in the highlight area at the left side of the image? Identify which areas of the image are the midtones.

FIGURE 3
Sampling the darkest area of the gradient

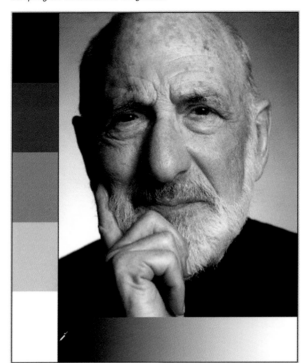

DESIGN*note*

The Posterize dialog box is the best feature in Photoshop for exploring the concept of grayscale. When you set an image to Grayscale mode, by definition, each pixel can be one of 256 shades of gray. The Posterize dialog box allows you to manipulate that number.

FIGURE 4

Posterizing to eight levels

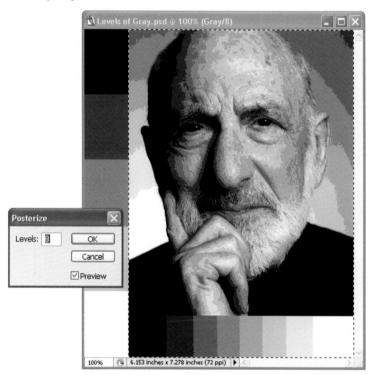

Modify the levels of gray in a grayscale image

1. Click **Select** on the menu bar, click **Load Selection**, click the **Channel list arrow**, click **Man and Gradient**, then click **OK**.

2. Click **Image** on the menu bar, point to **Adjustments**, then click **Posterize**.

3. Verify that the Preview check box is checked, type **8** in the Levels text box, then compare your artwork to Figure 4.

    With this value, each pixel can be one of only eight shades of gray. With only eight shades of gray available, there aren't enough grays to create the effect of a smooth transition from the shadow areas of the image to the highlight areas.

4. Float the pointer from left to right across the gradient at the bottom while noting the grayscale values in the Info palette.

    TIP The RGB section of the Info palette now shows two numbers separated by a forward slash for each value. The values to the left of the slash represent pixel values before posterizing, and the values on the right represent what the pixel values will be if you execute the posterize effect.

(continued)

DESIGN*note*

It's a pretty cool effect, don't you think? Posterizing an image is very popular—you've probably seen it many times. Now you have a better understanding of how it works. This is the first in what will be many examples that demystify Photoshop. Sorry. Hate to do it to you. But as a designer, you need to understand what Photoshop is doing. Does this mean you need to be a mathematical savant, like Dustin Hoffman in *Rain Man*? No. Absolutely not. But it does mean that some dazzling Photoshop effects are the result of relatively simple algorithms. Getting an intellectual grasp on how Photoshop is doing what it's doing is the first step to mastering this application.

5. Type **24** in the Levels text box, then compare your artwork to Figure 5.

   With only 24 shades of gray available per pixel, the image is surprisingly normal looking. It would be difficult to notice anything amiss in the man's face or in his hands. This is because these areas do not demand the effect of a smooth and graduated transition from light to dark. However, note that the shadow areas on the side of the man's face are posterized.

   Now look at the tones in the background: the posterize effect is immediately apparent and is mirrored in the gradient at the bottom of the canvas.

6. Type **64** in the Levels text box.

   At 64 levels, the posterize effect (often called *stair-stepping* because you can see the step from one gray level to another) is hardly visible. However, note the gradient at the bottom. The stair-stepping is still visible.

   (continued)

FIGURE 5
Posterizing to 24 levels

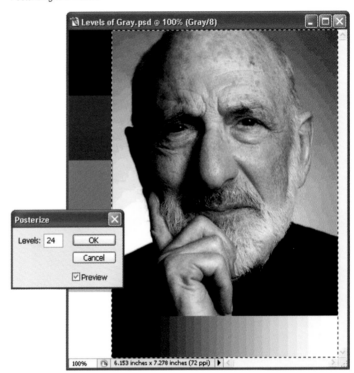

DESIGN*note*

Smooth gradients are the most challenging effect for Photoshop and the most challenging effect to reproduce on the Web and in a printed document. Using this exercise as an example, note that you need to quadruple the number of available grays—from 64 to 255—to create a gradient that not only looks good on screen, but will also print satisfactorily.

FIGURE 6

Posterizing to four levels

7. Type **255** in the Levels text box.

8. Type **4** in the Levels text box, click **OK**, then compare your artwork to Figure 6.

9. Deselect all, then save your work.

DESIGNnote

As part of your attempt to get an intellectual understanding of how Photoshop works, it's important to examine why this image looks the way it does. It started out with 256 grays available per pixel. Now it has only four grays available per pixel. So what? Why does the image look the way it does?

Here's what happened: Photoshop identified all the pixels whose value was from 0-63 and said, "You guys are 64 different shades of dark gray but now I only have four grays available. So you guys are all black, grayscale value 0. And 64-128? You're all dark gray—value 107. And 129-192? Now you're all light gray—value 187. And the rest of you, 193-255, you're all 255." When you look at it that way, the effect isn't quite so mystifying, is it?

USE THE
Tolerance-Based Tools

What You'll Do

How many times have you used the Magic Wand Tool? Too many to count, right? It was probably one of the first tools you played with because it is so cool. Now think about it: Did you ever change the value in the Tolerance text box before applying the Magic Wand Tool? Did you have any idea what tolerance meant at the time, and do you know what it means today? How much have you learned about tolerance since then? Could you explain it? Could you define it?

If you don't understand grayscale levels, then you don't really understand tolerance. At best, you understand that if you increase the tolerance value, the Magic Wand Tool selects more pixels. But how? And why? It's still a bit mysterious, isn't it?

If you do understand grayscale levels—which you now do—then tolerance becomes quite clear and simple. That's what this lesson is about: understanding how tolerance works with the Magic Wand Tool and the Paint Bucket Tool. When you understand how these tools *really* work, you'll be amazed at how empowered you'll feel the next time you use them.

FIGURE 7
Selecting only the white rectangle

1. Click the **Magic Wand Tool** ✎ then type **1** in the Tolerance text box in the Options bar.

2. Verify that the Anti-alias and the Sample All Layers check boxes are not checked, then verify that the Contiguous check box is checked.

3. Click the pointer in the white rectangle at the bottom left of the image.

   As shown in Figure 7, the white rectangle – and only the white rectangle – is selected. When you click the Magic Wand Tool on the image, you are clicking a single pixel. The Magic Wand Tool "reads" the grayscale value of that pixel, then selects contiguous pixels that fall within the range of tolerance that you set. In this case, you clicked a pixel with a grayscale value of 255. With a tolerance value of 1, the Magic Wand Tool can select adjacent pixels with a grayscale value of 255—the clicked pixel—and pixels with a grayscale value of 254—one level of gray away from the clicked pixel.

4. Change the Tolerance value to 0, then click in the white patch on the man's forehead.

(continued)

5. Click **Select** on the menu bar, then click **Similar**.

   As shown in Figure 8, all of the pixels whose value is 255—all of the white pixels—are selected.

   > **TIP** The Similar command overrides the Contiguous option that you checked in the Options bar.

6. Deselect, then click the **Contiguous check box** to remove the check mark.

7. Click the **black rectangle** at the upper left of the image.

   As shown in Figure 9, all of the black pixels in the image are selected. With the Contiguous option turned off, the Magic Wand Tool is free to select all the pixels in the image that fall within tolerance.

8. Deselect all.

9. Position the pointer over the white rectangle in the lower-left corner, then note in the Info palette that its grayscale value is 255.

10. Position the pointer over the light gray rectangle immediately above the white rectangle, then note that its grayscale value is 192.

   $255 - 192 = 63$. The grayscale values of the white rectangle and the light gray rectangle are 63 gray levels apart.

   If your pixel reads as a different grayscale value, see the Design Note on the next page.

   (continued)

FIGURE 8
Selecting all the white pixels

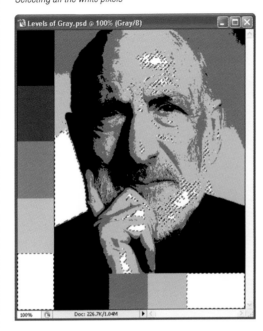

FIGURE 9
Selecting all the black pixels

FIGURE 10

Selecting two rectangles

11. Change the Tolerance value to **62**, then click the **Contiguous check box** in the Options bar.

12. Click the **white rectangle** in the lower-left corner.

    Only the white rectangle is selected.

13. Deselect all.

14. Change the Tolerance value to **63**, then click the same **white rectangle** again.

    As shown in Figure 10, both the white and the light gray rectangles are selected. You used the Magic Wand Tool with a tolerance setting of 63 and clicked a pixel whose value is 255. 255 - 63 = 192. The pixels in the light gray rectangle all have a grayscale value of 192. Since this value falls within tolerance, they are selected along with the white rectangle.

    TIP If this does not work for you, increase the tolerance setting until both rectangles are selected. See the Design Note on this page.

15. Click the **Contiguous check box** to remove the check mark.

(continued)

DESIGN*note*

When I created this exercise, it worked perfectly. However, when we tested it on different computers, sometimes it worked and sometimes it didn't. Also, we found that the grayscale values changed when the same file was opened on different computers. What's going on?

I think I can explain the changing grayscale values. An image's color information can change from computer to computer due to the number of color management profiles in the software. In the design firm where I work, this has caused an enormous amount of trouble and necessitated that all computers be set to the same color model. Yet we still have problems when we receive images from freelancers or others not working in our studio.

16. Click the **white patch** on the man's forehead.

As shown in Figure 11, all of the white pixels and all of the light gray pixels are selected.

17. Deselect all.

Use the Paint Bucket Tool

1. Click **Image** on the menu bar, point to **Mode**, then click **RGB Color**.

2. Click **Select** on the menu bar, click **Load Selection**, load Man Alone, then click **OK**.

3. Click **Image** on the menu bar, click **Crop**, then save your work.

Be sure to save here, because you will revert to this point later in the lesson.

4. Deselect.

5. Show the Swatches palette, then click a **bright yellow swatch** in the Swatches palette to change the foreground color to yellow.

(continued)

FIGURE 11
Selecting all the white and all the light gray pixels

FIGURE 12

Filling a single contiguous area of white with yellow

FIGURE 13

Filling all the white pixels with yellow

6. Click the **Paint Bucket Tool** then type **0** in the Tolerance text box in the Options bar.

   TIP The Paint Bucket Tool is hidden under the Gradient Tool.

7. Verify that the Anti-alias and the All Layers check boxes are not checked, then verify that the Contiguous check box is checked.

8. Position the pointer anywhere over the image, then press **[Caps Lock]**.

   TIP The [Caps Lock] key changes a tool pointer to a crosshair pointer, which is far more precise.

9. Position the crosshair over the white patch in the man's forehead, click, then compare your artwork to Figure 12.

   With a 0 tolerance value, only the contiguous white pixels are filled with yellow.

10. Click the **Contiguous check box** to remove the check mark, then click a **white patch** in the man's beard.

    As shown in Figure 13, with the Contiguous option turned off, all of the white pixels are filled with yellow.

11. Change the Tolerance value to 255, then click anywhere in the man's black sweater.

    With a tolerance value of 255, all of the pixels are within the tolerance; therefore, all are filled with yellow.

    (continued)

12. Undo your last step.

13. Change the Tolerance value to 16, check the **Contiguous check box**, then click a **light pink swatch** from the Swatches palette as a new foreground color.

14. Click the **light gray area** on the right side of the man's face so that your artwork resembles Figure 14.

(continued)

FIGURE 14
Filling with pink

DESIGN*note*

When the image was posterized in Grayscale Color mode, the resulting image only had four levels of gray. However, when you converted the mode to RGB Color, some pixels changed color very slightly. For example, if you float over the light gray areas of the man's face, you'll see that some pixels are lighter or darker than others, usually by only one grayscale value. There is no official reason for this; it just happened. This is why you increased the tolerance value to 16. Remember, whenever you switch color modes, unexpected and unexplainable things may occur.

FIGURE 15
Filling with orange

15. Click the **Contiguous check box** to remove the check mark, click a **bright orange swatch**, then fill the remaining light gray pixels so that your artwork resembles Figure 15.

Note how in the last two steps, by turning the Contiguous option on and off, you filled same-value light gray pixels with two different colors.

(continued)

16. Toggling the Contiguous check box on and off, fill all of the remaining gray pixels with any four colors you like, so that the final image contains a maximum of six colors (plus black, if you wish).

Figure 16 shows one example.

17. Click **File** on the menu bar, then click **Save As**.

18. Type **Color Man** in the File name text box (Win) or Save As text box (Mac), verify that the Format text box is set to the Photoshop format, check the **As a Copy check box**, then click **Save**.

The copy is saved and closed and the Levels of Gray document remains open. This is the best method to "save off a copy" of a file.

(continued)

FIGURE 16
A finished file

DESIGN*note*

This exercise is as much about choosing colors as it is about working with tolerance and the Paint Bucket Tool. Which colors work best in which areas of the image? How would the image look if you used light colors in the dark areas? Or dark colors in the light areas? If you replace the black pixels with dark blue, do you notice a loss in contrast?

FIGURE 17
Finished artwork

19. Click **File** on the menu bar, then click **Revert**.

20. Verify that the Tolerance value is set to 16 and that the Contiguous check box is not checked.

21. Fill the black areas with yellow.

22. Fill the dark gray areas with orange.

23. Fill the light gray areas with green.

24. Fill the white areas with dark blue, then compare your work to Figure 17.

    Note how the artwork appears inverted—as though it is an x-ray. Dark colors in the light areas and light colors in the dark areas created this effect.

25. Save your work, then close Levels of Gray.

WORK WITH HUE, SATURATION, AND
Brightness in the Color Picker Window

What You'll Do

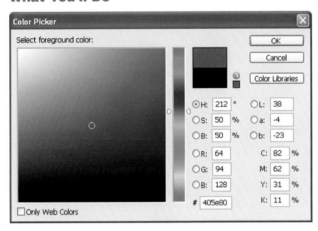

As a sophisticated photo manipulation application, Photoshop is fluent with a number of standard models for specifying color. The Color Picker window allows you to specify color in four color models: HSB, RGB, LAB, and CMYK. If you click the Color Libraries button, you can also specify a color using a spot color library.

Working with the Color Picker thrusts you into the fascinating world of color theory and the color models that Photoshop uses to define and display color. As you might imagine, this can get very mathematical, very theoretical, and very complex. But don't be intimidated. What's great about color theory is that you don't need to be a baby Einstein to learn a number of useful concepts. Even a little bit of information will go a long way in helping you to understand how Photoshop works with color.

Earlier in this chapter, you worked with the Grayscale mode. In this and the following lessons, you will define colors using hue, saturation, and brightness (HSB) values in the Color Picker. HSB is not a color mode; it is a color model that defines a range of color.

Regardless of the color mode of the file you are working in (usually Grayscale, RGB, or CMYK), Photoshop can define the color of any pixel in terms of HSB.

For you, the designer, an understanding of HSB is very empowering, because Photoshop offers a number of options for manipulating the hue, saturation, and brightness of an image. That's important, because manipulating HSB is something you'll want to do over and over again to achieve a number of effects, both practical and artistic. So, as you go through the upcoming lessons, you can certainly approach the content for its technical insights into color theory and how Photoshop assigns color to pixels. However, you should also keep your designer's eye open for the great number of cool effects that you can create with an understanding of HSB.

Identify the hue component of a color

1. Verify that no Photoshop documents are open.

2. Press [D] to access default foreground and background colors, then click the **Set foreground color button** on the toolbox to open the Color Picker.

   Note that the H, S, and B text boxes all read 0.

3. Drag the **circle** from the lower-left corner up to the upper-right corner so that your Color Picker resembles Figure 18.

   The upper-right corner of the Color Picker window represents a pure hue. A hue is the name of a color. Apples, tomatoes, and fire engines all have the same hue: red. In terms of HSB, a pure hue is a color whose saturation and brightness values are both 100%. Note in Figure 18 that the S and B text boxes both read 100 and the H text box reads 0. Note too the degrees symbol to the upper right of the H text box.

4. Drag the **triangles** at the base of the Hue slider slowly upward to the highest number you can see in the H text box, then compare your screen to Figure 19.

   TIP The Hue slider is the vertical bar in the middle of the Color Picker window that is filled with rainbow colors. It contains all the hues available in the Color Picker. Photoshop's Color Picker offers a total of 360 hues, from 0 to 359.

   (continued)

FIGURE 18
Color Picker at 0H/100S/100B

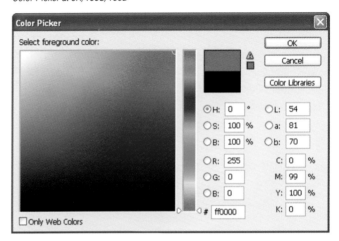

FIGURE 19
Viewing hue 359 as a pure hue

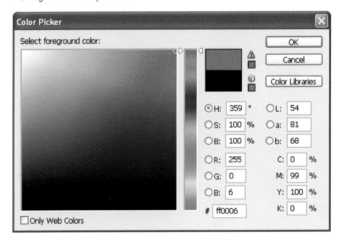

FIGURE 20
Color wheel

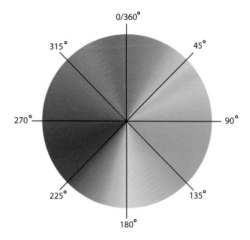

FIGURE 21
Viewing hue 212 as a pure hue

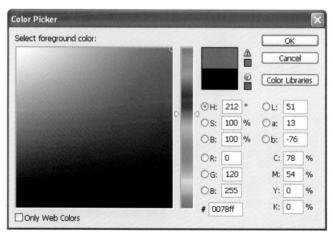

The highest numbered hue you will find on the Hue slider is 359 degrees. Despite the fact that the Hue slider is represented as a rectangle, it actually represents a standard color wheel. A color wheel, illustrated in Figure 20, is a 360-degree circle, with each degree representing a different hue.

5. Drag the **Hue slider** to hue 212, then compare your screen to Figure 21.

   Hue 212 is a bright light blue.

Identify the saturation and brightness components of a color

1. Drag the **circle** from the upper-right corner to the top left corner so that your Color Picker resembles Figure 22.

   The S (saturation) value changes to 0. Note, however, that the H (hue) value is still 212 degrees.

2. Slowly drag the **circle** along the top edge of the Color Picker window, from left to right, and note the change in the S (saturation) text box and the foreground color as you do so.

   In the Color Picker window, saturation is represented from the left edge of the window to the right edge of the window. The left edge represents 0 saturation; the right edge represents 100 saturation. Moving left to right, the saturation value increases.

   (continued)

FIGURE 22
Hue 212 with 0S/100B

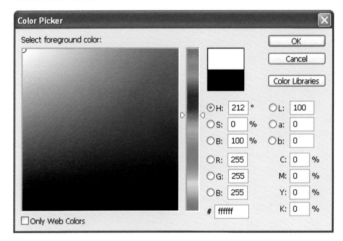

DESIGN*note*

Saturation is a measurement of the intensity of a color. A pure hue has a saturation value of 100. A saturation value of 0 is defined as no color. For example, the pixels in a grayscale image would all be defined as having zero saturation. A classic real-world analogy for saturation is that of a tomato versus a radish. In terms of hue, both have the same hue: they're both red. Their difference is in their saturation. The bright, vivid red of the tomato would be described in terms of HSB as being highly saturated, while the dull, muted red of the radish would be described as having low to moderate saturation.

3. Verify that the B value reads 100, then type **50** in the S text box.

As shown in Figure 23, hue 212 is far less intense—less vivid—at 50% saturation.

4. Drag the **Hue slider** to see the other hues on the color wheel at 50% saturation.

5. Drag the **Hue slider** back to hue 212.

(continued)

FIGURE 23

Hue 212 with 50S/100B

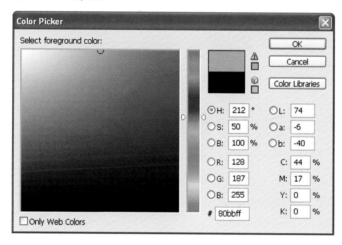

6. Type **50** in the B text box, then compare your screen to Figure 24.

   The hue is darkened dramatically because the brightness has been reduced to 50%.

7. Drag the **circle** up and down along the left edge of the Color Picker window.

   As you drag along the left edge, you see only different ranges of gray. This is the brightness range on its own—from black to white—with zero saturation.

FIGURE 24
Hue 212 with 50S/50B

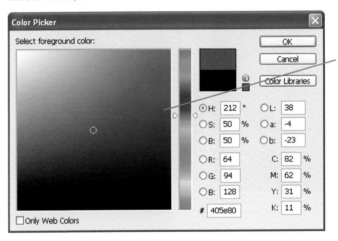

In the Color Picker window, brightness is represented from the bottom edge of the window to the top edge. The bottom edge represents 0 brightness, which is black. The top edge represents 100 brightness, which is white.

8. Type **0** in the S text box, type **50** in the B text box, then drag the **Hue slider** up and down, from top to bottom.

The foreground color remains a neutral gray. Regardless of the hue, there is no color because there is no saturation.

9. Type **100** in the B text box, then drag the **Hue slider** up and down, from top to bottom.

The foreground color remains white. 100% brightness with zero saturation is white, regardless of the hue.

10. Drag the **Hue slider** to 212, then drag the **circle** around in the Color Picker window, from top to bottom, from left to right, and note the effect on the foreground color.

In terms of HSB, every color you see as you drag around the window has the same hue—212. Photoshop's color wheel specifies 360 hues, but each of those hues is modified by 100 saturation values and 100 brightness values.

DESIGN*note*

Brightness is tricky to define, because all you can say is, "The brightness value represents the brightness of the hue." Here's a better way to understand brightness. Imagine you are on the beach at noon on a bright sunny day and you are wearing a lime green bathing suit. That green would be quite vivid, yes? Now, imagine that you stay on the beach past sunset into twilight. By the light of the moon, what does your bathing suit look like? Definitely not as vivid, because there isn't enough light—enough brightness—to reflect a vivid green. Instead, though it may be possible to identify the hue of the bathing suit as green, that green would be muted, like a forest green. Finally, if you had a black beach blanket and crawled underneath it, what would your lime green suit look like now? Like nothing, right, because there's no light underneath a black blanket at night. Therefore, a bright vivid color must have a high brightness value, while a dark muted color must have a low brightness value.

Identify gamut issues in the Color Picker window

1. Type **100** in both the Saturation and Brightness text boxes.

   Once again, the foreground color is the pure hue 212. Note that the Color Picker also defines this color in terms of the RGB color model and the CMYK color model.

2. Position your pointer over the Warning: out of gamut for printing button ⚠, as shown in Figure 25.

   The Warning: out of gamut for printing button means that the color cannot be printed as shown using the CMYK color model.The values in the RGB and CMYK text boxes on your screen may differ from the figure depending on the color settings you have chosen for the application.

3. Click ⚠, then compare your screen to Figure 26.

   The Color Picker identifies the closest color that can be achieved in the CMYK model. The HSB and RGB color models have a much larger gamut than the CMYK color model, with RGB

   (continued)

FIGURE 25
Warning: out of gamut for printing button

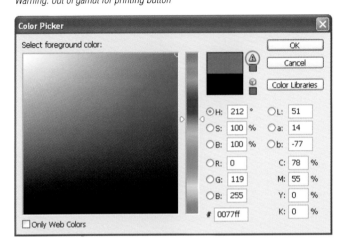

FIGURE 26
Viewing the closest in-gamut color

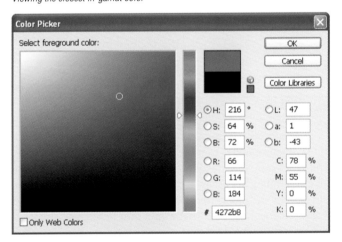

FIGURE 27

Warning: not a web safe color button

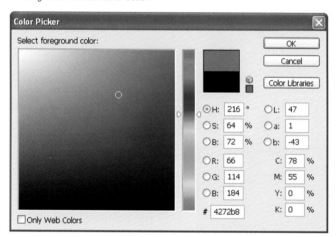

having by far the largest gamut. RGB theoretically defines over 16 million colors; HSB theoretically defines 3.5 million colors. The total number of distinctive colors that can be printed with CMYK inks is under 25,000.

4. Click the **Warning: not a web safe color button** , shown in Figure 27.

   Many Web sites are designed with a specific—and limited—color palette. This palette is composed of "web-safe" colors—colors that render accurately on the Web. When you specify colors for a Web site, use the warning button to be certain the colors you are choosing are Web safe.

5. Click **Cancel**.

DESIGN*note*

Does this mean that, as a designer, you should always specify in-gamut CMYK colors for jobs that will print? You could definitely find an argument for both sides, but I say no. If you are a designer in a professional agency or art department, it is your job to make art. If you want that art to be vibrant and intense, choose colors that are vibrant and intense. It is the production and print departments that have the responsibility of matching the color of your work as closely as they possibly can within the constraints of the CMYK gamut. Dealing with those constraints is their job, not yours. However, it is important that you understand the realities of working with color on a monitor versus reproducing that color in a printed document.

EXPLORE THE
Hue/Saturation Dialog Box

What You'll Do

The Hue/Saturation dialog box is a powerful Photoshop utility, one that you'll use over and over again. With it, you can saturate or desaturate an image, convert an image to black and white, and dramatically alter the hue of selected pixels. That's what you'll do in this lesson. You'll make a number of saturation and hue manipulations, and study the effect they have on an image.

FIGURE 28
Viewing modified hues

FIGURE 29
Comparing before/after for all hues

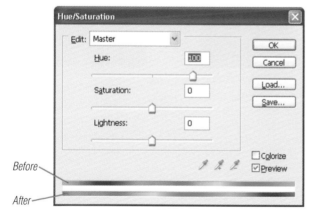

Before

After

1. Open AP 3-2.psd, then save it as **Crayons**.

2. Verify that the Info palette is visible.

3. Target the **Right** layer.

4. Press **[Ctrl][U]** (Win) or ⌘**[U]** (Mac) to open the Hue/Saturation dialog box.

   | **TIP** This is an easy quick key to memorize if you think of the *U* as *hue*.

5. Drag the **Hue slider** to the right so that its value reads 100, or simply type **100** in the Hue text box, then compare your artwork to Figure 28.

   The hue value—for every pixel in the image—has been moved 100 degrees on the color wheel.

6. Sample different pixels in the image, and note the before-and-after change in the hue value.

   For every pixel you click, the new value will be exactly the old value plus 100.

7. Note the two rainbow rectangles at the bottom of the dialog box, as shown in Figure 29.

   The top rainbow rectangle represents the original color wheel, and the bottom rectangle represents the color wheel as it is being modified.

   (continued)

8. Compare the red area at the center of the top rectangle to the same location in the bottom rectangle.

With the shift in hue, the areas of the image that were originally red are now green. The two rectangles in the Hue/Saturation dialog box are useful for predicting the results of modifying the Hue slider.

9. Click the **Preview check box** repeatedly to add and remove the check mark so that you can compare the red crayon in the original image to its modified version.

As shown in Figure 30, the red crayon is now green.

10. Compare different areas of the before-and-after rectangles to the before-and-after views of the image.

11. Drag the **Hue slider** to -100.

Though the hues in the Color Picker are shown from 0 to 359, in the Hue/Saturation dialog box, the slider moves in two directions, positive and negative. Starting with 0 degrees, 0 thru 180 represents a counterclockwise movement on the color wheel. 0 thru -180 represents a clockwise movement on the wheel.

12. Click **Cancel**.

FIGURE 30
Comparing before/after hues

FIGURE 31

Viewing the colorized image

Colorize an image

1. Display the Swatches palette, if necessary, then click the **RGB Green swatch** at the upper-left corner of the Swatches palette.

2. Click the **Set foreground color button** on the toolbox to open the Color Picker window.

3. Jot down the hue, saturation, and brightness values of the color.

   The values of this color are 120H/100S/100B.

4. Click **Cancel**.

5. Open the Hue/Saturation dialog box, click the **Colorize check box**, then compare your screen to Figure 31.

   When you click the Colorize check box, all of the pixels in the image take on the hue value of the foreground color.

6. Move your pointer over the modified pixels and note the before-and-after H values in the Info palette.

   The hue value for every pixel in the modified image is 120. The only thing that differentiates the pixels is their saturation and lightness values.

7. Note the bottom hue rectangle in the dialog box.

   Once colorized, every hue on the color wheel becomes the same hue—in this case hue 120. This is identical to what has happened to every pixel in the modified image.

   (continued)

8. Drag the **Hue slider** back and forth from left to right.

By moving the Hue slider, you can colorize the image with any of the 360 hues in the color wheel.

> **TIP** Note that, once colorized, the Hue slider specifies hues from 0 thru 360 rather than 0 thru 180 and 0 thru -180. This is a bit misleading, because 0–360 is actually a total of 361 hues. However, 0 and 360 represent the same location on the color wheel, and therefore the same hue.

9. Drag the **Hue slider** to 120.

Manipulate saturation

1. Drag the **Saturation slider** to 50, then compare your artwork to Figure 32.

The green hue is intensified.

2. Drag the **Saturation slider** to 75.

The green hue is further intensified.

3. Drag the **Hue slider** left and right to see the other hues at this saturation.

> **TIP** By definition, modifying hue and saturation will always have some impact on the lightness value.

4. Press and hold **[Alt]** (Win) or **[option]** (Mac) so that the Cancel button becomes the Reset button, then click **Reset**.

5. Click the **Colorize check box** to remove the check mark.

6. Drag the **Saturation slider** to 50, then compare your image to Figure 33.

(continued)

FIGURE 32
Increasing the saturation of the colorized image

FIGURE 33
Increasing saturation

original   *saturated*

DESIGN*note*

Note that, regardless of how you drag the Hue and Saturation sliders, the crayons always look like crayons. The darker crayons always stay darker than the lighter crayons. This is because you are not modifying the lightness values of the pixels. The lightness value defines the image—from shadow to highlight. So long as the overall lightness is maintained, the "reality" of the image will not change.

FIGURE 34
Reducing saturation

original   desaturated

FIGURE 35
Desaturating the image completely

original   completely desaturated

All the various hues are intensified. Note, however, that the gray crayon on the right hardly changes. This is because it originally had a low saturation value and the Saturation slider therefore has minimal impact. In other words, it's hard to increase saturation in a pixel that has little or no saturation to begin with.

7. Move your pointer over the modified image, and note the before-and-after values in the Info palette.

   Modifying saturation also affects the H and L values. The impact on the H values is minimal. However, an increase in saturation by definition requires an increase in lightness.

8. Drag the **Saturation slider** to -50, then compare your image to Figure 34.

   This decrease in saturation results in an image that clearly retains color, but that color is muted and not vibrant.

9. Drag the **Saturation slider** to –100, then compare your image to Figure 35.

   With no saturation, every pixel is and can only be a shade of gray.

10. Click **OK**, save your work, then close the Crayons document.

ADJUST HUE, SATURATION,
and Lightness

What You'll Do

In many projects, you will adjust and manipulate HSL to produce a variety of color effects. In other projects, you will adjust and manipulate HSL to achieve effects that are realistic. For example, if you were designing a catalog for a clothing company, they may supply you with a photograph of a green sweater then tell you that they want you to use the photo to also show a red and a blue sweater. Achieving a realistic result when modifying HSL is always interesting and often tricky. Lesson 5 focuses on that challenge. You will be given the task of modifying the color of articles of clothing, and your goal will be to manipulate HSL so that the modification is so realistic that nobody would notice that you've been up to your tricks.

FIGURE 36
Colorizing the yellow suit

1. Open AP 3-3.psd, save it as **Bathing Suits**, then verify that you are viewing the image at 100%.

2. Target the **First Red Suit layer**, make it visible, then open the Hue/Saturation dialog box.

3. Click the **Colorize check box**, drag the **Hue slider** to +355, drag the **Saturation slider** to +82, then compare your artwork to Figure 36.

   In terms of being realistic, the modification works—to a degree. The choice to colorize the image, however, was not a good one. The original (yellow) artwork contained a variety of hues—which is to be expected from a photograph taken in a real-world setting. Choosing to colorize the artwork converts all the hues to the same hue, which by definition is a movement away from reality.

   TIP When modifying HSL to achieve a realistic effect, colorizing the image is not a good choice for most cases.

4. Reset the Hue/Saturation dialog box, then remove the check mark in the Colorize check box.

5. Change the Hue value to -60, then modify the Saturation and Lightness values as you think best to achieve the brightest and most realistic red bathing suit.

   TIP Just preview, don't click OK.

   (continued)

6. Compare your artwork to Figure 37.

7. Set the Saturation value to +5 and the Lightness value to 0.

8. Click **OK**, target the **Second Red Suit layer**, make it visible, then open the Hue/Saturation dialog box.

9. Modify the orange suit so that it is the exact same red as the first suit.

(continued)

FIGURE 37

Making the yellow suit red

FIGURE 38

Making the orange suit red

10. Compare your artwork to Figure 38.

    I changed the HSL value to –5/+19/–15. What's interesting about those values is that the hue didn't change much, but it was necessary to both darken and saturate the image to achieve the red.

    > **TIP** When modifying HSL to achieve a realistic effect, increasing the lightness usually makes the image less realistic but decreasing the lightness seldom detracts from the illusion of realism.

11. Click **OK**, then hide the First Red Suit layer.

12. Target the **Turquoise Suit layer**, make it visible, then open the Hue/Saturation dialog box.

(continued)

13. Modify HSL as you think best to achieve turquoise, then compare your artwork to Figure 39.

Surprisingly, I found that I needed only to modify the hue. I set the hue value to 90, then found that the result was already so saturated that it required no further saturation. In fact, I found that increasing the saturation had almost no visible effect on the color.

14. Click **OK**, target the **Royal Blue Suit layer**, make it visible, then open the Hue/Saturation dialog box.

(continued)

FIGURE 39
Making the yellow suit turquoise

FIGURE 40

Making the yellow suit royal blue

15. Modify HSL to achieve your idea of a royal blue bathing suit, then compare your artwork to Figure 40.

    This is a fine example of how subjective color modifications can be. Your choice will almost certainly vary from the figures, because everybody has their own idea of what royal blue looks like, especially in a sunny beach setting with shiny bathing suit fabric. All of those factors come into play. Note that I both desaturated and darkened when I chose +153/-15/-13.

16. Click **OK**, target the **Chocolate Brown Suit layer**, make it visible, then create a new Hue/Saturation adjustment layer named **Brown**.

    TIP Be sure to click the Use Previous Layer to Create Clipping Mask check box when you create the adjustment layer.

    (continued)

17. Modify HSL as you think best to achieve chocolate brown.

This one will probably be a challenge. Here are a couple of hints if you want them: Clearly, brown is a dark color, so creating it will involve reducing lightness. On the other hand, brown is indeed a color; it's not gray. Therefore the color will require some saturation, especially since chocolate brown connotes a warm brown. But more than S and L, choosing the right H to begin with will be the key to achieving the brown.

18. Compare your artwork to Figure 41.

I identify a basic brown hue as being somewhere between a dark maroon and a dark mustard. Therefore, I moved the hue to +18, which gave me a reddish yellow to start with, as shown in Figure 42. I then darkened the hue by reducing the lightness to -67. This achieved a brown. I then experimented with increasing the saturation to create a warmer, more vibrant brown. This move was by far the most subjective. I chose a saturation value of +40.

(continued)

FIGURE 41
Making the orange suit chocolate brown

FIGURE 42
Choosing the starting hue for brown

FIGURE 43

Comparing the yellow suit to the chocolate brown suit

19. Type **18**, **40**, and **-67** in the H, S, and L text boxes; click **OK**, hide the Royal Blue Suit layer and the Turquoise Suit layer, then compare your artwork to Figure 43.

    Compare the bright areas of the chocolate brown suit to the bright areas of the yellow suit. Even though both have minimal shadow areas and almost no detail in the bright areas, the yellow suit appears more realistic than does the chocolate brown suit, which is just barely passing for real.

20. Target the **Navy Blue Suit layer**, then make it visible.

    TIP Note the shadow under the woman's arm and the shadow her hand casts on the yellow suit.

21. Create a new Hue/Saturation adjustment layer named **Navy Blue**.

    TIP Be sure to click the Use Previous Layer to Create Clipping Mask check box when you create the adjustment layer.

(continued)

22. Set the hue to +170, then experiment with reducing the lightness value to create a dark navy blue.

23. Reduce the Lightness value to -80, click **OK**, then compare your artwork to Figure 44.

Because the original artwork was so bright and light, it is difficult if not impossible to achieve a realistic color as dark as navy blue. At -80 lightness, the color is dark enough to resemble a dark navy blue, but the suit no longer looks realistic—it looks like a selection filled with a single color. If you compare it to the brown bathing suit, you can see that the navy blue suit is flat. This is because the new hue is darker than the original shadows in the image. Note that the shadow under the arm and even the shadow from the hand are nearly indistinguishable from the rest of the suit. Because there are no shadows, there's no range from dark to light, and therefore no shape. When there's no shape, there's no realism.

(continued)

FIGURE 44
Losing shadow detail

FIGURE 45
Retaining shadow detail

24. Open the Navy Blue adjustment layer, change the Lightness value to -45, change the Saturation value to -15, click **OK**, then compare your artwork to Figure 45.

    This is the darkest blue I could achieve while maintaining distinct shadows for shape—and realism—in the image.

25. Undo and redo to see the difference between the unrealistic and the realistic modification.

    TIP Whenever you are asked to undo and redo a change, be sure that you redo the change before you move forward.

26. Save your work, then close the file.

Adjust HSL in dark areas

1. Open AP 3-4.psd, then save it as **Sweater**.

2. Show the Sweater 1 layer and the Navy Blue adjustment layer, then double-click the **Layer thumbnail** on the Navy Blue layer.

3. Drag the **Hue slider** back and forth to see the sweater as different hues.

   Regardless of what hue you set, the color of the sweater looks realistic.

4. Drag the **Hue slider** to -180, drag the **Saturation slider** to +30, then compare your artwork to Figure 46.

   When you are working with darker images, it's easier to modify the hue and keep the image looking real. This is because, by definition, a darker image has broad shadow areas that clearly define the shape of the image. In this case, because the entire sweater is one big shadow area, all of the pixels that make up the sweater have a low saturation and a low lightness value, which keeps the colors muted and less saturated—and therefore realistic.

   (continued)

FIGURE 46
Making the sweater navy blue

FIGURE 47
Making the sweater black

5. Click **OK**, show the Sweater 2 layer and the Black layer, then double-click the **Layer thumbnail** on the Black layer

6. Modify HSL to achieve the effect that the woman is wearing a black (not just dark gray) sweater, as shown in Figure 47.

7. Set the Saturation value to -100, set the Lightness value to -40, then click **OK**.

   First, I dragged the Saturation slider all the way left to desaturate the image entirely. From there, I lowered the Lightness value to -40. Note how easy it was to achieve the black effect with this image, as opposed to the image of the yellow bathing suit, which we weren't even able to darken to a navy blue.

   (continued)

8. Target the **Sweater 2 layer**, click the **Lock transparent pixels button**  on the Layers palette, press **[D]**, then fill the image with the black foreground color.

Compare your screen to Figure 48.

Undo and redo to see the difference between the "black" sweater we created and the shape filled with 100% black. In our first black sweater, we left a range of tone, with areas that were darker than others, such as the folds in the sleeves and under the arm. Note too that you can see a dark black line where the turtleneck folds over and meets the sweater. Compare this to the all-black sweater. This is a great example of how you always want to maintain detail and a range of tone in the dark areas of a realistic image, even an image that is supposed to register as black.

9. Show the Sweater 3 layer and the Red layer, then double-click the **Layer thumbnail** on the Red layer.

(continued)

FIGURE 48
Filling the sweater with black

FIGURE 49
Making the sweater red

10. Modifying only the Hue and Saturation sliders, experiment with different values and try to make the sweater the most vivid red that you can while maintaining realism.

11. Drag the **Hue slider** to -98, drag the Saturation slider to +80, then compare your result to Figure 49.

    This is as bright and vivid a red sweater as you'll be able to create while maintaining realism. If you push the saturation value past 80, the highlights on the shoulders get hot and start to pop, creating an unrealistic effect.

    (continued)

Lesson 5   Adjust Hue, Saturation, and Lightness

11. Drag the **Lightness slider** to +20, then compare your result to Figure 50.

The increase in lightness detracts from the color of the image and makes it look unrealistic. See the Design Note below.

(continued)

FIGURE 50
Increasing lightness in the Hue/Saturation dialog box

DESIGN*note*

This is an important footnote to this entire chapter. The Lightness slider in the Hue/Saturation dialog box is not intended to be used to brighten or darken an image. It was not designed for that purpose. Photoshop has a number of other dialog boxes that brighten and darken an image using far more sophisticated algorithms. As you saw in this lesson, the Lightness slider was not at all a good choice for brightening the image. On the other hand, you can use the Lightness slider to darken an image; for example, it did a good job modifying the sweater to black. However, again, other features will do an even better job.

FIGURE 51
A brighter and more vivid red created using other Photoshop utilities

12. Drag the **Lightness slider** to 0, click **OK**, then compare your image to Figure 51.

The image on your screen will not resemble Figure 51. The red sweater in the figure was achieved by brightening the image using the Curves dialog box. In Photoshop, there are many ways to brighten an image, with the Curves dialog box being the most sophisticated. However, the Hue/Saturation dialog box is not designed to brighten an image in this manner; the Hue/Saturation dialog box cannot achieve this effect.

13. Save your work, then close the Sweater document.

Adjust HSL in hard-to-select areas

1. Open AP 3-5.psd, then save it as **Replace Color**.

   Imagine for a moment that your client supplies you with this photo and says, "I want you to use this photo, but I need you to make all the purple elements blue so they work better with the head scarf." How in the world would you select those purple parts of the costume? Cutting a path around all that embroidered detail would be a nightmare. A layer mask might work, but it too would be terribly time consuming.

2. Show the Go Blue layer, target the **Go Blue layer**, then press **[D]** to access default foreground and background colors.

3. Click **Image** on the menu bar, point to **Adjustments**, then click **Replace Color**.

   The Replace Color dialog box, shown in Figure 52, is one of the coolest features in Photoshop and is extremely powerful for manipulating HSL in hard-to-select areas. What's even better—it's something of a well-kept secret. Most designers don't use it because they either don't know about it or they don't know how it works.

4. Drag the **Fuzziness slider** to 40.

   (continued)

FIGURE 52
Replace Color dialog box

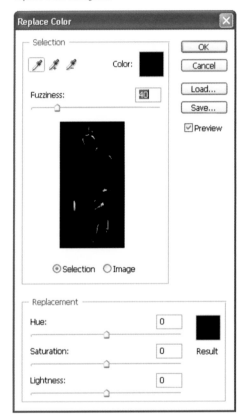

FIGURE 53
Sampling the light purple area

5. Click the **Eyedropper Tool** in the light purple area shown in Figure 53, then note the result in the Replace Color dialog box.

A mask is being created.

(continued)

6. Drag the **Fuzziness slider** to 4, then compare your dialog box to Figure 54.

The white pixels in the mask represent the selected areas of the image. The Fuzziness value controls how large the selection range is from the location that you clicked. In this case, with the low Fuzziness value, only a very small area where you clicked is selected.

7. Drag the **Fuzziness slider** to 80, then compare your dialog box to Figure 55.

The increased Fuzziness value greatly expands the white areas of the mask.

TIP Feel free to think of *fuzziness* as being the same thing as *tolerance*. With the Magic Wand Tool, tolerance determines how far from where you click the selection will be created. In the Replace Color dialog box, fuzziness determines how far from where you click the Eyedropper Tool the selected areas of the mask will be created. They are quite similar, with the only apparent difference being that fuzziness can be manipulated dynamically with a slider.

(continued)

FIGURE 54
Reducing fuzziness reduces area to be modified

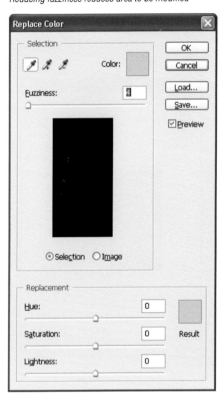

FIGURE 55
Increasing fuzziness increases area to be modified

FIGURE 56
Adding a dark purple area to the sample

8. Drag the **Fuzziness slider** to 36, then click the **Add to Sample Tool** .

9. Click in the dark purple area shown in Figure 56.

   The white areas of the mask are expanded by the new sample and the current fuzziness value.

   I prefer to maintain a relatively low fuzziness value and extend a sample with the Add to Sample Tool because I like the control that it offers. Increasing fuzziness means increasing the selection based on the original sample. But with the Add to Sample Tool, you can create a selection from multiple original samples. For example, with these two clicks, we have sampled both a light purple and a dark purple to modify, and the fuzziness extends from both, creating a layer mask that targets a broad range or purple tones.

   (continued)

Lesson 5   Adjust Hue, Saturation, and Lightness

10. Drag the **Hue slider** to +180, drag the **Saturation slider** to +50, then compare your screen to Figure 57.

Although our goal is to convert these areas to blue, we changed them to a saturated green for the time being so they will be easy to differentiate from the purple areas that have so far escaped our sampling.

(continued)

FIGURE 57
Modifying the hue and saturation

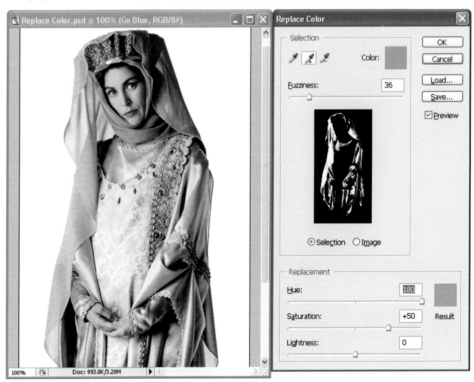

FIGURE 58

Adding more purple areas to the sample

11. Position ![dropper] in the location shown in Figure 58, then click to add that range of tone to the sample.

The Replace Color dialog box is dynamic. When you click the Add to Sample Tool in the image, the mask is updated and the modification is updated immediately.

(continued)

12. Click in other purple areas to add them to the sample so that your screen resembles Figure 59.

   TIP Be judicious when you click. Don't overlook the darker purple areas in the shadowy parts of the image. However, be careful not to click neutral shadows. The neutral shadows in the purple areas are not the only neutral shadows in the image. If you add neutral shadows to the sample, the woman's hair and eyebrows will become green!

   TIP You can always undo if you don't like the result of a sample. Also, the Subtract from Sample Tool also allows you to remove areas from the sample.

13. Drag the **Hue slider** slowly to the left to see all the other hues available to you.

(continued)

FIGURE 59
Replacing all the purple areas

FIGURE 60

The image before and after

14. Set the Hue to -87, set the Saturation to +19, then click **OK**.

15. Undo and redo to see the change, then compare your results to Figure 60.

How amazing is that? A global color change in nonspecific areas made without a selection in a matter of minutes if not seconds. What's really stunning is how seamless the modification is—nobody would ever guess. Of course, this image was perfect for this modification, because the purple areas in the costume were the only purple areas in the image. If the damsel were astride a purple horse, things wouldn't have been so easy, because the purple horse would have gone blue with the dress; there would have been no way for the Replace Color dialog box to distinguish them. However, that problem would have been easily remedied by masking out the modified horse to show the original horse on the background layer. Make a big note to remember the Replace Color dialog box. It's a tremendously powerful skill to have in your skills set.

16. Save your work, then close all open files.

1. Open AP 3-6.psd, then save it as **Color Woman**.

2. Posterize the image to six levels.

3. Select all the black areas, then fill them with a different color.

4. Select all the white areas, then fill them with a different color.

5. Fill each of the other four levels with four different colors so that each level is all one color.

6. Use the Paint Bucket Tool to add other colors to the artwork.

7. Compare your artwork to Figure 61.

8. Save your work, then close the Color Woman document

FIGURE 61
Completed Project Builder 1

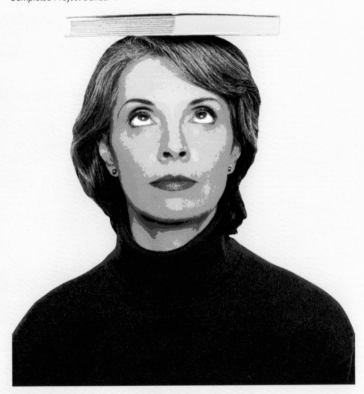

1. Open AP 3-7.psd, then save it as **Seeing Red**. (*Hint*: The goal in this exercise is to use the Replace Color dialog box to make both the purple areas of the dress and the head scarf red.)

2. Target the Go Red layer.

3. Open the Replace Color dialog box, then sample a light area in the blue head scarf.

4. Click the Add to Sample Tool, then sample a darker area of the blue head scarf.

5. Drag the Hue slider to 151.

6. Add additional samples until the scarf and the blue jewels are red.

7. Increase the Saturation to +10.

8. Click OK, then open the Replace Color dialog box again.

9. Click the Eyedropper Tool, then sample a light area of the purple veil.

10. Convert all the purple areas to red, then compare your screen to Figure 62.

11. Save your work, then close the Seeing Red document.

FIGURE 62
Completed Project Builder 2

chapter

4

TACKLING LEVELS
and Curves

1. Adjust levels.

2. Adjust curves.

3. Analyze an RGB image.

ADJUST
Levels

What You'll Do

Now that you have a thorough understanding of grayscale and levels, you are ready to manipulate the color of pixels with the Levels dialog box. The Levels dialog box is a great place to analyze the tonal range of your file, from shadows to highlights. Quite literally, the Levels dialog box shows every pixel in the image using a diagram based on grayscale values. While you can use levels to adjust the color of an image, the dialog box is best used to specify the basic tonal range of the image: the shadow point, the highlight point, and the midpoint.

FIGURE 1

Levels dialog box showing histogram

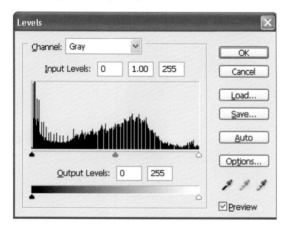

1. Open AP 4-1.psd, then save it as **Levels Intro**.

2. Load the selection named Man Alone.

3. Click **Image** on the menu bar, point to **Adjustments**, then click **Levels**.

   TIP Be sure to read the Design Note on this page about histograms.

   (continued)

DESIGNnote

As shown in Figure 1, the most striking component of the Levels dialog box is the histogram. The *histogram* is a visual reference of every pixel in the selection—in this case, the selection of the man. Here's a good analogy for understanding the histogram: Imagine that the histogram has 256 slots, one for each of the 256 available colors in the grayscale image. The slot for the 0-value pixels is on the left, and the slot for the 255-value pixels is on the right. Imagine that there are a total of 1000 pixels in the image with a grayscale value of 64. Using a black marble to represent each pixel, imagine that you drop 1000 marbles into the 64 slot on the slider. Next, imagine that the image contains 1500 pixels with a grayscale value of 72, and you drop 1500 black marbles into the 72 slot. Imagine that you do this for each of the 256 colors in the image. Your result would be the histogram—exactly what you see in the Levels dialog box. The height of the histogram, from left to right, shows the relative number of pixels that the file—or in this case, the selected pixels—has in each of the 256 grayscale values.

4. Verify that the Preview check box is checked, then view the Levels dialog box beside the image, as shown in Figure 2.

   Figure 2 is an approximate representation of the histogram's relation to areas of the image. The dark pixels in the image are represented by the yellow area in the histogram. The far fewer light pixels are represented by red. And the majority of the image is composed of midrange pixels, represented by blue.

5. Click **Cancel**.

6. Click **Window** on the menu bar, then click **Info** to show the Info palette.

7. Click the **Info palette list arrow**, then click **Palette Options**.

8. Click the **Mode list arrow** in the First Color Readout section, then click **RGB Color**.

9. Click the **Mode list arrow** in the Second Color Readout section, then click **HSB Color**.

   TIP The two eyedropper icons in the Info palette are called Tracks actual color values and Tracks user chosen color values, respectively. Clicking the eyedroppers is another way to choose the desired color mode.

10. Click **Image** on the menu bar, point to **Adjustments**, then click **Posterize**.

(continued)

FIGURE 2
Approximate representation of the histogram's relation to areas of the image

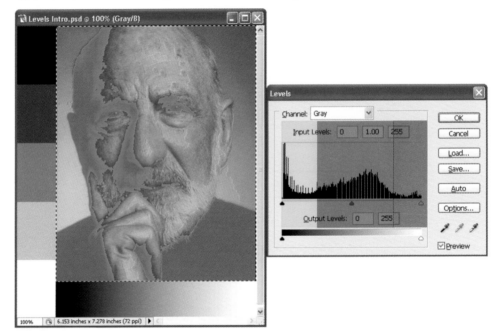

FIGURE 3

Levels dialog box showing only 4 gray values

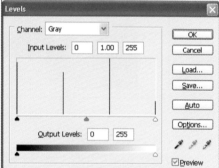

11. Type **4** in the Levels text box, if necessary, click **OK**, then float your pointer over the image to sample the four grayscale values that now compose the image.

    The image is composed of pixels that have grayscale values of 0, 107, 187, or 255.

12. Open the Levels dialog box, then compare it to Figure 3.

    The histogram precisely reflects the change in the image, with pixels represented only at the 0, 107, 187, and 255 points on the Levels slider. To extend the previous analogy, all of the "marbles" now fall into one of four "slots."

13. Click **OK**, then revert the file.

Analyze fundamental moves in the Levels dialog box

1. Load the saved selection named Half Gradient, then verify that your Info palette is positioned as shown in Figure 4.

2. Open the Levels dialog box, then position it as shown in Figure 5.

   The histogram describing the gradient is pretty much what you'd expect: a relatively even dispersion of pixels across the levels ramp. Note that not one area—from shadows to midtones to highlights—dominates the histogram.

3. Click **Cancel**.

4. Click **Select** on the menu bar, then click **Load Selection**.

(continued)

FIGURE 4
Positioning the Info palette

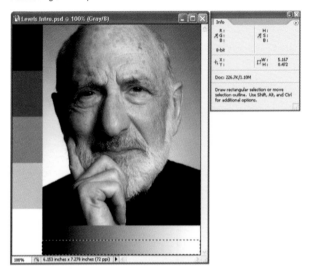

FIGURE 5
Positioning the Levels dialog box

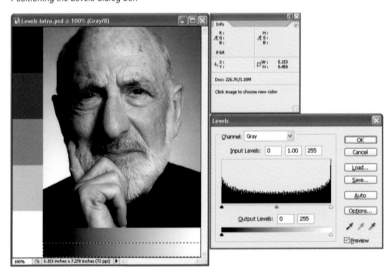

FIGURE 6

Loading a selection to be added to an existing selection

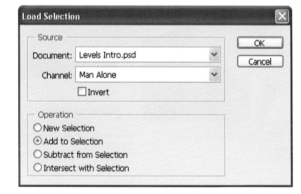

5. Click the **Channel list arrow**, click **Man Alone**, then click **Add to Selection**, so that your Load Selection dialog box resembles Figure 6.

6. Click **OK**, then hide the selection by clicking **View** on the menu bar, pointing to **Show**, then clicking **Selection Edges** to remove the check mark.

7. Open the Levels dialog box.

   The histogram has changed because it now represents the pixels in the two selections.

8. Note the three triangles at the base of the Levels slider.

   The black triangle on the left represents all black pixels in the selection—those with a grayscale value of 0. The white triangle on the right represents all white pixels in the image—those with a grayscale value of 255. The gray triangle in the middle represents the middle value of all the selected pixels.

(continued)

9. Drag the **white triangle** to the left until the third Input text box reads 128, then compare your screen to Figure 7.

The movement of the triangle has had a very specific effect on the selection. All of the pixels in the selection that were originally 128—middle gray—are now 255. Therefore, any pixel that was originally 128 or higher is now white. Note that the gray triangle moved with the white triangle, and the transition of black pixels to white pixels now happens in a much shortened range. In the gradient, the shortened transition from black to white then the "blow out" to white in the second half is analogous to what is happening to the image of the man above.

TIP See the Design Note at the bottom of this page.

10. Float your pointer over the image, then note in the Info palette the before/after grayscale values.

TIP Moving the white triangle to the left reduces the total number of pixels available to transition from black to white (shadow to highlight).

FIGURE 7

Viewing the result of moving the highlight point

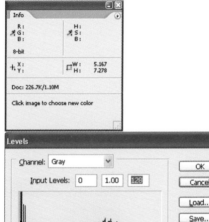

DESIGN*note*

It is important that you understand that the move affected all of the pixels in the image—not just those in the "upper half" of the histogram. All of the pixels in the upper half have been changed to 255 *and* all of the pixels in the lower half have changed as well, because they are now used to make the transition from black to white. In terms of grayscale value, the pixels that were 0–128 in the original are now 0–255. Get it? The only pixels that didn't change are the black pixels—they were 0 in the original, and they are 0 with the adjustment.

FIGURE 8

Viewing the result of moving the shadow point

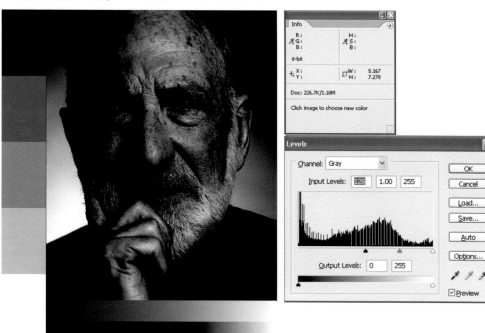

11. Press and hold **[Alt]**(Win) or **[option]**(Mac) so that the Cancel button changes to Reset, then click **Reset**.

12. Drag the **black triangle** to the right until the first Input text box reads 128, then compare your screen to Figure 8.

    This step has the exact opposite effect on the selection. The pixels that were originally 0–128 are all now 0. The transition from black to white now occurs in the pixels that were originally 129–255. This is illustrated in the gradient: the left half is entirely black, and the right half now transitions from black to white.

    > **TIP** Moving the black triangle to the right increases the total number of pixels whose grayscale value is 0 and reduces the total number of pixels available to transition from shadow to highlight.

13. Reset the Levels dialog box.

(continued)

14. Drag the **gray triangle** left until the middle Input text box reads 1.92, then compare your screen to Figure 9.

The effect on the image is far less drastic, but just as specific. Looking at the histogram, note how many more pixels are now positioned between the midpoint value—the gray triangle—and the white triangle. In other words, much more of the image now falls in the lighter half of the grayscale. Note how the image of the man was substantially brightened. In the gradient, note how short the range is from shadow to midpoint, while the midpoint to highlight point has been lengthened.

TIP Moving the gray midpoint triangle to the left brightens the middle range of a selection.

(continued)

(continued)

FIGURE 9
Viewing the result of moving the midpoint to the left

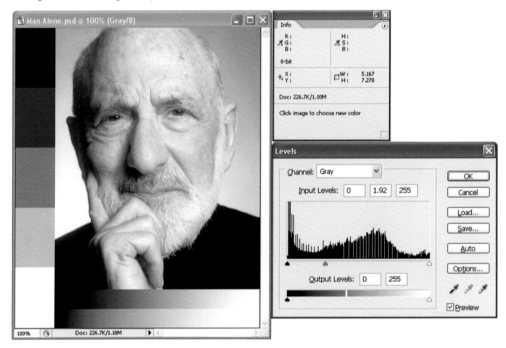

Tackling Levels and Curves   Chapter 4

FIGURE 10

Viewing the result of moving the midpoint to the right

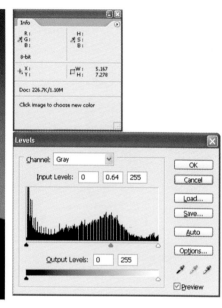

15. Reset the Levels dialog box.

16. Drag the **gray triangle** right until the middle Input text box reads 0.64, then compare your screen to Figure 10.

   Looking at the histogram, note how many more pixels are now positioned between the midpoint value and the black triangle. More of the image now falls in the darker half of the grayscale. Note how the image of the man was substantially darkened. In the gradient, note how long the range is from shadow to midpoint, while the midpoint to highlight point has been shortened.

   TIP Moving the gray midpoint triangle to the right darkens the middle range of a selection.

17. Click **Cancel** to close the Levels dialog box, save your work, then close Levels Intro.

Use Levels to set the shadow point and the highlight point

1. Open AP 4-2.psd, then save it as **Shadow & Highlight Points**.

2. Open the Levels dialog box, compare your histogram to Figure 11, then float around the image to sample the darkest and lightest pixels anywhere on the canvas.

   This file has been manipulated to show an example of "weak" shadow and highlight points.

   Weak shadow points occur when dark areas of an image are composed of pixels whose grayscale values aren't dark enough. Conversely, weak highlight points occur when light areas of the image aren't light enough.

   To create an image with a dynamic range from highlight to shadow, you want the pixels in the image to utilize the entire grayscale. However, as often happens when you scan your own images on relatively less sophisticated equipment, the blacks aren't black enough and the whites aren't white enough.

   (continued)

FIGURE 11
Viewing a histogram with "weak" shadow and highlight points

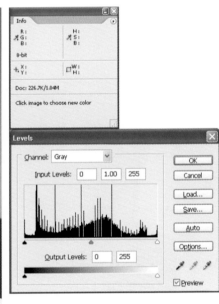

FIGURE 12

Sampling the lightest areas of the image

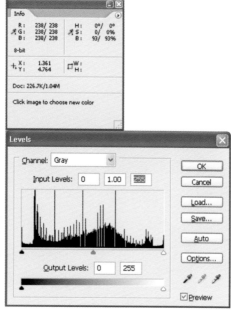

If you look at the histogram, you can clearly see that although the entire range is being utilized very few pixels are at the low end and the high end of the grayscale. This is reflected in the image as well. If you sample the man's sweater, or the left side of the gradient, or the dark rectangle in the upper-left corner, you would want to find pixels whose grayscale values range from 0–10. However, you'll note that the grayscale values in these areas are much higher.

On the other side of the grayscale, the areas that should be 250 or higher are hovering somewhere in the 230 range. Because of weak highlight and shadow points, the image appears flat and lacks contrast.

3. Float your pointer in the lightest area of the image—over the man's shoulder—as shown in Figure 12.

4. Look for the lightest pixel you can find.

   The lightest pixel you can find is grayscale value 238.

(continued)

5. In the Levels dialog box, drag the **white triangle** left until the far-right Input text box reads 235, as shown in Figure 13.

6. Position your pointer over the far-right end of the gradient to verify that the lightest pixel has been brightened to 255.

7. Float your pointer in the darkest area of the image—in the man's sweater—looking for the darkest pixel you can find.

   The darkest pixel to find is grayscale value 31.

   TIP Because you have modified the highlight point, the Info palette now shows before and after values when you sample the image. Note only the before values when you sample.

   (continued)

FIGURE 13
Moving the highlight point

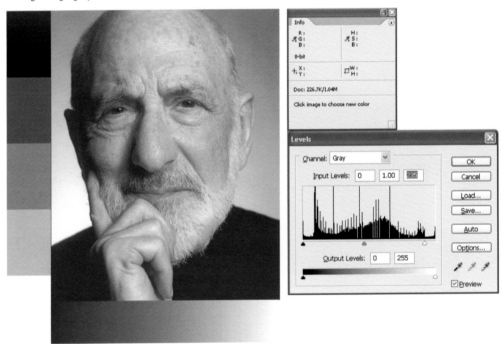

Tackling Levels and Curves   Chapter 4

8. In the Levels dialog box, drag the **black triangle** right until the far-left Input text box reads 31, as shown in Figure 14.

(continued)

FIGURE 14
Moving the shadow point

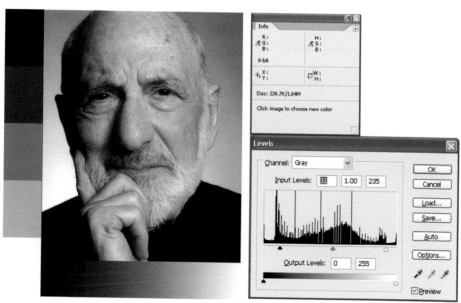

DESIGN*note*

As a designer, you want to educate your eye to look for the kind of improvements that you just applied to this image. The original image was flat. Designers use that term to refer to an image in which the tonal range from shadow to highlight is underwhelming. The corrected image has "snap"—a certain vitality to it—as though you can almost feel the energy of the transition from the dramatic dark areas to the clean white areas.

Note that, in the original, it's not only the shadows and highlights that are weak. The middle range also suffers from a lack of contrast, say from the three-quarter tones to the quarter tones. In the corrected image, note how the man's face suddenly takes shape. His nose becomes more prominent, the lines in his face show greater detail, and overall the face becomes much more three-dimensional. It's as though you were looking at the image through a dirty glass pane, and the adjustment allowed the true image to show through.

9. Click **OK**, then undo and redo the change to see the dramatic change to the image, as shown in Figure 15.

> **TIP** Throughout this book, when you are asked to undo and redo to see a change, always end by redoing the change—in other words, when you are done viewing, be sure that the change has been executed.

10. Save your work.

FIGURE 15
Comparing before and after examples of the image

FIGURE 16
"Opening" the midtones

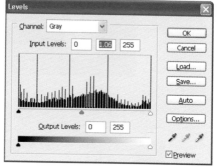

Adjust midtones and specific areas of an image

1. Open the Levels dialog box, drag the **midpoint triangle** left until the middle Input Levels text box reads 1.06, then click **OK**, as shown in Figure 16.

   Designers often refer to making the midtones brighter as opening the midtones.

2. Undo and redo to see the change.

3. Float your pointer over the man's face and beard, and try to find the brightest pixels that you can find.

   The brightest pixel you can find is 240, which is in the man's beard.

4. Float your pointer in the white background area over the man's shoulder to sample that area.

   The pixels in the white background area do not need to be lightened—they are all in the high range of the grayscale. Despite setting the shadow and highlight points and opening the midtones, the man's face still fails to reach its potential. The white area over the man's shoulder is the brightest area in the image. In other words, most of the highlights aren't even in the man's face, they're in the background.

   (continued)

DESIGN*note*

Whereas setting shadow and highlight points is often based on pixel data in the image, lightening or darkening midtones is usually a very subjective choice. An image that looks just fine to one designer may need brightening in the eyes of another designer, whereas a third designer might find the image too light already. In the case of this image, where the overall tone of the face fell on the darker side, a slight brightening was arguably the right move.

5. Show the Layers palette, duplicate the Background layer, then name the new layer **White Beard**.

6. Open the Levels dialog box, then drag the **white triangle** left until the third Input text box reads 236, as shown in Figure 17.

7. Click **OK**, then undo and redo to see the change.

The choice was a good one. The tonal range of the face was increased, making the transition from shadow to highlight—in the face—more dramatic. The white beard is now the highlight area on the face, and it provides contrast to the dark areas on the shadowed side of the face. However, notice the highlights on the hands. Most designers and photographers would agree that the highlights on the hands are getting hot and starting to pop. Because they are in the foreground of the image and because they are close to being white patches, they are stealing focus from the main interest of the image—the man's face and eyes.

8. Add a layer mask to the White Beard layer, then mask the entire hand on the White Beard layer so that your Layers palette resembles Figure 18.

The move was subtle but nevertheless important. Note how the highlights in the hands do not compete with the highlights in the man's beard. This is an excellent example of how you can use layer masks in conjunction with the Levels dialog box to adjust color only in specific areas of an image.

(continued)

FIGURE 17
Moving the highlight point

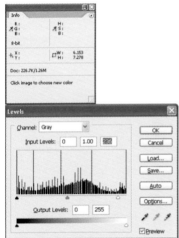

FIGURE 18
Masking the brightened hand

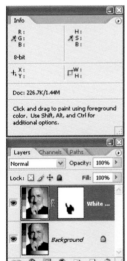

10. Load the selection named Man Alone, click
Image on the menu bar, click **Crop**, deselect,
then compare your work to Figure 19.

11. Save your work, then close Shadow &
Highlight Points.

FIGURE 19

Viewing the final adjusted image

ADJUST
Curves

What You'll Do

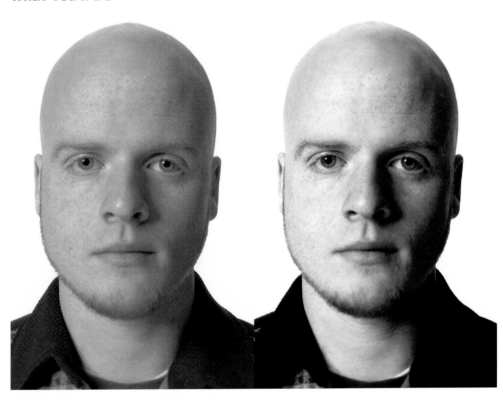

When it comes to adjusting color, the Curves dialog box is the most sophisticated utility that Photoshop has to offer. Quite literally, you can use a curve to manipulate each and every level of gray in an image—it's that precise.

Mastering the Curves dialog box is one of the great challenges in Photoshop. It is an art, it is a craft, and it is a major technical challenge as well. In fact, you can base an entire career on mastering the Curves dialog box, and many people do.

As a designer, you don't need to be a color technician, and you don't need to master curves and color retouching. But you most certainly do need to work with curves and to understand the basics of how they control the color and the tonal range of the image.

Your understanding of grayscale is the key to working with curves effectively. You may have played around with curves before—brightening or darkening an image or manipulating contrast—but how much did you understand about what you were doing? Once you do understand what you're doing, your ability to manipulate an image will grow exponentially.

DESIGN*note*

If you've walked through the color department of a design firm, advertising agency, or offset printer, you've probably seen men and women in a dark room staring intently at images on their monitors.

These are the people who are responsible for the color quality of a job; these are the people who make sure that the client's million-dollar print campaign looks great when it's printed. These people—scanners, retouchers, and color specialists—spend much of their well-paid days working with curves.

You could spend years learning about curves and still not know everything there is to know. You're not going to learn everything in the next five lessons. However, you are going to learn basic curve adjustments, and it's important to understand that you can use these skills in the real world, when you're designing and creating artwork.

Professional designers use these same skills every day. However, designing something that looks great on your monitor is completely different from getting that something to look as great when it's printed. So understand that the skills you are about to learn are only the tip of the proverbial iceberg, and they don't factor in the exacting standards and tough realities of the offset printing world. For that, you'll need a professional to help you translate your artwork to the printed page.

Should you worry about this? The answer is an emphatic No. As a designer, it's your job to create great artwork, and if you use curves to create that artwork, good for you. It's not your job to worry about making the image print-ready. In most professional settings, designers are free to create artwork to the best of their skills, and it is the job of the retoucher or the color specialist to translate that artwork into something that can be reproduced.

So in a professional setting, you're usually covered. In a freelance setting, however, or if you're in charge of the whole project, be sure to factor in a color professional somewhere in the process.

Invert an image using curves

1. Open AP 4-3.psd, then save it as **Curves**.

2. Target the **Original layer** in the Layers palette.

3. Click **Image** on the menu bar, point to **Adjustments**, then click **Invert** so that your image resembles Figure 20.

(continued)

FIGURE 20
Viewing the result of the Invert command

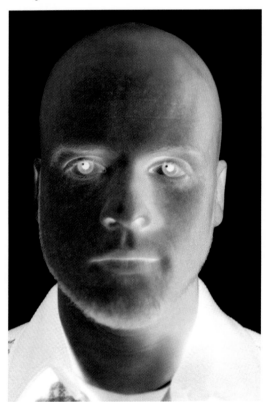

DESIGNnote

How does the Invert command work? Earlier, this chapter discussed the need to demystify Photoshop—to at least try to understand how the application does some of the things that it does. Before going forward, take a moment to try to answer the question. In terms of grayscale values, what happens to the image when you use the Invert command? The hint in that sentence is the phrase "In terms of grayscale values…."

FIGURE 21

Curves dialog box

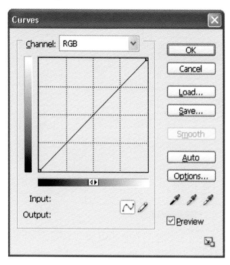

4. Undo your last step.

5. Click **Image** on the menu bar, point to **Adjustments**, then click **Curves**.

6. Verify that the Channel list is set to RGB so that your Curves dialog box resembles Figure 21.

When the Curves dialog box is set to an RGB channel, the lower-left point is the black point or the shadow point—its grayscale value is 0, and it represents the black pixels in the image.

The upper-right point is the white point or the highlight point—its value is 255, and its value represents all the white pixels in the image.

The line between the two points is called the **curve** (even though it's not curved when you open the dialog box). The curve represents every pixel value between 0 and 255.

> **TIP** The terms "black point" and "shadow point" are interchangeable. The same is true of the terms "white point" and "highlight" point."

(continued)

DESIGNnote

Stop. Take a moment to look at the Curves dialog box. Note the grid behind the curve—it will help you to identify points on the curve. Note too the blends at the bottom and left side of the grid. They show that, from left to right and bottom to top, the grayscale moves from black to white.

7. Position your pointer over the shadow point, click to select it, then compare your Curves dialog box to Figure 22.

Notice the Input and Output text boxes in the Curves dialog box. Think of Input and Output values as the before and after values of points on the curve and the pixels in the image that those points represent. At this point, the Input/Output values for the selected shadow point both read 0, 0, which makes sense, given that you haven't moved the point or changed the curve. In other words, the pixels in the image that had a grayscale value of 0 still have a grayscale value of 0.

(continued)

FIGURE 22
Identifying the grayscale value of the shadow point

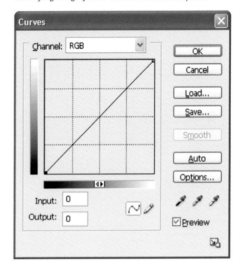

FIGURE 23

Relocating the black point

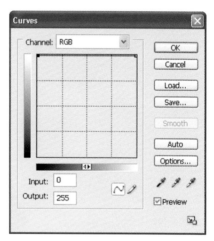

8. Drag the **shadow point** up to the upper-left corner so that your image and your Curves dialog box resemble Figure 23.

> **TIP** Verify that the Preview check box is checked, and position the Curves dialog box so that you can see the image better, if necessary.

The Output value changes to 255. This means that all the black pixels are white. But it means more than that—because the curve moved with the shadow point. With the curve at the top of the grid, every pixel—regardless of its input value—now has an output value of 255. In other words, every pixel is now white.

(continued)

9. Drag the **highlight point** to the lower-right corner so that your image and your Curves dialog box resemble Figure 24.

   The image is inverted. All of the white pixels are now black.

   (continued)

(continued)

FIGURE 24
Relocating the white point

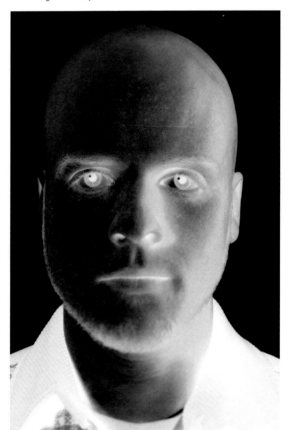

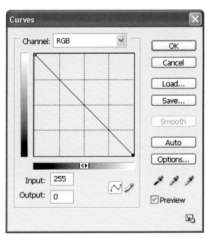

FIGURE 25

Viewing the change to pixel 191

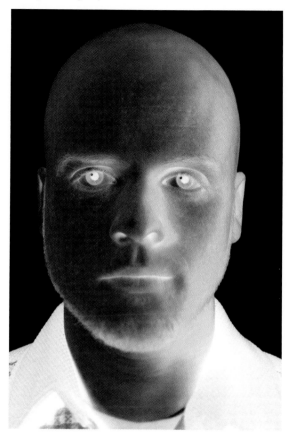

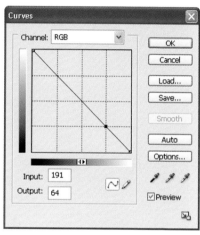

10. Position your pointer over the curve, then click to add a point in the location shown in Figure 25.

    Pixel 191—a light gray pixel—will be output as 64, a dark gray pixel.

    (continued)

DESIGN*note*

When working with curves, keep in mind that wherever the curve changes, all the points on the curve change, not just the specific point you are moving.

11. Position your pointer over the curve, then click to add a point in the location shown in Figure 26.

Pixel 64 is now being output as 191.

Stop for a moment and ask yourself this question about Figure 26: If you were to click to add a point in the exact middle of the curve, what would the input value be, and what would the output value be? Take the time to figure it out before moving ahead.

12. Position your pointer as shown in Figure 27.

13. Click to add a point.

Pixel 128 is the middle gray pixel—128 is the median point between 0 and 255. The curve has not changed location at the 128 point on the grid—only the 128 point on the grid has not changed. All the other pixels have swapped values with their counterparts on the other side of the midpoint. 129 is 127. 130 is 126. 131 is 125, and so on.

14. Click **OK**.

Ask yourself: If you were to open the Curves dialog box right now, what would the curve look like? Take a minute to think about it before moving ahead.

15. Open the Curves dialog box.

Did you guess correctly? The curve is reset. The Curves dialog box doesn't keep an ongoing record of the moves you make. As far as it's concerned, the black pixels in the image are 0—which indeed they are. The Curves dialog box doesn't remember and doesn't care that they were once white—the curve represents the pixels as they are now.

(continued)

FIGURE 26
Viewing the change to pixel 64

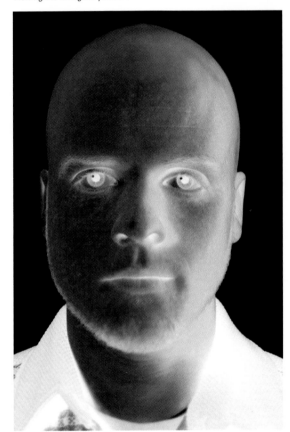

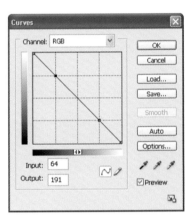

FIGURE 27

Positioning the cursor at the middle of the grid

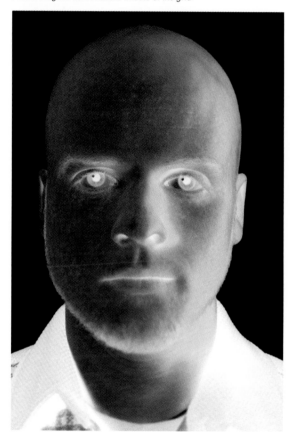

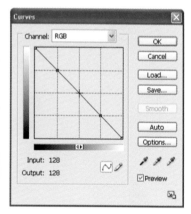

16. Close the Curves dialog box, click **File** on the menu bar, then click **Revert**.

17. Click **Layer** on the menu bar, point to **New Adjustment Layer**, then click **Curves**.

18. Type **Invert** in the New Layer dialog box, then click **OK**.

19. Invert the curve as you did before, then click **OK**.

Ask yourself: If you were to re-open the Invert adjustment layer right now, what would the curve look like?

20. Double-click the **Layer thumbnail** on the **Invert layer**.

Yet another example—and a good one—of the beauty of adjustment layers. The curve adjustment that you made is maintained in the dialog box and able to be readjusted.

21. Close the Curves dialog box, hide the Invert layer, then save your work.

Improve shadow points, white points, and midtones with curves

1. Hide every layer except for the Weak Highlights and Shadows layer, then target the **Weak Highlights and Shadows**.

   The image on this layer has been manipulated to show an example of weak shadow and highlight points—the darkest pixels need to be darker, and the lightest pixels need to be lighter.

2. Float your pointer around over the image and try to find the lightest grayscale value that you can.

   The light background contains the lightest pixels to be found—those with a grayscale value of 235. This means that there are 20 lighter pixels available on the grayscale that this image is not using.

3. Float your pointer over the image and try to find the darkest grayscale value that you can.

   The darkest pixels to be found are in the shadows underneath the man's collar—those with a grayscale value of 26. This means that there are 26 darker pixels available on the grayscale that this image is not using.

4. Create a new curves adjustment layer named **Improve Highlight/Shadow Points**.

5. Drag the **highlight point** to the left, so that your Input/Output values are the same as those in Figure 28.

   (continued)

FIGURE 28
Relocating the white point

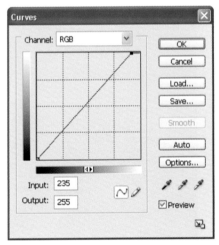

DESIGN*note*

When sampling for highlights, don't sample the white circles that usually appear in the center of a subject's eyes, as they do in this image. These highlights are created from a reflection of the camera's flash. In other words, they are artificial, and therefore shouldn't be used as part of your sample when adjusting highlights. Printers and retouchers refer to these highlights as *spectral* highlights.

FIGURE 29
Relocating the black point

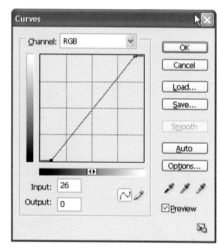

With this move, the pixels that were originally 235 are now 255. That's the move that you made to the white point. But remember the big point with curves: wherever the curve moves, all of the pixels on the curve change. Look carefully at the curve—at no point is it in the same location as it was originally. At every point, it is slightly above its original location. This makes sense. From your sampling, you know that the grayscale range of the original image was approximately 26–235. By relocating the white point to 235, you have taken all of those pixels and redistributed them from 26–255. If you look again at the curve, you can see that the lighter areas of the curve—in the upper-right quadrant—are much further above the location of the original curve then the darker areas of the curve. Put another way, the lighter areas of the image lightened up more than the darker areas of the image. However, it is important to note that the shadow point did not change. You cannot change the shadow point by moving the white point.

6. Drag the **shadow point** to the right, so that your Input/Output values are the same as those in Figure 29.

   With this move, the pixels that were originally 26 are now 0. Note the change to the curve. In the lower-left quadrant, the curve is below its original location—the dark half got darker. In the upper-right quadrant, the curve is above its original location—the lighter half got lighter. Note especially that the middle areas of the curve moved the least.

(continued)

7. Click to add a point anywhere on the curve, then move the point to the center so that your dialog box resembles Figure 30.

TIP If you like, you may enter numbers directly into the Input and Output text boxes.

FIGURE 30
Positioning the midpoint

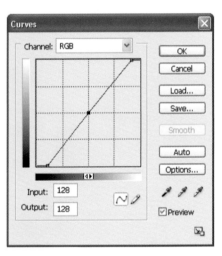

FIGURE 31
Darkening the midtones

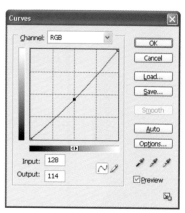

FIGURE 32
Brightening the midtones

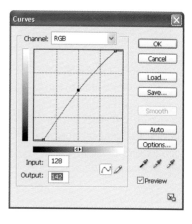

8. Drag the **midpoint** straight down so that your dialog box resembles Figure 31.

   The middle area of the curve—and the middle range of the image—are darkened.

9. Drag the **midpoint** straight up so that your dialog box resembles Figure 32.

   The midtones are lightened.

10. Remove the midpoint by dragging it out of the Curves dialog box.

11. Click **OK**, then save your work.

Improve contrast with curves

1. Hide every layer except for the Poor Contrast layer, then target the **Poor Contrast layer**.

2. Float your pointer over the image and try to find the lightest grayscale value and the darkest grayscale value that you can.

   The image on this layer has been manipulated to show an example of poor contrast in the dark gray to light gray range. Don't confuse this with the shadow point and the highlight point. In this image, the shadow and highlight points are set properly. The darkest pixels are in the single-digit area of the grayscale, and the lightest pixels are 250 or over. The poor contrast is in the range from the dark grays (grayscale value 64) and the light grays (grayscale value 191).

   (continued)

3. Position your Eyedropper Tool ✎ as shown in Figure 33.

   The pixels on the light side of the face are in the 165–195 range.

4. Position your Eyedropper Tool as shown in Figure 34.

   The pixels on the dark side of the face are in the 65–85 range.

5. Create a new curves adjustment layer named **Improve Contrast**.

   (continued)

Do not get your terms mixed up. *Highlights* are light gray areas of the image. The *highlight point*—or *white point*—is the whitest area of the image. *Shadows* are the dark gray areas of the image. The *shadow point*—or *black point*—is the blackest area of the image. This is all lingo, and none of it is official. The design and print worlds are replete with lingo, jargon, and catchphrases. It is important that you develop your own set of terminology that you can use to clearly identify specific areas of an image. Consider using the following five terms: *black point, shadows, midtones, highlights, white point.*

FIGURE 33
Sampling a highlight area

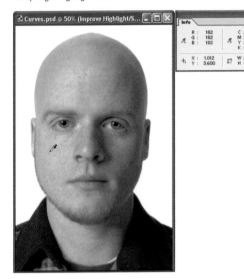

FIGURE 34
Sampling a shadow area

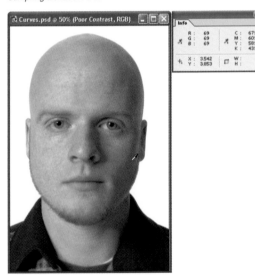

FIGURE 35

Identifying the 64 grayscale value on the curve

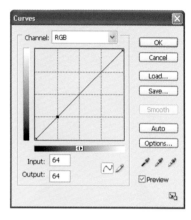

FIGURE 36

Identifying the 191 grayscale value on the curve

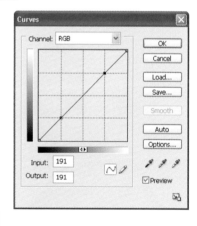

6. Add a point to the curve in the location shown in Figure 35.

   Grayscale 64 is commonly recognized as the central area of the shadows in an image, because 64 is exactly between 0 and 128.

7. Add a second point to the curve in the location shown in Figure 36.

   Grayscale 191 is commonly recognized as the central area of the highlights in an image, because 191 is exactly between 128 and 255.

   (continued)

8. Drag the **191 point** straight up so that your dialog box resembles Figure 37.

   Note the curve from the midpoint of the grid to the white point. With this move, every pixel in the "upper half" of the grayscale has been brightened.

9. Drag the **64 point** straight down so that your dialog box resembles Figure 38.

   Very important: Note the shape of the curve. It is a very subtle S-curve. An S-curve in the Curves dialog box always "bumps" contrast, meaning it increases the range from shadows to highlights.

10. Click the **Preview check box** on and off to see the change to the image.

11. Verify that the Preview check box is checked.

12. Drag the **64 point** in a southeast direction, and experiment with how far you can "push" the shadows without the image becoming too dark.

   Moving in a southeast direction, the input value is increasing and the output value is decreasing. This means that lighter and lighter original pixels are getting substantially darker and darker. Thus, darkening of the image becomes more dramatic, over an increased range.

   (continued)

FIGURE 37
Relocating the 191 point

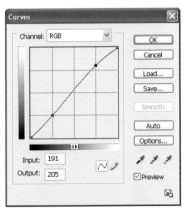

FIGURE 38
Relocating the 64 point

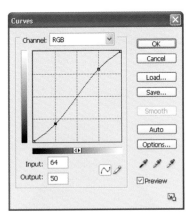

FIGURE 39
Deepening shadows further

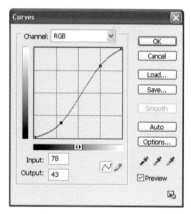

13. Set the Input/Output values as shown in Figure 39.

This is a great opportunity to consider an important concept about curves. The first move you made was from 64 to 50. This move is 78 to 43. Take a minute to think about the differences between those two moves. With the second move, a lighter range of pixels darkened more dramatically. The second move is a "bigger move."

14. Drag the **191 point** in a northwest direction, and experiment with how far you can push the highlights without them becoming too white.

Moving in a northwest direction, the input value is decreasing and the output value is increasing. This means that darker and darker original pixels are getting substantially lighter and lighter.

(continued)

DESIGNnote

Don't just accept cookie-cutter contrast bumps. Being willing and able to experiment with curves will empower you enormously. The best Photoshop designers are those who know how to use the software to achieve a specific look. With curves and your artist's eye, you can bring an image to life, convey a mood, or emphasize an emotion.

15. Set the Input/Output values as shown in Figure 40.

This S-curve is a dramatic increase in contrast. In a real-world project, the shadows might be considered too dark. However, note that the zigzag in the shirt collar is still visible. Note too that, although the light side of the face has become substantially lighter, its range maxes out in the 230 range—it is very distinct from the white background.

16. Drag the **Eyedropper Tool** 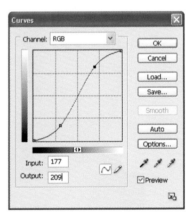 and note the response in the Curves dialog box.

A small circle appears on the curve indicating where the pixels the Eyedropper is sampling are located on the curve.

17. Click **OK**, then hide and show the adjustment layer to see the dramatic before-and-after comparison.

It's as though you were looking at the image through a dirty window that's been suddenly wiped clean. When working with contrast, it's often the case that you don't realize how bad the original image is until you make the change. If you analyze the curve in Figure 40, you'll see that every pixel above the midpoint is lighter, and every pixel below the midpoint is darker. But there's something else that's important for you to note: you have increased the distance between the two points that you added. Thus you have increased the range between shadows to highlights.

(continued)

FIGURE 40
Brightening highlights further

FIGURE 41

Viewing shadows that are too dark

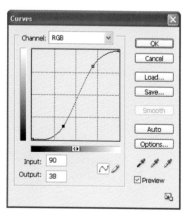

18. Double-click the **Layer thumbnail** on the Improve Contrast layer, then set the Input/Output values as shown in Figure 41.

The shadows become too dark. Note that the bottom range of the curve has flattened out—all of those pixels are black. The image reflects this problem: note how the shadow areas have no range—they're just black patches.

(continued)

DESIGN*note*

Note the lack of detail in the dark side of the face. There's no longer any range—it appears to be an area filled with a single dark gray or black color. Note how there's no distinction from the collar on the right where it meets the shadow on the neck. It's just all black.

19. Set the Input/Output values as shown in Figure 42.

The highlights are "blown out." Note the lack of detail in the light side of the face, and note the flat white patch in the forehead. If you sampled those areas, you would find pixels with a grayscale value of 255—way too bright for flesh tones. Also, note how the ear is disappearing into the white background.

20. Click **Cancel**, then save your work.

FIGURE 42

Viewing an image with too much contrast

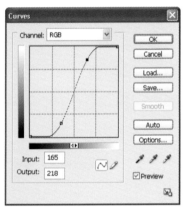

DESIGN*note*

Pushing too far is often a smart move. In other words, experimenting to see what too much contrast looks like will help you identify what too little contrast and just right contrast look like as well.

FIGURE 43

Specifying the threshold level

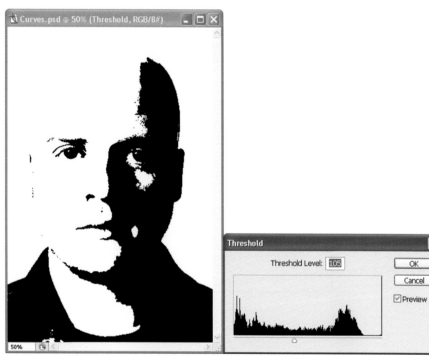

Draw a Threshold curve

1. Hide all layers except the Threshold layer, then target the **Threshold layer**.

2. Click **Image** on the menu bar, point to **Adjustments**, then click **Threshold**.

3. Verify that the Preview check box is checked, then view the image as you drag the **slider** in the Threshold dialog box.

   With a threshold effect, pixels are either black or white. The slider allows you to determine where your pixels become either white or black.

4. Drag the **slider** so that the Threshold Level text box reads 105, as shown in Figure 43.

   At 105, this means that all pixels whose grayscale values are 105 or below are now black. All pixels that were 106 or above are now white.

5. Click **OK**, click **Image** on the menu bar, click **Duplicate**, type **Threshold Copy**, then click **OK**.

6. Minimize the Threshold Copy window, return to the Curves document, click **Edit** on the menu bar, then click **Undo Threshold**.

(continued)

7. Create a new curves adjustment layer named **Threshold Curve**.

   How do you recreate the threshold effect with a curve? Remember, you want the point where pixels go from black to white to be at 105. What would that curve look like? Try to picture it in your mind before moving on.

8. Click the **pencil icon** 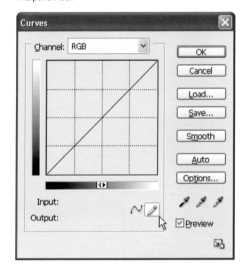 in the Curves dialog box, shown in Figure 44.

   (continued)

FIGURE 44
The pencil icon

FIGURE 45
Clicking the shadow point

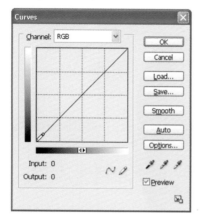

FIGURE 46
Clicking 105/0

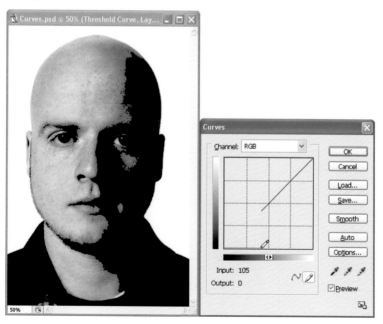

9. Position the pencil over the shadow point, as shown in Figure 45, then click.

10. Press and hold **[Shift]**, position the pencil at Input/Output location 105/0, then click so that your screen resembles Figure 46.

You have drawn a straight line from 0 to 105. This means that all the pixels whose input value were 0–105 now have an output value of 0; they're all black.

TIP The curve's color has been changed to red so that you can see them better.

(continued)

11. Release [Shift], position the pencil at Input/Output location 106/255, then click so that your screen resembles Figure 47.

Note the white pixels that now dot the image. The pencil in the Curves dialog box is extremely powerful. It allows you to specify a new output value for a *single* grayscale value. With this last move, the pixels with an input value of 106—*and only those pixels*—are now white. The white pixels you see dotting the image are those that were originally 106.

12. Press and hold [Shift], position the pencil at Input/Output location 255/255, then click so that your screen resembles Figure 48.

You have drawn a straight line from 106 to 255. This introduces an entirely new concept so far: the broken curve. The first half of the curve is a straight line from 0 to 105. The second half of the curve is a straight line from 106 to 255. Thus the threshold effect has been achieved.

13. Click **OK**.

(continued)

FIGURE 47
Clicking 106/255

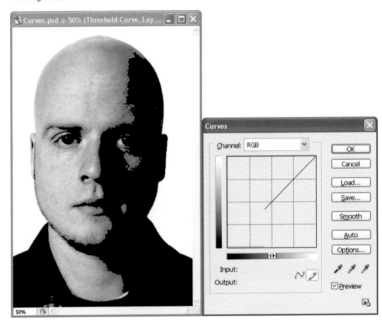

FIGURE 48
Clicking the white point

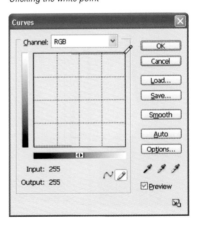

FIGURE 49

Comparing two threshold effects

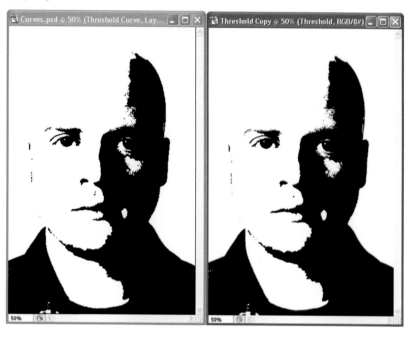

14. Maximize the Threshold Copy document, click **Window** on the menu bar, point to **Arrange**, click **Tile Vertically**, then compare your screen to Figure 49.

Threshold Copy, the effect you created with the menu command, is nearly identical to the effect you created in the Curves document.

15. Close Threshold Copy without saving changes to it.

16. Save your work.

DESIGN*note*

Don't miss the big picture here. Curves were used here to reproduce an effect that can be created with a menu command. You'd never do that for real; why would you, when it's so much easier to just use the menu command? The point here is that you *can* do it. If you can use curves to duplicate an effect done with a menu command, then it follows logically that you can use curves to slightly modify the effect. In other words, where most designers would be stuck with the result of the menu command, now that you know how to use curves to achieve that effect, you can create your own unique version of the effect. And even if you don't want to go that extra mile, you now have a much better understanding of what a threshold effect is and how Photoshop itself uses Curves algorithms to create it.

Draw a Posterize curve

1. Hide all layers except for the Posterize layer, then target the **Posterize layer**.

   First, you will posterize the image using the menu command.

2. Click **Image** on the menu bar, point to **Adjustments**, then click **Posterize**.

3. Type **4** in the Levels text box, if necessary, then click **OK**.

   Your screen should resemble Figure 50.

4. Click **Image** on the menu bar, click **Duplicate**, type **Posterize Copy**, then click **OK**.

5. Minimize the Posterize Copy document, return to the Curves document, click **Edit** on the menu bar, then click **Undo Posterize**.

6. Create a new curves adjustment layer named **Posterize Curve**.

   Why does the posterized image appear the way it does? Because all the pixels from 0–63 are now black. The pixels from 64–127 are now dark gray. The pixels from 128–190 are light gray, and the pixels from 191–255 are now white. So here's the question: If you were to duplicate this effect using a curve, what would you do? What would the curve look like? Take some time to think about it before moving on. Sketch it out on a piece of paper. Apply everything you've learned about grayscale and how the Curves dialog box functions. Test yourself. How would you do it?

7. Click the **pencil icon** [pencil] in the Curves dialog box, if necessary, then click the **shadow point**.

   (continued)

FIGURE 50
Posterizing with the menu command

FIGURE 51
Viewing the posterize curve

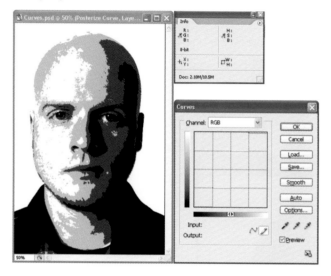

FIGURE 52
Comparing two posterize effects

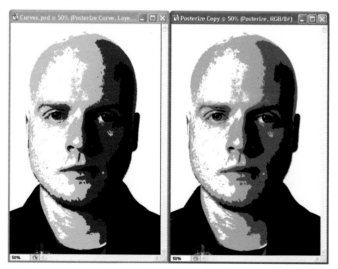

8. Press and hold **[Shift]**, then click the **64/0 point** on the grid.

   All pixels input from 0–64 are now 0.

9. Click the **64/64 point** on the grid.

   The 64 point is returned to its original value.

10. Press and hold **[Shift]**, then click the **128/64 point** on the grid.

    All pixels from 64–128 are now 64.

11. Click the **128/191 point** on the grid.

12. Press and hold **[Shift]**, then click the **191/191 point** on the grid.

    All the pixels from 128–191 are now 191.

13. Click the **191/255 point** on the grid.

14. Press and hold **[Shift]**, click the **white point (255/255)**, compare your screen to Figure 51, then click **OK**.

15. Maximize the Posterize Copy document, click **Window** on the menu bar, point to **Arrange**, click **Tile Vertically**, then compare your screen to Figure 52.

    The two effects are nearly identical.

16. Close the Posterize Copy document without saving changes to it.

17. Save your work.

ANALYZE AN
RGB Image

What You'll Do

This lesson was inevitable, don't you think? Up to this point, you've been studying grayscale and gray levels and how to manipulate them with levels and curves. And you've been working with black-and-white images. Now it's time to take what you've learned and apply it to a color image. With color, the whole concept gets a lot bigger. Actually, the concept is cubed! With black and white, you're dealing with 256 colors. With color, you're dealing with 256 colors in the Red channel, in the Green channel, and in the Blue channel. That's $256 \times 256 \times 256$. That's around 16.7 million colors. But here's the important point: Everything that you learned about grayscale and gray levels up to this point applies directly to working with color images. Use that knowledge as your first key to working with color.

FIGURE 53
Sampling color pixels

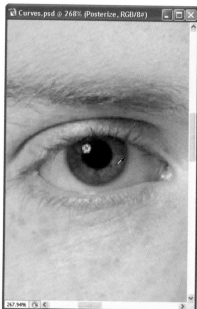

FIGURE 54

Sampling pixels in the Red channel

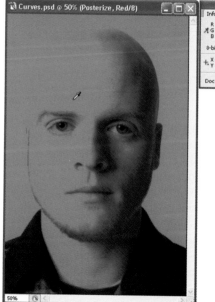

Analyze grayscale channels in a color image

1. Hide all layers except for the Color Image layer, then target the **Color Image layer**.

2. Zoom in on the left eye, sample pixels with the **Eyedropper Tool** 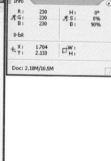, then compare your Info palette to Figure 53.

   Remember the #1 rule about pixels: pixels are only one color. When you sample color pixels, you'll note that they have an R value, a G value, and a B value. Those three values *together* define the pixel's color.

3. Return the view of the image to 50%.

4. Click **Edit** (Win) or **Photoshop** (Mac) on the menu bar, point to **Preferences**, then click **Display & Cursors**.

5. In the Display section, click the **Color Channels in Color check box**, then click **OK**.

6. Show the Channels palette, then click the **Red channel**.

7. Float the **Eyedropper Tool** over the image, then compare what you find to Figure 54.

   Because you are sampling in the Red channel, you are sampling only the red component of the pixels. The three numbers in the R, G, and B text boxes actually refer only to the red component of the pixels you are sampling. This can be a bit misleading, because you are not sampling G or B at all, and the numbers in the G and B text boxes of the Info palette have nothing to do with G and B, even though the palette says so.

(continued)

Lesson 3   Analyze an RGB Image

8. Sample the background area of the channel.

   Each channel—in this case, the Red channel—is a grayscale image. Each pixel can be one of 256 colors, from 0 (black) to 255 (red).

9. Click the **Green channel**, then sample different areas of the channel.

10. Click the **Blue channel**, then different areas of the image.

11. Click the **RGB channel**, sample the image, then compare your screen to Figure 55.

   In the RGB channel, the Eyedropper Tool samples each color component from each channel that makes up the image.

   TIP When viewing the RGB channel, you are viewing the actual color of the pixels—the color that is derived from the three component colors.

   (continued)

FIGURE 55
Sampling pixels in the RGB channel

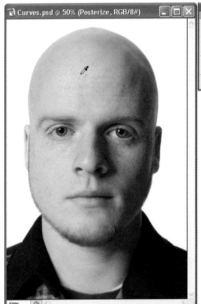

DESIGN*note*

Think about the pixels in an RGB image compared to those in a grayscale image. In Grayscale mode, there's only one channel. There are 256 colors available per pixel in the one channel. So there are 256 colors available in total. In an RGB image, there are 256 colors available for the red component of the pixel, 256 colors available for the green component of the pixel, and 256 colors available for the blue component of the pixel. This means that there are a total of over 16 million different colors that each pixel could potentially be ($256 \times 256 \times 256$). If you had two versions of the same image, one in Grayscale mode and one in RGB mode, the RGB file would be three times the file size (in memory) than the grayscale file, even though they have the same total number of pixels. This is because, in the RGB file, each pixel requires three times the amount of data than in the single channel image.

FIGURE 56
Sampling a white pixel

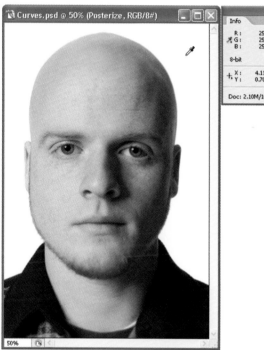

12. Position the Eyedropper Tool over the background area of the image, then compare your screen to Figure 56.

The pixel itself is white because its value is 255 in each of the three channels.

13. Save your work.

DESIGN*note*

Together, 255 Red, 255 Green, and 255 Blue make a white pixel. Remember, whenever the R, G, and B values are the same, the pixel has no chromatic color. It can only be a neutral gray in the range from black to white. 128, 128, 128 is a middle gray. 191, 191, 191 is a light gray, and so on.

Posterize a color image

1. Verify that the Color Image layer is targeted.

2. Click **Image** on the menu bar, point to **Adjustments**, click **Posterize**, type **4** in the Levels text box, then click **OK**.

3. In the Channels menu, click the **Red channel**, compare it to Figure 57, then sample the four gray levels created from the Posterize command.

   The Red channel contains four gray levels: 0, 85, 170, and 255.

4. Click the **Green channel**, then sample the levels.

5. Click the **Blue channel**, then sample the levels.

   The Green and Blue channels contain the same four gray levels as the Red channel.

6. Click through the three channels to see how the Posterize command affected each channel.

   Though the three channels have the same four levels, the Posterize command affected different areas differently in each channel.

7. Click the **RGB channel**, then sample different areas.

(continued)

FIGURE 57
Viewing the posterized Red channel

FIGURE 58

Sampling the red pixels

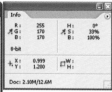

FIGURE 59

Sampling the yellow pixels

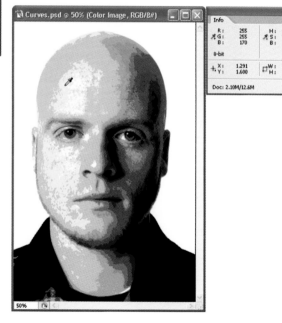

8. Position your pointer over the light red area in the forehead, as shown in Figure 58.

   When the Posterize command was applied, the pixels in this area changed to grayscale value 255. However, in the Green and Blue channels, the same area switched to the light gray value of 170. Therefore, the higher red value dominates the pixels in this area.

9. Position your pointer over the yellow area in the forehead, as shown in Figure 59.

   The pixels in this area changed to grayscale value 255 in *both* the Red and Green channels. In the Blue channel, the same area changed to the light gray value of 170. The higher red and green values dominate these pixels, giving them a yellow hue.

(continued)

Lesson 3   Analyze an RGB Image

10. Position your pointer over the dark yellow area on the head, as shown in Figure 60.

Again, the red and green values both dominate the blue. Therefore, these pixels also have a yellow hue. However because the three RGB components are darker than in the previous sample, the yellow created is also darker.

(continued)

FIGURE 60
Sampling the dark yellow pixels

DESIGNnote

Be sure you get the central point of this lesson. Unless you become a professional color retoucher, when you're working with an RGB image, you're not going to be concentrating on the grayscale values in each channel and why they are creating the pixel colors that you see in the RGB channel. With over 16 million pixel colors available, you'd have to be "Rain Man" to figure it out. But as a designer, it is important that you have an intellectual understanding that the color of every pixel in the RGB channel is derived from combining the grayscale values in the Red, Green, and Blue channels. Use this lesson as a clear example of that concept.

11. Position your pointer over the dark gray pixels in the chin, as shown in Figure 61.

    When posterized, this area was changed to grayscale value 85 in all three channels. Whenever the RGB values are the same, the pixel color must be black, white, or a neutral gray.

12. Save your work, then close the Curves document.

FIGURE 61

Sampling the dark gray pixels

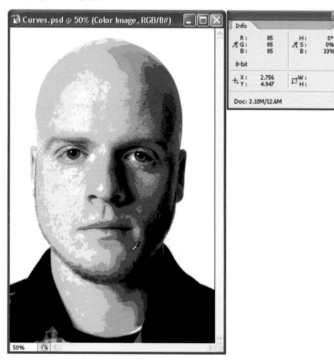

Part 1

1. Open AP 4-4.psd, then save it as **Levels Review.**
2. Fit the entire image on your monitor screen, decide which of the four you think has the best tonal range, and be prepared to explain your decision.
3. Make only the Top Left layer visible, target it in the Layers palette, then zoom in so that you are viewing the image at 50%.
4. Posterize the image to six levels.
5. Use the Magic Wand Tool to select all of the white pixels with one click.
6. Fill the selection with a color of your choosing.
7. Use the Magic Wand Tool to select the light gray pixels only in the neck, then fill that selection with a color of your choosing.
8. Use the Paint Bucket Tool to fill the remaining areas of the image. Use no more than eight colors (plus black, if you wish).

Part 2

1. Show the Top Right layer, target it, then zoom in so that you are viewing the image at 50%.
2. Use the Eyedropper Tool to find the brightest pixels in the image, then write down that grayscale value on a piece of paper.
3. Use the Eyedropper Tool to find the darkest pixel, then write down that number.

4. Click Layer on the menu bar, point to New Adjustment Layer, then click Levels.
5. Name the new adjustment layer **White/Black Point**, and be sure to use the previous layer as a clipping mask. (*Hint*: Be sure to click the Use Previous Layer as Clipping Mask check box whenever you create a new adjustment layer in the remainder of this Project Builder.)
6. Click OK.
7. In the Levels dialog box, improve the image by resetting the white point and the black point.

Part 3

1. Show the Bottom Left layer, target it, then zoom in so that you are viewing the image at 50%.
2. Find the brightest pixel in the image.
3. Find the darkest pixel.
4. Create a new levels adjustment layer named **Midtone Adjustment**.
5. Improve the image by correcting the white point and the black point.
6. Lighten or darken the midtones to a level that you think looks best.

Part 4

1. Show the Bottom Right layer, target it, then zoom in so that you are viewing the image at 50%.
2. Use the Magic Wand Tool to select only the white background of the image.
3. Click Select on the menu bar, click Inverse, then hide the selection marquee.
4. Create a new levels adjustment layer named **Head Selection**.
5. Make the image look the best you think it can look.
6. Compare your artwork to Figure 62.
7. Save and close Levels Review.

FIGURE 62
Completed Project Builder 1

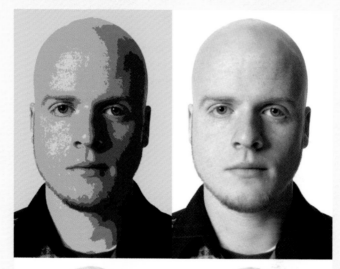

Part 1

1. Open AP 4-5.psd, then save it as **Curves Review.**
2. Fit the image on your computer screen.
3. Target the layer named Left Side.
4. Create a new curves adjustment layer named **Left Side Curves.**
5. In the Curves dialog box, fix only the white point and the black point, and brighten the midtones until you think the left side looks good.
6. Target the layer named Right Side.
7. Create a new curves adjustment layer named **Right Side Curves**, and be sure to click the Use Previous Layer as Clipping Mask check box.
8. Use the curve to improve the contrast only until you think the right side looks good. Don't yet try to match the two sides.
9. Adjust either side or both sides until the two halves can pass for one image, as shown in Figure 63.
10. Save and close Curves Review.

FIGURE 63
Completed Project Builder 2

LAURA KENT
ANTHONY BURTON
BLACK KNIGHT
THEATRUM MUNDI PICTURES PRESENTS
MIRIBILE VISU AND THEATRUM MUNDI PRESENT IN ASSOCIATION WITH AD ASTRA AND AD CROMENUM A ALEA IACTA EST PRODUCTION "IPSISSIMA VERBA"
DUX FEMINA FACTI PLACENS UXOR AND DRAMATIS PERSONAE INTER PARES SIMPLEX MUNDITISS VESTITUS AMPLUS IGNIS FATUUS
TOTIDEM VERBIS FIAT LUX SCHOLA CANTORUM DATA ET ACCEPTA "IPSISSIMA VERBA" BY EDITO PRINCEPS FATA VIAM INVENIENT
OPUS ARTIFICEM PROBAT NIHIL QUOD TETIGIT NON ORNAVIT LAPSUS CALAM
HOLLYWOOD STUDIO

5

DESIGNING WITH
Multiple Images

1. Create a concept for a poster.

2. Assess supplied images.

3. Position images for a background setting.

4. Integrate multiple images into a single background image.

5. Position foreground images.

6. Merge two images.

7. Integrate foreground images.

8. Finish artwork.

CREATE A CONCEPT
for a Poster

What You'll Do

Fasten your seatbelts; you're in for a great ride. Throughout the eight lessons in this chapter, you're going to build a movie poster—from scratch. Actually, you're going to build the movie poster that I built when I first wrote this chapter. The design dialog that runs throughout the chapter will be first-person commentary from me, sharing with you the decisions I made—and why I made them—as I created this poster.

Step by step, you'll build the poster with me, just as I did the first time around. You'll even make the mistakes that I made and take the same wrong turns that I took. And then you'll backtrack and fix your mistakes just like I did. My goal here was to create as much of a real-world project as I could, and then strap you in beside me—my designer copilot—as I retrace my steps.

Real-world is the key here. The images you'll use are stock images that I researched myself—having no idea if they'd actually work together for the concept I had in mind. About the only thing that I created in advance was the concept.

The concept is this: We are art directors working for a Hollywood agency that designs and produces first-run movie posters. We've just been brought in on a new project: *Black Knight*. Here's what the client has told us about *Black Knight*.

- It's an American-produced film, but it was shot in England.
- It stars two respected actors.
- The actress has the leading role. She is played by a very popular American actress (doing a solid English accent).
- The actor is British, well-respected for both his stage and film work.

- The plot, in a nutshell, is as follows: The king has been away at battle for months. The queen falls in love with another man—a knight, believing that her jealous king is far away and may never return. Unknown to her, he has actually returned and is masquerading as a servant in the castle. The queen's handmaiden alerts the queen to the King's ruse. Before the king can confront the queen about her admirer, she has him jailed as a thief who has invaded the castle. A battle of wills

develops between the royals—she knows that he knows, and he knows that she knows that he knows. Trying to test her, he sentences the man to death, believing the queen will have no choice but to confess her infidelity. To his surprise, the defiant queen accepts his gambit. Vowing vengeance, the "thief" is suited in armor and burned at the stake. His silver armor is blackened. After his death, stories begin circulating that a mysterious black knight has been seen in the dark of night. The royals dismiss this as mere hysteria— until the queen's handmaiden is found dead.

■ The marketing team has positioned this film in two important ways: first, as an historical thriller, with lots of action, suspense, and sword battles between mounted knights and kings; however, it's also positioned as a costume-drama-romance. The client's marketing team wants your agency to design a poster expressing both these approaches.

After coming up with this concept, I sketched out the thumbnails shown in Figures 1, 2, and 3. Based on the marketing strategy, I determined that I wanted the following five elements in the poster: the queen, the king, the black knight, a sword, and a castle. The king and queen are the "star sell"—the famous people that everybody likes and wants to pay money to see. The black knight is the title character.

FIGURE 1
Poster thumbnail

A black knight is so visually interesting that I knew it alone would define the mysterious, menacing quality that I wanted the poster to have. Working in concert with the beautiful queen, it would also generate the romantic aspect that I needed to convey: a dangerous story of forbidden love, passion, and revenge.

I knew immediately that I wanted to use a castle somewhere in the poster. I need it to establish a sense of place and time—nothing says medieval England like a castle. Finally, the sword plays a central role in the poster. As a visual cue, it signals both the action/battle and the history/romance that the client desires.

FIGURE 2
Thumbnail of castle and knight

FIGURE 3
Thumbnail of sword

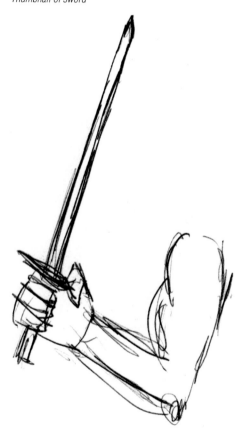

ASSESS SUPPLIED
Images

What You'll Do

Before I even think about starting to design a poster, I prepare myself for at least a few hours of assessing, retouching, and preparing my supplied images to be used as artwork.

You've probably heard thousands of times that "those beautiful people in the ads don't really look like that." Well guess what…it's true. In every case, posters, advertisements, magazine covers, you name it, the final images you see have gone through substantial amounts of preparation and retouching.

As a designer, this stage for you has two components. First you must assess the images to get a sense of how they can be positioned and combined to achieve the look that you are working toward. It's one thing to sketch out a concept, but it's another thing to utilize actual photography that will work within that concept. Second, you must "clean up" the raw materials.

Whenever you're working with photographs that show people, some amount of retouching will be involved. It may be minor, or it may be extensive, but it will always be necessary.

When retouching, I approach an image from three perspectives. From the cosmetic perspective, I work to hide flaws. Those flaws might be problems with the photograph such as dust or hairs in the image, or they might be problems with the subject, such as skin imperfections.

From the enhancement perspective, I work to improve the effect of the image. Especially when you are working on a project like this, which is romantic and atmospheric, it's important that your artwork be effective. This type of retouching would include making the color of the image more vivid, the eyes more entrancing, and so on.

Finally, from the realistic perspective, I try to identify problems with the originals that won't work realistically within my concept. There could be any number of problems from this perspective, and they're not always easy to identify before you start working.

One example would be lighting. If I'm planning to combine two headshots of two different actors, it will be a realistic problem if one is lit from the right and the other from the left. Or if one has a blue highlight and the other has a red highlight.

In this lesson, you will examine three photographs to see the changes and retouching that I applied. You won't actually do the retouching—that's something you'll do in an upcoming chapter—but you will be able to see the work that I did to the images long before I began designing the poster. I timed myself, and in total, I spent about 2.5 hours working on the images you're about to assess.

Assess the image of the big knight

1. Open Big Knight.psd, shown in Figure 4.

2. Hide and show the Adjust Levels layer.

   This was a simple move in which I darkened the shadow point to increase contrast and to improve the depth of the shadows. When you are done examining the change, verify that the Adjust Levels layer is showing.

   > **TIP** Throughout this chapter, you will be asked to hide and show layers to see a before and after effect. In every case, verify that the layer is showing when you are done.

3. Hide and show the Remove Sword layer.

   As shown in Figure 5, I removed the sword entirely using the Clone Stamp Tool. Where the sword overlapped the armor was difficult and time consuming. If you look closely, however, you'll see that I wasn't overly concerned with making the armor "perfect." This is because I knew in advance that the knight will be very dark against a very dark background and that not too much detail would be visible.

   (continued)

FIGURE 4
Big Knight.psd original

FIGURE 5
Removing the sword

FIGURE 6
The silhouette

FIGURE 7
Actress.psd original

4. Target and show only the Silo layer.

   Because the background was basically one color, I was able to use the Magic Wand Tool to create the silhouette shown in Figure 6. This made the task quick and easy.

5. Verify that all layers are showing, save your work, then close Big Knight.psd.

Assess the image of the actress

1. Open Actress.psd, shown in Figure 7.

2. Verify that the Background layer is the only layer visible and that it is targeted.

   The very first problem I noticed was a big one—my lead actress was not in costume. Often, actors and actresses are photographed in their street clothes simply for a face shot. Another model is then photographed in the costume for the movie. As the poster designer, you're expected to merge the face of the actor into the costume.

   (continued)

3. Open Damsel.psd, shown in Figure 8.

   I chose this image for the costume. Eventually, I'll need to replace the damsel's face with the actress's face. I must keep this in mind as I assess the photo of the actress.

4. Return to the Actress.psd file, then click the **Zoom Tool** 🔍 on her nose until you are viewing the entire head at 100%.

   The blue highlight on the right side of her face will present a problem when she's copied into the damsel's costume. There will be no reason for the actress to have a blue highlight on her face. In fact, because of the scarf that will be "put on" her head, her face will be shadowed rather than highlighted.

5. Show the No Highlight layer.

   As shown in Figure 9, this change involved replacing the soft, highlighted edge of her face. This involved creating a path to define the edge of her face, and about 45 minutes of cloning with the Clone Stamp Tool to create a flesh tone that was continuous with the rest of her face.

6. Show the Remove Scar layer.

   An excellent example that nobody's perfect.

   (continued)

FIGURE 8
Damsel.psd original

FIGURE 9
Removing a highlight from the face

FIGURE 10
Enhancing the eyes

7. Show the Reduce Eyeshadow layer.

   Conceptually, this one was trickier than it seems. A woman in medieval times wouldn't have had such dramatic eyeshadow, if any at all. However, this is a romantic Hollywood movie and she's a glamorous actress—not a plain Jane. As a designer, my choice was to keep her beautiful and glamorous, but to reduce the extreme touches.

8. Show the Reduce Lip Gloss layer.

9. Show the Shadow Right Side layer.

   The face that I cloned in was starting to look strange to me. Nobody's face exists on a flat plane, so I added shadow to convey a sense of dimension. Also, I knew in advance that her face would be shadowed on the sides when she's pasted into the damsel's costume.

10. Show the Whiten Eyes, Outline Iris, and Eye Power layers.

   As shown in Figure 10, these standard moves can make the eyes far more interesting and entrancing. Again, since this is a romantic movie about kings, queens, and knights, these changes are that much more useful for the overall effect.

11. Show the Darken Eyebrows layer.

   From reading the script, I know that the character of the queen is both the heroine and the villain. Darkening the brows adds intensity and an edge to her features.

(continued)

12. Target the **No Highlight layer**, press and hold **[Shift]**, then select all the layers above it.

> **TIP** Only the Background layer should not be selected.

13. Click the **Layers palette list arrow**, click **New Group from Layers**, accept the default name, then click **OK** to close the New Group from Layers dialog box.

    The selected layers are collected into a single folder named Group 1.

14. Hide and show the Group 1 layer to see a before-and-after comparison of all the retouching changes applied to the image.

15. Keep the Actress file open but do not save changes at this point.

16. Close the Damsel.psd document.

Assess the image of the king

1. Open King.psd, then zoom in so that you are viewing his face at 100%.

2. Target the **Background layer**, then verify that the Background layer is the only layer visible.

3. Arrange the King.psd and the Actress.psd documents side by side, if possible.

    The focus and the lighting on the king image is very different from that of the actress image. Since they will be positioned side by side in the final poster, I needed to make the two images as similar in tonal range as possible.

    (continued)

FIGURE 11
Lightening the king to match the actress

FIGURE 12

Smoothing the king's face

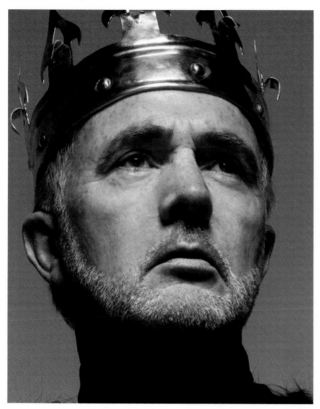

4. Show the No Sword layer.

5. Show the Match Actress layer.

   As shown in Figure 11, I lightened the highlights and midtones dramatically to improve contrast and to mimic the overall lightness of the actress image.

6. Show the Lighten eyes layer.

7. Show the Soften pockmarks layer.

   As shown in Figure 12, the face is smoothed out overall.

8. Show the next three layers to see the same standard eye retouches as you saw in the actress file.

9. Show the Add Grain layer.

   The Actress.psd document has a distinct grainy quality that the King.psd photo lacks.

10. Create a new layer group with all the retouched layers, then hide and show the new group for a before-and-after view of all the changes.

11. Close King.psd and Actress.psd, without saving changes to either.

DESIGN*note*

Nobody's perfect, but alas some are closer to perfect than others. Our older actor lacks the near-flawless complexion of our youthful actress. That's not such a big deal, as he is indeed older and, as a king, he's rugged and manly. However, twenty minutes with the Clone Stamp Tool softens the harsh texture overall and helps to make our leading man just a bit more Hollywood handsome.

POSITION IMAGES FOR
a Background Setting

What You'll Do

The great thing about designing movie posters is that you need to tell a story. Sometimes, when there's a really big star in the movie, all you need to do is run a picture of the star and the title. Any poster for a movie with Jim Carrey would be a good example of this. For most titles, however, the poster needs to convey some aspect of the story. For a designer, this is an opportunity to get creative and to design some interesting, evocative artwork.

But make no mistake, in today's Hollywood the movie poster is usually a "star sell." Not always, of course, but if there's a recognizable star in the movie, the studio usually wants that star in the poster. For you the designer, this means that telling the story will happen in the background, usually behind a big headshot of the big movie star.

With this type of poster, the challenge for you is to design the poster as a world unto itself. It's almost as if the poster is a glimpse into the world of the movie. This means that much of your work will be focused on the background imagery of the poster—and that's usually the place you start to work.

FIGURE 13

Stars.psd image in the poster file

Position images

1. Open AP 5-1.psd, then save it as **Black Knight Poster**.

2. If necessary, resize the window so that you can see the entire canvas.

3. Open Stars.psd, select all, copy, then close the file.

4. Paste the selection into the poster, then name the new layer **Stars**.

   TIP   If the Paste Profile Mismatch dialog box appears, click the Don't show again check box, then click OK.

5. Compare your canvas to Figure 13.

6. Sample the blacks in the Stars image to verify that they are truly black.

   This is an example of how you need to be conscious of grayscale values while you work. In our concept, this is a deep, dark black night's sky. An alert designer will take the time to sample the image to verify that it is as black as can be, which in this case, it is.

7. Open Billing.psd, select all, copy, then close the file.

(continued)

8. Paste the selection into the poster, then name the new layer **Billing**.

> **TIP** Be sure to name layers with descriptive names. By the end of this chapter, this file will have about 50 layers, and you'll be so thankful when you're scrolling through the Layers palette that you took the time to name each individual layer.

9. In the Layers palette, change the blending mode for the Billing layer to Screen, then compare your canvas to Figure 14.

The Screen blending mode makes black pixels completely transparent. This is a great example of how useful this blending mode can be. As a designer, you will use the Screen blending mode frequently.

10. Save your work.

FIGURE 14
Result of the Screen blending mode

DESIGN*note*

When I design posters, one of the first things I do is position the important text elements. The type elements do a lot to define the look of the piece. Already, this looks like a movie poster, and that helps me to visualize the final poster while I'm working. Also, I place the type elements in the beginning of the project simply to reserve space for them while I'm working. Otherwise, I might create a great piece of artwork then realize I've not left enough room for the billing block!

FIGURE 15

The Big Knight artwork pasted on the Big Knight layer

1. Target the **Stars layer**.

2. Open Big Knight.psd, target the **Silo layer**, select all, copy, then close the file.

3. Paste the selection, then name the new layer **Big Knight**.

   Your canvas should resemble Figure 15.

4. Hide the Billing layer.

5. Display the Options bar, if necessary, then verify that the center point is selected in the Reference point location in the Options bar.

6. Press **[Ctrl][T]** (Win) or ⌘**[T]** (Mac) to scale the image.

   Once you press **[Ctrl][T]** (Win) or ⌘**[T]** (Mac), the Options bar displays the physical attributes of the image within the bounding box, such as its X and Y locations, and its horizontal and vertical scale.

7. Moving left to right, type **555.7** in the X text box, press **[Tab]**, type **514.7** in the Y text box, press **[Tab]**, type **80** in the W text box, press **[Tab]**, type **80** in the H text box, then press **[Tab]**.

(continued)

DESIGNnote

Throughout this chapter, you will scale and position images exactly as I did when I designed the poster. Not only will this help us to avoid potential problems with your images being a slightly different size or a slightly different location than mine, it offers the opportunity for you to learn to use the Options bar to position the images in a specific location.

8. Click the **Move Tool** ⊕ , click **Apply** to execute the transformation, then compare your screen to Figure 16.

   The Big Knight image was scaled 80%; the location of its center point is 555.7 pixels from the left edge of the canvas and 514.7 pixels from the top.

9. Save your work.

FIGURE 16
Positioning the big knight

DESIGN*note*

At this point, an alert is sounding in my head. I'm thinking that the knight is looking a lot like Darth Vader, especially against that black starry sky that looks so much like outer space. This is not a big shock—Darth Vader really does look a lot like a knight. From my design perspective, this is first a bad thing, but also a good thing. It's bad because I don't want the final image to look silly or like a cheap knock-off of *Star Wars*. It's a good thing because I remember the great *Star Wars* posters and how Darth Vader was used so effectively as a background image.

FIGURE 17

Hard Light blending mode

1. Verify that the Big Knight layer is targeted.

2. Experiment with all of the blending modes in the Layers palette.

   So much of working in modern day Photoshop involves blending modes, and so much of working with blending modes involves experimentation. Through experimentation, you can become familiar with the basic functions of the major blending modes. Be sure to take note of how they are grouped in the palette menu. Modes that generally lighten an image are grouped together, as are modes that generally darken an image.

3. Choose the Hard Light blending mode, then compare your screen to Figure 17.

4. Click **Layer** on the menu bar, point to **New Adjustment Layer**, then click **Hue/Saturation**.

(continued)

5. Type **Desaturate** in the Name text box, click the **Use Previous Layer to Create Clipping Mask check box**, then click **OK**.

> **TIP** Whenever you are asked to create an adjustment layer, always click the Use Previous Layer to Create Clipping Mask check box unless you are instructed not to.

6. Drag the **Saturation slider** to –50, click **OK**, then compare your screen to Figure 18.

   Because the Hard Light blending mode made the knight artwork transparent, we can now see the stars artwork through the knight artwork, which is not an effect I want.

7. Press and hold **[Ctrl]** (Win) or ⌘ (Mac), then click the **Layer thumbnail** on the Big Knight layer to load its selection.

8. Click the **Rectangular Marquee Tool** [⬚], press and hold **[Shift]**, then add the bottom of the canvas to the selection so that your screen resembles Figure 19.

9. Target the **Stars layer**.

(continued)

FIGURE 18
Desaturating the big knight

FIGURE 19
Selecting areas for a mask

FIGURE 20

Masking out the stars where they overlap the big knight

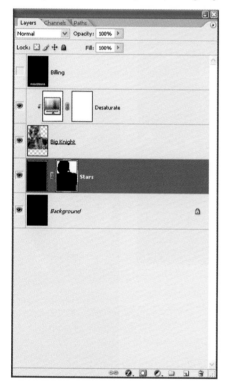

10. Press and hold **[Alt]** (Win) or **[option]** (Mac) then click the **Add layer mask button** on the Layers palette.

As shown in Figure 20, a layer mask is added with the selected area automatically filled with black. Everything is automatically deselected.

> **TIP** When any selection is loaded, pressing and holding [Alt] (Win) or [option] (Mac), then clicking the Add layer mask button creates a layer mask in which the selected pixels are filled with black. If you are not holding [Alt] (Win) or [option] (Mac) when you click the Add layer mask button, the selected pixels will be filled with white in the layer mask.

11. Target the **Big Knight layer**, press and hold **[Shift]**, then click to select the adjustment layer above it.

12. Click the **Layers palette list arrow**, then click **New Group from Layers**.

13. Type **Black Knight Group** in the Name text box, then click **OK**.

14. Show the Billing layer to see how things are looking, then hide it again.

15. Save your work.

Control the effect of the Hard Light blending mode

1. Sample the image, then note in the Info palette that the black areas of the image are pure black.

(continued)

From my design perspective, the knight is too black, so much so that he's mostly invisible against the black background and difficult to identify as a knight. Since there's no way to control the degree to which the Hard Light blending mode affects the artwork, I'm going to use a work-around technique.

2. Click the **gray triangle** to expand the Black Knight Group, then target the **Big Knight layer**.

3. Press and hold **[Ctrl]** (Win) or [⌘] (Mac), then click the **Create a new layer button** 🗐 on the Layers palette.

   A new empty layer is added *below* the Big Knight layer.

4. Name the new layer **White**.

5. Press and hold **[Ctrl]** (Win) or [⌘] (Mac), then click the **Layer thumbnail** on the Big Knight layer to load its selection.

6. Press **[X]** to change the foreground color to white, fill the selection, deselect, then compare your screen to Figure 21.

7. Reduce the opacity of the White layer to 30%, then compare your screen to Figure 22.

   With this method, we can use the White layer as an artificial way to control the effect that the Hard Light blending mode has on the knight image.

   (continued)

FIGURE 21

Filling white behind the Hard Light blending mode

FIGURE 22

Reducing the opacity of the White layer

FIGURE 23
Masking the white copy

FIGURE 24
The final effect

8. Add a layer mask to the White layer.

9. Click the **Brush Tool** , type **[X]** to switch to a black foreground color, verify that the Opacity is set to 100%, then choose a medium-sized hard brush.

10. Mask out every area of the White layer except the head.

 Your artwork should resemble Figure 23.

11. Add a layer mask to the Big Knight layer, then mask the same area as you did in the White mask so that only the knight's head is visible.

12. Reduce the opacity of the White layer to 5%, then compare your screen to Figure 24.

13. Collapse the Black Knight Group layer.

14. Save your work.

Position three background images

1. Verify that the **Black Knight Group layer** is targeted.

2. Open Castle.psd, target the **Silo layer**, select all, copy, then close the file.

3. Paste the selection, then name the new layer **Castle**.

   TIP The new layer should be immediately above the Black Knight Group layer.

4. Press **[Ctrl][T]** (Win) or ⌘[T] (Mac) to scale the image.

5. Type **692** in the X text box, press **[Tab]**, type **1283** in the Y text box, press **[Tab]**, type **63** in the W text box, press **[Tab]**, type **63** in the H text box, then press **[Tab]**.

6. Click the **Move Tool**  to execute the transformation, click **Apply**, then compare your screen to Figure 25.

(continued)

FIGURE 25
Positioning the castle

DESIGN*note*

The castle plays such an important role. First, it identifies a recognizable place. Second, it provides depth to the background. The black grass provides a much-needed foreground object, which also adds to the sense of depth.

FIGURE 26

Pasting the Moon artwork

7. Target the **Black Knight Group layer**.

8. Open Moon.psd, target the **Silo layer**, select all, copy, then close the file.

9. Paste the selection into the poster, then name the new layer **Moon**.

   Your canvas should resemble Figure 26.

10. Press **[Ctrl][T]** (Win) or ⌘**[T]** (Mac) to scale the image.

11. Type **881** in the X text box, press **[Tab]**, type **843** in the Y text box, press **[Tab]**, type **52** in the W text box, press **[Tab]**, type **52** in the H text box, then press **[Tab]**.

(continued)

Lesson 3   Position Images for a Background Setting

12. Click  to execute the transformation, click **Apply**, then compare your screen to Figure 27.

I'm already thinking that the moon is a wrong turn. To my eye, it's making the whole concept look more like sci-fi, which makes the knight look more like Darth Vader. I don't like the way the moon mimics the roundness of the knight's helmet, and I don't like that it adds such a distinctive geometric element to the piece either. However, it's still worth a try, and I don't have any other ideas at this point.

13. Open Small Knight.psd, target the **Silo layer**, select all, copy, then close the file.

14. Verify that the **Moon layer** is targeted, paste the selection, then name the new layer **Small Knight**.

15. Press **[Ctrl][T]** (Win) or ⌘[T] (Mac) to scale the image.

(continued)

FIGURE 27
Positioning the moon

FIGURE 28
Positioning the small knight

18. Type **824.1** in the X text box, press **[Tab]**, type **731.3** in the Y text box, press **[Tab]**, type **40** in the W text box, press **[Tab]**, type **40** in the H text box, then press **[Tab]**.

19. Click ➤✥ to execute the transformation, click **Apply**, then compare your screen to Figure 28.

20. Save your work.

INTEGRATE MULTIPLE IMAGES INTO A
Single Background Image

What You'll Do

Once you've positioned the images that you want to use in a poster, there always comes this critical point where this hodge-podge needs to be integrated so that it becomes one piece of art. This is often a strange, exciting, and nerve-wracking transition. Positioning the images is a challenge for a designer's layout skills. Integrating the images challenges a whole different set of skills. This is where your individuality as a designer really comes into play. Given the layout in this chapter, 10 different designers would create 10 different pieces of artwork—even though they're all working with the same base imagery. And that's great—because design is all about individuality, and there's never a right solution. However, the challenge itself is always that same one: How do you use a bunch of photos to make one piece of art?

FIGURE 29

Painting black to convey depth and distance

Create depth between placed images

1. Assess the relationship between the castle and the small knight behind it.

   Together, these two images are a great example of one of the toughest challenges you'll face when working with multiple images: the need to create a sense of depth. First, look at the castle. Behind it is the small knight, and behind the small knight is the moon. Note how much imagery is in front of the castle: the bridge, the water, the shadows, the foliage in the foreground, and so on. But there's nothing behind the castle. Note the relationship between the castle and the knight. Clearly, the knight is behind the castle, but how far behind it? They appear to be on the same plane. These issues are typical of the problems you'll confront when creating composite art.

2. Click the **Brush Tool** 🖌, then press **[X]** to specify a black foreground color.

3. Choose the Soft Round 200 pixels brush, then target the **Small Knight layer**.

4. Paint a black streak across the bottom half of the small knight, below his belt, as shown in Figure 29.

   The simple black streak creates the illusion that the knight is farther back behind the castle. This is a standard technique that designers use: put some color between the two overlapping images to create depth. It's just an illusion, but the eye registers it instantly as depth.

(continued)

5. Undo and redo to see the effect.

6. Click **Edit** on the menu bar, then click **Undo Brush Tool**.

7. Open Small Knight.psd.

8. Target the **Knight and Trees layer**, select all, copy, then close the document.

9. Paste the selection into the poster, then name the new layer **Knight and Trees**.

   | **TIP** The new layer should be immediately above the Small Knight layer in the Layers palette.

10. Scale the small knight in the Knight and Trees layer 40%, then align him to the previous copy of the small knight.

    Your screen should resemble Figure 30.

    (continued)

FIGURE 30
Scaling and aligning the second small knight

FIGURE 31
Moving the layer

11. Change the blending mode on the Knight and Trees layer to Multiply.

   Multiply is one of the most commonly used blending modes. Pixels retain their color, but they become completely transparent and therefore blend with the pixels of images behind them.

   > **TIP** Because Multiply makes pixels transparent, designers often use it to align two overlapping images, as with this case of the two small knights.

12. Zoom in and verify that the two knights are perfectly aligned.

   > **TIP** Use the arrow keys to move the top image one pixel at a time. When the details are in focus, the images are aligned.

13. Zoom out so that you can see the entire canvas.

14. In the Layers palette, drag the **Knight and Trees layer** below the Small Knight layer, then compare your screen to Figure 31.

(continued)

DESIGNnote

The trees resolved the depth issue between the small knight and the moon, but not between the small knight and the castle in front of him.

15. Target the **Small Knight layer**, click the **Create a new layer button**  on the Layers palette, then name the new layer **Darken Small Knight**.

16. Click the **Brush Tool** , then paint with black to create a shadow below the knight's belt, as shown in Figure 32.

17. Press and hold **[Alt]** (Win) or **[option]** (Mac), position your pointer between the Darken Small Knight and the Small Knight layers, then click to clip the Darken Small Knight layer into the Small Knight layer beneath it.

    Your screen should resemble Figure 33.

18. Select the three Small Knight layers, make a new layer group, then name the new group **Small Knight Group**.

19. Save your work.

FIGURE 32
Shadowing the small knight

FIGURE 33
Clipping the layers to create the effect

FIGURE 34
Desaturating the castle

Use adjustment layers to integrate artwork

1. Target the **Castle layer**.

2. Click **Layer** on the menu bar, point to **New Adjustment Layer**, then click **Hue/Saturation**.

3. Type **Desaturate Background** in the Name text box, do not check the Use Previous layer to Create Clipping Mask check box, then click **OK**.

4. Drag the **Saturation slider** to −80, click **OK**, then compare your canvas to Figure 34.

5. Undo and redo to examine how this simple move does so much to integrate the artwork.

(continued)

DESIGN*note*

Desaturated, the images all share a common look. Also, the setting is more realistic with the images desaturated. This is a night setting—a very dark night at that. It's not possible that the knight's garment could appear as such a bright red in the pale light of the moon. With the desaturation adjustment layer, it is reasonable to believe that both the castle and the knight are illuminated by the moon.

6. Display the Info palette, then sample the shadow areas on the small knight.

   The small knight suffers from weak shadows. Note how the streak of black paint is so much darker than the shadow areas of the small knight.

7. Expand the Small Knight Group layer, then target the **Small Knight layer**.

8. Click **Layer** on the menu bar, point to **New Adjustment Layer**, then click **Levels**.

9. Type **Deepen Shadows** in the Name text box, check the **Use Previous Layer to Create Clipping Mask check box**, then click **OK**.

10. Drag the **black triangle** to the right until the far-left Input text box reads 22, then click **OK**.

    The deepened shadows dramatically increase the sense of depth between the castle and the knight and make the knight more scary and menacing.

11. Target the **Knight and Trees layer**, apply the exact same levels adjustment to it, then compare your Layers palette to Figure 35 and your artwork to Figure 36.

(continued)

FIGURE 35
Layers palette

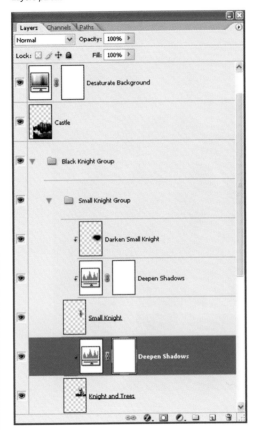

FIGURE 36
Darkened shadows in small knight artwork

FIGURE 37
Adjusting levels

12. Collapse the Small Knight Group layer, then target the **Castle layer**.

    As a foreground image, both the castle and the water in front of it should be brighter, sharper, and more distinct than the shadowy knight.

13. Apply a Levels adjustment layer named **Brighten Castle**.

    TIP Be sure to click the Use Previous Layer to Create Clipping Mask check box.

14. Type **32** in the left Input text box, type **1.4** in the middle text box, type **180** in the right text box, click **OK**, then compare your artwork to Figure 37.

15. Make a new layer group named **Castle Group** for the Castle layer and its adjustment layer.

16. Target the **Moon layer**.

(continued)

17. Apply a Levels adjustment layer named **Brighten Moon**.

   | **TIP** Be sure to click the Use Previous Layer to Create Clipping Mask check box.

18. Drag the **white triangle** in the Input Levels section left until the far-right text box reads 160, click **OK**, then compare your artwork to Figure 38.

19. Make a new layer group named **Moon Group** for the Moon layer and its adjustment layer.

20. Save your work.

FIGURE 38
Brightening the moon

FIGURE 39
Specifying the fill adjustment layer

FIGURE 40
The background

1. Target the **Desaturate Background layer**.

2. Click **Layer** on the menu bar, point to **New Fill Layer**, then click **Solid Color**.

3. Type **Colorize Background** in the Name text box, do not click the Use Previous Layer to Create Clipping Mask check box, then click **OK**.

4. Type **84** in the R text box, type **110** in the G text box, type **179** in the B text box, then click **OK**.

5. Change the blending mode to Multiply so that the blue fill layer becomes transparent.

6. Reduce the opacity to 70%, then compare your screen to Figure 39.

7. Show the Billing layer, then compare your screen to Figure 40.

8. Save your work.

POSITION FOREGROUND
Images

What You'll Do

Transitioning from background to foreground is always an interesting step when building a composite image. In many ways, it's like shifting gears.

When working on the background, the focus of your work usually involves pushing things back, making them less distinct, blurring the line between one image and another, muting colors, and so on. The opposite is usually true when working with the foreground. With this type of poster—a lush, romantic thriller—I think of the foreground as the "eye candy." The foreground sells the poster, it sells the story, and it sells the movie.

This lesson is about positioning the foreground elements. Note how you'll use bright colors and central locations to make these elements the focus of the poster.

FIGURE 41
Positioning the sword

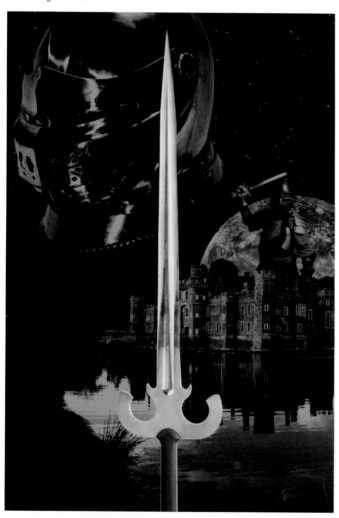

Position the sword

1. Hide the Billing layer.

2. Open Sword.psd, then show the White and Silo layers to see the retouching that was done.

   The original sword had a rounded edge. For this poster, a sharp point for the sword will be a subtle but necessary component to the concept as a whole.

3. Target the **Silo layer**, select all, copy, then close the file.

4. Target the **Colorize Background layer**, paste, then name the new layer **Sword**.

5. Click **Edit** on the menu bar, point to **Transform**, then click **Rotate 180°**.

6. Press **[Ctrl][T]** (Win) or ⌘**[T]** (Mac) to scale the image.

7. Type **506** in the X text box, press **[Tab]**, type **833** in the Y text box, press **[Tab]**, type **37** in the W text box, press **[Tab]**, type **37** in the H text box, then press **[Tab]**.

8. Click the **Move Tool** ⊹, click **Apply**, then compare your screen to Figure 41.

9. Save your work.

Enhance the sword

1. Click **Layer** on the menu bar, point to **Layer Style**, click **Bevel and Emboss**, then verify that the Preview check box is checked.

2. Verify that the Style is set to Inner Bevel and that Technique is set to Smooth.

3. Set the depth to 750%.

4. Set the Size to 11 px.

5. Set the Opacity of the Highlight Mode and Shadow Mode to 90%.

6. Click the **Gloss Contour list arrow**, double-click the eighth contour named **Ring**, click the **Anti-aliased check box**, then compare your dialog box to Figure 42.

7. Click **OK**, then compare your artwork to Figure 43.

8. Click **Layer** on the menu bar, point to **New Adjustment Layer**, then click **Levels**.

9. Type **Brighten Sword** in the Name text box, click the **Use Previous Layer to Create Clipping Mask check box**, then click **OK**.

(continued)

FIGURE 42
Layer Style dialog box

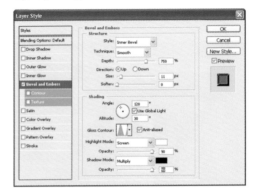

FIGURE 43
The sword enhanced with a layer style

FIGURE 44

Brightening the sword with an adjustment layer

FIGURE 45

Selecting the sword

10. Drag the **black triangle** in the Input Levels section to the right until the far-left Input text box reads 18, drag the **white triangle** left until the far-right Input text box reads 220.

11. Click **OK**, then compare your screen to Figure 44.

12. Target the **Sword layer**.

13. Drag a rectangular selection marquee around the sword but not the handle, as shown in Figure 45.

14. Feather the selection using 6 pixels, click **Filter** on the menu bar, point to **Sharpen**, then click **Unsharp Mask**.

15. Type **100** in the Amount text box, then click **OK**.

    The tones in the sword become much more distinct and hard edged. You will study sharpening techniques in more detail in upcoming chapters.

16. Deselect, then create a new layer group for the Sword and its adjustment layer, then name the new group **Sword Group**.

17. Save your work.

Place the king

1. Target the **Colorize Background layer**.

2. Open King.psd, make all layers visible except for the top layer named Silo, then target the **Background layer**.

3. Press and hold **[Ctrl]** (Win) or ⌘ (Mac), then click the **Layer thumbnail** on the Silo layer to load its selection.

    The selection is loaded but the Silo layer remains hidden.

4. Click **Edit** on the menu bar, then click **Copy Merged**.

    The Copy Merged command is very useful if you want to copy an image on your screen that is being created from multiple layers. The Copy Merged command copies all the visible layers as though they were a single, merged layer.

5. Close King.psd, switch to the Black Knight Poster document, paste, then name the new layer **King**.

6. Click **Edit** on the menu bar, point to **Transform**, then click **Flip Horizontal**.

7. Press **[Ctrl][T]** (Win) or ⌘**[T]** (Mac) to scale the image.

8. Type **426** in the X text box, press **[Tab]**, type **947** in the Y text box, then press **[Tab]**.

9. Click the **Move Tool** ⊹, click **Apply**, then compare your screen to Figure 46.

    (continued)

FIGURE 46
Positioning the king

FIGURE 47
Masking an unintended white line

It's difficult to see, but a horizontal white line above the king's head was inadvertently copied from the King.psd file. If you zoom in or move the image of the king around, you'll see it more clearly. There's no reason for this to have happened; we loaded the silo selection and applied the Copy Merged command. These inexplicable glitches happen often, and you must keep an eye out for them.

10. Add a layer mask to the King layer, make the selection shown in Figure 47, then fill the selection in the layer mask with black.

11. Deselect, then save your work.

Mask the king

1. Select the entire right half of the canvas, then mask out all elements of the king image that are on the right side of the sword.

2. Deselect all, then compare your screen to Figure 48.

(continued)

FIGURE 48
Masking the king to the right of the sword

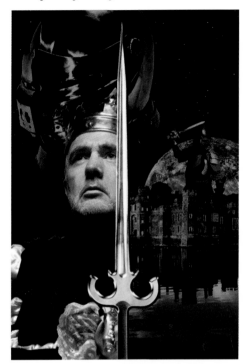

FIGURE 49
A poor design for a mask

DESIGN*note*

The king is a major foreground element and a major character in the concept. He must stand out from the background, but he must also be integrated with the background so that the entire poster eventually works together to create a single piece of art. This is one of the toughest challenges a designer faces when working with multiple images: how to make many images become one image. In Figure 49, I masked out the king's entire body to show you what not to do. This has reduced the king to a disembodied floating head, and it's a fundamental mistake that junior designers tend to make.

FIGURE 50

Masking the white, light, and bright areas

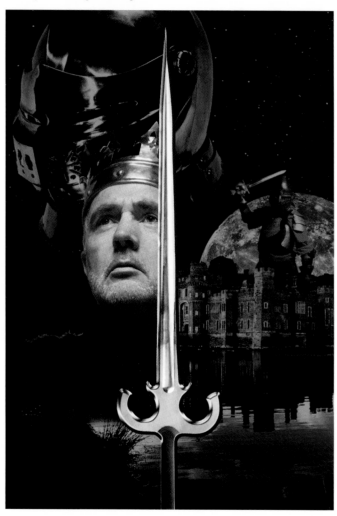

3. Click the **Brush Tool** , choose the Soft Round 100 pixels brush, then mask out only the hand, the gold handle and white areas of the costume so that your canvas resembles Figure 50.

4. Moving upward slowly and making small moves, mask the king's black costume so that it merges with the shadows that surround the blue water.

(continued)

5. Compare your result to Figure 51.

(continued)

FIGURE 51
Merging the king's clothes with the water

DESIGNnote

As shown in Figure 51, the king's costume merges seamlessly with the shadows in the water. Rather than a floating head, we now recognize the king's shoulder, his collar, and the shiny detail on his chest and sleeve. However, those elements transition into the shadows in a way that you really can't tell where the king ends and the shadows on the water begin.

FIGURE 52

Masking the Big Knight elements

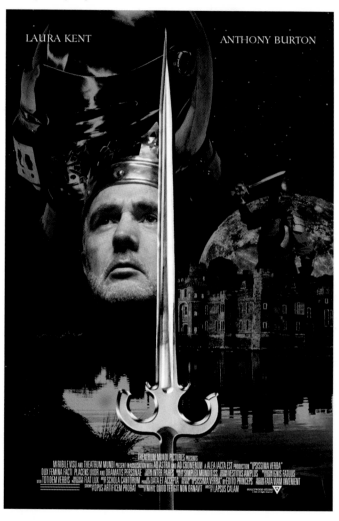

6. Show the Billing layer so that your artwork resembles Figure 52.

7. Hide the Billing layer, then save your work.

MERGE TWO
Images

What You'll Do

Merging two images to create a third image is perhaps the most delicate surgery you can do in Photoshop, especially when it involves somebody's face. It's one thing to paste a tree into a field; it's a whole different thing to take the eyes from one photo and paste them onto the face in another photo—with nobody catching on. You might be surprised at how often it's done. I do a lot of work with movie posters, and in most cases, the actor's head and the actor's body are from two different original photos. This happens because, when choosing from originals, the face in one photo might be perfect for the concept, but the body might be in the wrong position. But in another photo, the body is in a great position, but the actor won't approve the face shot. So a merge is necessary —put this head on that body.

Sometimes, as you'll see in this lesson, it's not even the actor's body. This happens all the time at the agency where I work. We have an in-house photo studio and a professional photographer on staff. When we come up with a concept, we get the studio to send over costumes, then we hire models to pose in the position that we need to work with. Sometimes,

Designing with Multiple Images   Chapter 5

we don't even hire models—we shoot our coworkers, our friends, even our brothers and sisters. Then we paste the actor's head onto the body. This is so standard that the studio always provides the actors' measurements—height, weight, and so on—so that we can use models with similar body types. In many ways, this type of work involves the true magic of Photoshop. Magic is all about illusion, and you're trying to create the illusion that this is just one photo. If you're really good and you do it well, the best compliment is no compliment at all—because nobody realizes the tricks you've been playing.

Prepare the base image for merging

1. Open Actress.psd.

2. Open Damsel.psd, then position it beside Actress.psd so that you can see both images.

   The angles in the two photographs aren't compatible. In the Actress photo, the model's head tilts slightly right. In the Damsel photo, the model's head tilts left.

3. Click the **Damsel.psd window**, click **Image** on the menu bar, point to **Rotate Canvas**, then click **Flip Canvas Horizontal**.

4. Show the Final layer to see the retouching that was done.

   As shown in Figure 53, the veil was removed from the side of the face and the cloth on her chest was brought up so that it meets the scarf around her head.

5. Click **Select** on the menu bar, then load the selection named **Head and Shoulders**.

(continued)

FIGURE 53
Retouching applied to Damsel.psd

DESIGN*note*

When merging photos, it's very important that you think ahead. It would be very easy to jump in and paste the actress into the damsel image. If you did so, you'd need to scale down the actress's head, and you'd need to rotate her head counterclockwise. But here's the problem: Damsel.psd is not the final image. The poster is the final image. At this point, you have no idea how Damsel.psd will fit into the poster image. In fact, it is too small for the poster and will need to be scaled up. Therefore, this means you would have scaled the actress down only to scale her back up again in the poster file. Not a good idea.

FIGURE 54

Assessing the size of the damsel image

6. Target the **Final layer**, click **Edit** on the menu bar, then click **Copy**.

7. Switch to the Black Knight Poster document, then target the **Sword Group layer**.

8. Click **Edit** on the menu bar, click **Paste**, then move the damsel image to the right.

   As shown in Figure 54, the damsel's head is too small and tilts too far to the right in comparison to the king.

9. Press **[Ctrl][T]** (Win) or ⌘**[T]** (Mac) to scale the image.

10. Type **150** in the W text box, press **[Tab]**, type **150** in the H text box, press **[Tab]**, type **−12** in the Rotate text box, then press **[Tab]**.

(continued)

11. Click the **Move Tool**  to execute the transformation, click **Apply**, then compare your screen to Figure 55.

These scale and rotation values work for the damsel image in relation to the image of the king.

12. Delete the new layer, then return to Damsel.psd.

13. Deselect.

14. Click **Image** on the menu bar, then click **Image Size**.

15. Verify that the Constrain Proportions and Resample Image check boxes are both checked.

(continued)

FIGURE 55
Transforming the image

FIGURE 56

Scaling the file

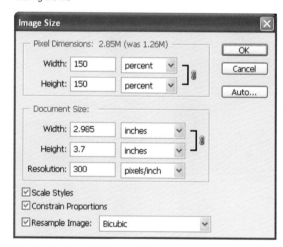

16. In the Pixel Dimensions section, change the Width and Height list arrows to **percent**.

17. Type **150** in the Width text box so that your dialog box resembles Figure 56.

18. Click **OK**.

The file is scaled 150%.

19. Press **[D]** to access a white background color.

20. Click **Image** on the menu bar, point to **Rotate Canvas**, then click **Arbitrary**.

(continued)

21. Type **11.5** in the Angle text box, click **CCW**, then click **OK**.

   As shown in Figure 57, the image is rotated –11.5 degrees.

22. Save the file as **Actress Damsel Merge.**

Remove the face in the base image

1. Show the Green Screen layer, then add a layer mask to the Final layer.

2. Zoom in on the face, click the **Brush Tool** ✏️, then choose the **Hard Round 19 pixels brush**.

3. Mask out the entire face, using Figure 58 as a guide.

   Try to paint as close to the blue scarf as possible so that you don't leave a black line around the perimeter. Don't worry about the hair in the upper-right corner—we will address that later.

4. Save your work.

FIGURE 57
Rotating the canvas

FIGURE 58
Masking the face

Designing with Multiple Images   Chapter 5

FIGURE 59
Positioning the artwork before scaling

FIGURE 60
Positioning the scaled artwork

Place the paste image behind the base image

1. Switch to the Actress.psd file, then make every layer visible.

2. Display the Paths palette, press and hold **[Ctrl]** (Win) or ⌘ (Mac), then click **Path 1**. Path 1 is loaded as a selection.

3. Click **Edit** on the menu bar, then click **Copy Merged**.

4. Switch to the Actress Damsel Merge file, then target the **Green Screen layer**.

5. Paste.

6. Name the new layer **Actress**.

7. Click the **Move Tool** , then position the actress artwork as shown in Figure 59.

8. Press **[Ctrl][T]** (Win) or ⌘**[T]** (Mac) to scale the image.

9. Type **588** in the X text box, press **[Tab]**, type **469** in the Y text box, press **[Tab]**, type **77** in the W text box, press **[Tab]**, type **77** in the H text box, then press **[Tab]**.

10. Click , click **Apply**, then compare your screen to Figure 60.

11. Target the **layer mask** in the Final layer, choose a small soft paint brush and a white foreground color, then smooth the transition between the damsel's dark hair and the actress's blond hair.

12. Hide the Green Screen layer.

(continued)

Lesson 6   Merge Two Images

ADVANCED PHOTOSHOP 5-55

13. Target the **Background layer**, click the **Layers palette list arrow**, then click **Duplicate Layer**.

14. Accept the default layer name, then click **OK**.

15. Click ✛, then click ← four times so that it "patches" the hole at the right side of the actress's face, as shown in Figure 61.

16. Save your work.

Create a shadow for the paste image

1. Delete the Green Screen layer.

2. Duplicate the Actress layer, name it **Shadow**, then move it to the top of the Layers palette.

3. Click **Image** on the menu bar, point to **Adjustments**, then click **Levels**.

4. Drag the **middle triangle** to the right until the middle Input value reads 0.65.

5. Click **OK**.

6. Click **Image** on the menu bar, point to **Adjustments**, then click **Hue/Saturation**.

7. Reduce the saturation to −30, then click **OK**.

   Your artwork should resemble Figure 62.

   (continued)

FIGURE 61
Hiding a bare spot

FIGURE 62
Darkening and desaturating the image

FIGURE 63

Removing areas that will not be shadowed

FIGURE 64

Final shadow effect

8. Press and hold **[Ctrl]** (Win) or ⌘ (Mac), then click the **layer mask** in the Final layer.

    When you load the selection of a layer mask, all of the white areas of the layer mask are selected. In this case, this means that the center of the actress's face, her eyes, nose, mouth, and so on, are not selected.

9. Click **Select** on the menu bar, then click **Inverse**.

    The actress's face is now selected.

10. Click **Select** on the menu bar, point to **Modify**, then click **Contract**.

11. Type **12** in the Contract By text box, then click **OK**.

12. Click **Select** on the menu bar, then click **Feather**.

13. Type **12**, then click **OK**.

14. Show only the Shadow layer.

15. Click **Edit** on the menu bar, then click **Cut**.

    Compare your screen to Figure 63.

16. Show all layers.

17. Drag the **Shadow layer** beneath the Final layer, then compare your artwork to Figure 64.

18. Hide and show the Shadow layer to see the impact of your work.

19. Save your work.

INTEGRATE FOREGROUND
Images

What You'll Do

When finishing the background art, we responded to a central challenge: How do you use a bunch of photos to make one piece of art? For the background, that meant creating a night world of stars and a black sky, a shadowy castle and menacing knights, barely visible. This night world is dark, and we used the concept of darkness to integrate the artwork. Now, with the foreground, we need to switch gears. The challenge is the same: use the photos of the sword, the king, and the queen to make one piece of art. But in this case, the art is foreground art. It needs to be bright and eye-catching. It needs to sell the concept. Darkening, desaturating, muting, blurring—none of these useful techniques are the answer for the foreground images—at least not in the way they were used for the background art. In this lesson, you will utilize the power of blending modes to integrate the foreground artwork while maintaining brightness and color.

FIGURE 65
Positioning the queen

Position the queen

1. Verify that the top layer is targeted in Actress Damsel Merge.psd. and that all the layers are showing.

2. Click **Select** on the menu bar, click **Load Selection**, then load the Head and Shoulders selection.

3. Click **Edit** on the menu bar, then click **Copy Merged**.

4. Switch to the Black Knight Poster file, make the Billing layer visible, then target the **King layer**.

5. Paste, then name the new layer **Queen**.

6. Press **[Ctrl][T]** (Win) or **⌘[T]** (Mac).

7. Type **640** in the X text box, press **[Tab]**, type **747** in the Y text box, then press **[Tab]**.

8. Click the **Move Tool** ⊕, click **Apply**, then compare your screen to Figure 65.

9. Save your work.

Lesson 7   Integrate Foreground Images

Mask the queen

1. Add a layer mask to the Queen layer.

2. Select the entire left half of the canvas, then mask out all elements of the queen image that are on the left side of the sword so that your canvas resembles Figure 66.

3. Deselect all.

4. Click the **Brush Tool** 🖌, choose the Soft Round 100 pixels brush, then mask the queen's dress so that your artwork resembles Figure 67.

(continued)

FIGURE 66
Masking the queen against the sword

FIGURE 67
Masking the queen's dress

FIGURE 68
Masking the satin

5. Using the same brush, mask the pink satin so that your screen resembles Figure 68.

6. Save your work.

Use smart groups

1. Target the **King layer**, press **[Shift]** and click the **Queen layer**, then create a new layer group named **Royals**.

2. Duplicate the layer group, then name the new group **Royals Copy 1**.

3. Click **Layer** on the menu bar, point to **New Adjustment Layer**, then click **Hue/Saturation**.

4. Note that you do not have the option to click the Use Previous Layer to Create Clipping Mask check box.

   This is a problem. We want to desaturate both the king and queen images, but we don't have the option of applying one adjustment layer to both images in the group.

5. Click **Cancel**, then click the **Layers palette list arrow**.

6. Choose **Group into New Smart Object**.

   The Royals Copy 1 group is now a single object on a single layer. Smart objects are new to Photoshop CS2, and this is a great example of how they come in very handy. Simply put, smart objects allow you to work with a layer group as though it were a single image on a single layer.

(continued)

7. Click **Layer** on the menu bar, point to **New Adjustment Layer**, then click **Hue/Saturation**.

8. Type **Desaturate Royals** in the name text box, click the **Use Previous Layer to Create Clipping Mask check box**, then click **OK**.

9. Drag the **Saturation slider** to −90, click **OK**, then compare your canvas to Figure 69.

10. Click **Layer** on the menu bar, point to **New Adjustment Layer**, then click **Levels**.

11. Type **Blow Out Highlights** in the Name text box, click the **Use Previous Layer to Create Clipping Mask check box**, then click **OK**.

12. Drag the **white triangle** left to 195, drag the **black triangle** right to 16, then click **OK**.

13. Select all three layers, click the **Layers palette list arrow**, then click **New Group from Layers**.

14. Name the new group **Royals Hard Light**, then click OK.

FIGURE 69
Desaturating the copy

FIGURE 70
Hard Light effect

1. Target the **Royals Hard Light layer group**, then change the blending mode to Hard Light.

2. Change the opacity to 90%, then compare your screen to Figure 70.

3. Hide and show the Royals Hard Light layer group to see the effect.

(continued)

DESIGN*note*

Understanding why the effect appears the way it does is a bit tricky. For one thing, it seems illogical: how is it that a desaturated, black-and-white layer is creating this effect? Think of it in terms of light and dark. the Hard Light mode was applied, the white areas drastically brightened the areas of the original beneath. The dark areas made the colors on the layer beneath them darker and more intense.

4. Duplicate the Royals Hard Light layer group, then name the new group **Royals Multiply**.

   Doubling the layer group doubles the Hard Light effect.

5. Change the blending mode to Multiply.

   In Multiply mode, white pixels become invisible. Every other pixel retains its color but becomes transparent. The result is that all the shadow areas become darker and deeper—in this case, too much so.

6. Reduce the opacity to 50%, then compare your screen to Figure 71.

7. Save your work.

Position the title

1. Open Title.psd.

2. Target the **Title layer**, select all, copy, then close the file.

3. In the Black Knight Poster file, target the **Billing layer**.

(continued)

FIGURE 71
Multiply effect

Designing with Multiple Images   Chapter 5

FIGURE 72
Positioning the title

4. Paste, then name the new layer **Title**.

5. Press **[Ctrl][T]** (Win) or ⌘**[T]** (Mac) to scale the image.

6. Type **503** in the X text box, press **[Tab]**, type **1056** in the Y text box, then press **[Tab]**.

7. Click the **Move Tool** ⊕, click **Apply**, then compare your screen to Figure 72.

8. Save your work.

FINISH
Artwork

What You'll Do

Finish artwork may sound like, *Get it done*. But in the design world, *finish* is used the way a carpenter would apply a finish to a table. Finishing artwork is the final design stage of a project.

In a way, finishing is everything, and everything leads up to finishing. It is the point at which you as a designer must distill your work into one piece of art, which is always the central challenge throughout this work. If you like, we can take it even one step further. Finishing is the point at which you as a designer must bring your artwork to life.

FIGURE 73

Scaling and repositioning the castle, small knight, and moon

Reposition elements

1. Assess the poster in terms of layout—the position of elements and how they relate to each other.

   At this point, the poster is working well. I like the diagonal movement that begins with the knight in the upper-left corner and moves down and to the right with the king and queen, and then to the small knight and castle. I also like how this diagonal plays off the hard vertical line created by the sword. However, there are issues that need to be addressed. First and foremost, the queen is covering the castle and is in conflict with the small knight. Overall, the poster is a bit top-heavy. I still don't like the moon—I'm feeling that it makes the top half of the poster crowded and congested.

2. Target the **Castle Group layer**, press and hold ⌘ **[Shift]**, then click the **Small Knight Group** and **Moon Group layer groups**.

3. Press **[Ctrl][T]** (Win) or ⌘**[T]** (Mac).

4. Type **680** in the X text box, press **[Tab]**, type **979** in the Y text box, press **[Tab]**, type **92** in the W text box, press **[Tab]**, type **92** in the H text box, then press **[Tab]**.

5. Click the **Move Tool** ⊹, click **Apply**, then compare your screen to Figure 73.

   (continued)

6. Target the **Royals layer group**, press and hold **[Ctrl]** (Win) or ⌘ (Mac), then target the **Royals Hard Light** and **Royals Multiply groups** so that all three are selected.

7. Press and hold **[Shift]**, then press ↓ one time.

   The royals are moved down 10 pixels.

8. Compare your artwork to Figure 74.

   (continued)

FIGURE 74
Repositioning the royals

LAURA KENT   ANTHONY BURTON

BLACK KNIGHT

DESIGN*note*

The move brings our focus more toward the vertical center of the poster, which is a good thing. It also creates a much-needed relationship between the king and the title. However, now I'm finding the moon even more annoying because it's butting up against the queen's scarf.

FIGURE 75
Hiding the moon

9. Hide the Moon Group layer, then compare your work to Figure 75.

10. Save your work.

Use shadows to increase depth

1. Expand the Sword Group layer.

2. Double-click the **Bevel and Emboss effect** to open the dialog box.

3. In the Styles list on the left, click **Outer Glow**.

4. Click the **Set color of glow button** to open the Color Picker.

5. Type **0** in the R, G, and B text boxes, then click **OK**.

6. Change the blending mode to Multiply.

(continued)

DESIGN*note*

It's amazing how sometimes taking something away adds so much to a concept. Without the moon, the entire top half of the poster feels lighter and the night sky feels more open. The diagonal that we discussed earlier now flows more easily from the upper-left corner down to the small knight. Removing the bright moon also has a substantial effect on the overall tone of the poster. The royals are now the only bright characters in the piece, which seems right, and the small knight is so much more creepy now that he appears to be emerging from the shadows.

7. Change the Spread value to 8, change the Size value to 24, click **OK**, then compare your artwork to Figure 76.

8. Press and hold **[Alt]** (Win) or **[option]** (Mac), then drag the **Outer Glow effect** up to the Title layer so that the title too has the same effect.

9. Double-click the **Outer Glow effect** on the Title layer to open its dialog box.

(continued)

FIGURE 76
Applying an outer glow effect to the sword

FIGURE 77

Applying an outer glow effect to the title

10. Reduce the Opacity setting to 50%, click **OK**, then compare your artwork to Figure 77.

11. Save your work.

Mask multiple layer groups

1. Assess the relationship between the queen and the small knight.

2. Target the **Royals layer**, press and hold **[Ctrl]** (Win) or ⌘ (Mac), then click the **Royals Hard Light** and **Royals Multiply layers**.

3. Click the **Layers palette list arrow**, then click **New Group from Layers**.

(continued)

4. Name the new group **Royal Mask**, then click **OK**.

5. Add a layer mask to the Royal Mask layer.

6. Paint with a large soft brush and a low opacity to fade the queen's blue scarf, so that your artwork resembles Figure 78.

   I used the Soft Round 100 pixels brush at 20% opacity and made about 30 moves to get the effect.

   | **TIP** Feel free to also mask the queen's pink scarf so that it too fades into the background. Be sure that none of your moves accidentally fade the king's face.

7. Save your work.

FIGURE 78
Masking three layer groups with a single mask

DESIGN*note*

With the moon now gone, I felt that the queen's blue scarf was too bright to have such a hard edge. That led me to notice that I thought the pink scarf over her head had too hard an edge as well. I decided to use a layer mask to fade it down a bit. Masking at this late stage at the project can get very tricky. For example, in this case, the image of the queen is the result of three layer groups interacting with blending modes. Fortunately, Photoshop CS2's upgraded Layers palette offers the ability to apply one mask to multiple layer groups.

FIGURE 79
Lens Flare dialog box

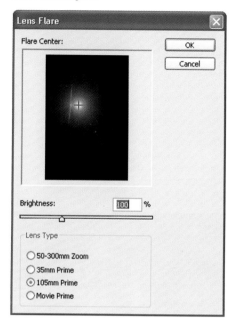

FIGURE 80
Lens flare layer

Add a lens flare effect

1. Hide the Billing and Title layers.

2. Target the **Sword Group layer**, verify that it is compressed, then click the **Create a new layer button** ⬚ on the Layers palette.

3. Name the new layer **Lens Flare**, press **[D]**, then fill the layer with the black foreground color.

4. Click **Filter** on the menu bar, point to **Render**, then click **Lens Flare**.

5. Click **105mm Prime**, as shown in Figure 79.

6. Click **OK**.

7. Click **Layer** on the menu bar, point to **New Adjustment Layer**, then click **Levels**.

8. Type **Screen Flare** in the Name text box, click the **Use Previous Layer to Create Clipping Mask check box**, then click **OK**.

9. Drag the **black triangle** to the right until the first input value reads 111, then click **OK**.

10. Target the **Lens Flare layer**, then paint everything black except for the central flare so that your layer resembles Figure 80.

(continued)

11. Change the blending mode to Screen, then change the Opacity of the layer to 90.

12. Click the **Move Tool**, then position the flare as shown in Figure 81.

Integrate the entire concept

1. Show the Billing layer and the Title layer.

2. Open Smoke.psd.

   Smoke.psd is a photograph that I shot with my own camera. I lit a cigar and positioned it against a large piece of black foam core. I then shined a bright spotlight on the setting to illuminate the smoke.

3. Select all, copy, then close Smoke.psd.

4. Target the **Title layer** in the Black Knight Poster file.

5. Paste, then name the new layer **Smoke**.

6. Press **[Ctrl][T]** (Win) or ⌘ **[T]** (Mac).

7. Type **600** in the X text box, press **[Tab]**, type **752** in the Y text box, press **[Tab]**, type **53** in the W text box, press **[Tab]**, type **53** in the H text box, then press **[Tab]**.

8. Click the **Move Tool**, then click **Apply**.

9. Change the blending mode to Screen, then compare your artwork to Figure 82.

   With the Screen blending mode, the black areas become invisible. This is why I shot the smoke against the black background. I knew I could remove the black background and show only the smoke.

   (continued)

FIGURE 81
Positioning the lens flare

FIGURE 82
Screening the smoke

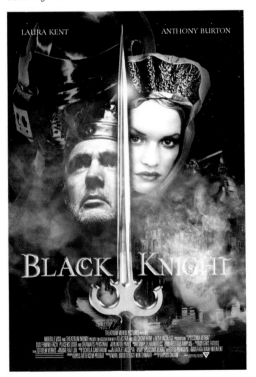

FIGURE 83

The final poster

10. Drag the **Smoke layer** down below the Colorize Background layer in the Layers palette.

11. Change the opacity to 55%.

12. Compare your screen to Figure 83.

13. Save your work.

14. Close the Black Knight Poster document.

15. Close any other documents that are open.

1. Open AP 5-2.psd, then save it as **Project Builder 1**.
2. Hide the All Type group layer, then target the Lens Flare group layer.
3. Press [Shift][Alt][Ctrl][N] (Win) or [Shift][option][Macintosh Command key][N] (Mac).
4. Press [Shift][Alt][Ctrl][E] (Win) or [Shift][option][Macintosh Command key][E] (Mac).
5. Name the new layer **Stamped Art**.
6. Open the Channels palette, then duplicate the Green channel by dragging it down to the Create a new channel button.
7. Select all in the Green copy channel, then copy.
8. Target the RGB channel, then return to the Layers palette and verify that the Stamped Art layer is targeted.
9. Paste, then name the new layer **Green Channel**.
10. Change the blending mode to Screen, then duplicate Green Channel.
11. Move the Stamped Art layer above the Green Channel copy layer.
12. Change the Stamped Art layer's blending mode to Soft Light.
13. Click the Add layer mask button to add a layer mask to the Stamped Art layer.
14. Press and hold [Alt] (Win) or [option] (Mac), then click the layer mask. (*Hint*: The all-white layer mask becomes visible on the canvas.)
15. Select all, click Edit on the menu bar, then click Paste Into. (*Hint*: The green channel art is pasted into the mask.)
16. Click Image on the menu bar, point to Adjustments, then click Invert. (*Hint*: Remember, this artwork is being used as a mask. Note the white areas.)
17. Click the Layer thumbnail on the Stamped Art layer so that you can see the artwork again.
18. Drag the Sword Group above the Stamped Art layer.
19. Drag the Lens Flare group above the Sword Group, make the All Type group layer visible, then compare your artwork to Figure 84.
20. Hide and show the Stamped Art and the two Green Channel layers to see the impact they've had on the original artwork.
21. Save your work, then close Project Builder 1.

FIGURE 84
Completed Project Builder 1

1. Open AP 5-3.psd, then save it as **Project Builder 2**.
2. Duplicate the Stamped Art layer, then rename it **Screen**.
3. Verify that the Screen layer is targeted, then change the blending mode to Screen.
4. Add a new Hue/Saturation adjustment layer, accept the default name, and be sure to click the Use Previous Layer to Create Clipping Mask check box. (*Hint*: If you use the Create new fill or adjustment layer button on the Layers panel, press and hold [Alt] (Win) or [option] (Mac) when you click the button.)
5. In the Hue/Saturation dialog box, click the Colorize check box, drag the Hue slider to 150, drag the Saturation slider to 50, then click OK.
6. Change the blending mode on the Hue/Saturation adjustment layer to Multiply.
7. Select both the Screen layer and the adjustment layer, then create a new layer group named **Screen Group**.
8. Duplicate the Screen Group layer, then name the new group **Screen Group 2**.
9. Drag the Lens Flare layer below the Screen Group layer.
10. Drag the Sword Group layer below the Lens Flare layer.
11. Compare your screen to Figure 85.
12. Save your work, the close Project Builder 2.

FIGURE 85
Completed Project Builder 2

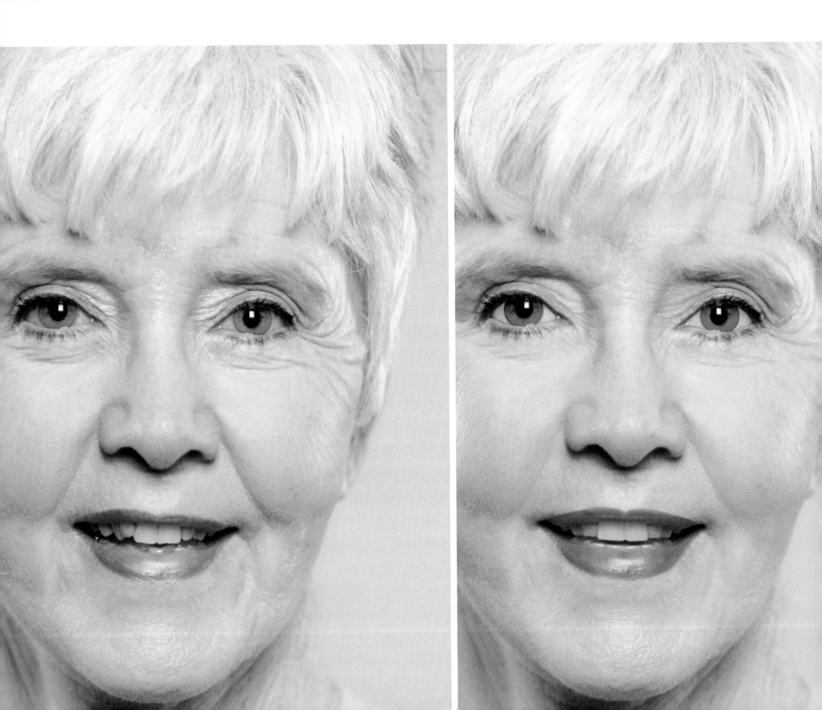

chapter

6

RETOUCHING AND
Enhancing Images

1. Whiten eyes.

2. Use the Sponge Tool.

3. Investigate the Overlay blending mode.

4. Overlay detail.

5. Use a channel as a mask.

6. Use the cloning tools.

7. Retouch teeth.

WHITEN
Eyes

What You'll Do

Whitening eyes is a standard move in almost every retouching project that involves a person's face. In fact, if you think of the thousands of faces you've seen in magazines over the years, chances are that in only a very few are the eyes not retouched.

People's eyes are seldom perfect. That's right, even the "perfect" models in the magazines get bloodshot eyes. However, it's not only for cosmetic reasons that eyes usually require retouching. In actuality, it's difficult to photograph a subject in a way that the whites of eyes are white, as opposed to a dull bluish gray. Because of eyelids and eyebrows, eyes are usually in shadow, and it usually requires professional lighting techniques to capture a vivid bright white eye on film.

There are many techniques for whitening eyes, and it seems like every retoucher has his or her own tricks. The technique we're going to execute in this lesson is a standard approach that retouchers use as a baseline—meaning that this technique gets you to a point that the eyes are white enough that they can be cloned or further retouched.

FIGURE 1
Assessing levels

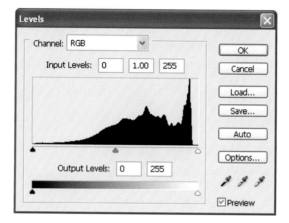

Whiten eyes

1. Open AP 6-1.psd, then save it as **Bright Eyes**.

2. Assess the image.

   This is an image that has very few obvious problems. The model is young; he has no wrinkles, no age spots, no pock marks, and so on. His mouth is closed, so if he has chipped yellow teeth, it's not our problem. If you were asked to retouch this image, what is the first thing your eye would go to? Perhaps the most obvious retouching issue would be his red cheeks. Is that the first thing you noticed, or did your eye find other problems with the image?

3. Verify that the Background layer is targeted, add a new Levels adjustment layer named **Basic**, then compare your histogram to Figure 1.

   (continued)

DESIGNnote

Before you do any retouching, it is critical that you know the context in which an image is to be used. This is the major determining factor of the artistic goal that you set for the retouching. For example, if this image were to be used to profile a new young author in the Sunday section of the *New York Times Book Review*, that fact would have enormous impact on how I want the final image to appear. I would retouch only obvious flaws in the image, with the goal of keeping the image very realistic and not stylized. When an author—even a hip young author—is being profiled in the *New York Times*, that author wants to be taken seriously. For this project, the image is being used to profile a rap star in a weekly news magazine, like *Time* or *Newsweek*. With that in mind, we're going to use techniques that exaggerate and define elements of the image so that the photo is vivid and eye-catching, with the rap star appearing just a bit bigger than life. However, we're not going to overdo it—we do not want the final image to be obviously retouched or to look like a computer-generated special effect.

The first step in retouching is adjusting levels and curves to create the best image to start with. Most images, whether they come from a stock house or from a photographer that you work with, require some degree of adjustment. In the case of this photograph, a stock photo that has not been modified, the histogram shows that there is minimal detail in the shadow areas, which explains why the image is flat and has weak shadows.

4. Drag the **black triangle** to 33, drag the **white triangle** to 243, click **OK**, then compare your screen to Figure 2.

5. Undo and redo to see the change.

6. Press and hold **[Shift][Ctrl][Alt][N]**(Win) or **[Shift][option]** ⌘ **[N]** (Mac) to create a new layer, then press and hold **[Shift][Ctrl][Alt][E]**(Win) or **[Shift][option]** ⌘ **[E]** (Mac) to stamp all visible layers.

Stamping the visible layers gives us the color-adjusted layer to work with without having to flatten the entire image.

> **TIP** For the remainder of this chapter, I will refer to this move as "Create a new stamp visible layer."

(continued)

FIGURE 2
Adjusted levels

7. Name the new layer **Start**.

8. Duplicate the Start layer, then name the new layer **Whiten Eyes**.

9. Zoom in to 200% and position the eyes in the document window so that you have a good view of them.

   Both eyes are noticeably bloodshot, especially at the outer sides. Note too the red line in the left eye, just below and left of the iris.

(continued)

10. Click the **Brush Tool** , select a small soft brush, then using Figure 3 as an example, paint the white areas of the eyes white.

In Figure 3, the Soft Round 5 pixels brush was used. For the corner areas, I reduced it to 2 pixels.

> **TIP** Be sure to paint up to but not over the iris. Note too that the pink corners of the eye were not painted.

(continued)

FIGURE 3
Painting the whites white

FIGURE 4

Reducing opacity for realism

11. Zoom out so that you are viewing the image at 50%, reduce the opacity of the Whiten Eyes layer to what you think is the best whitening you can achieve while still maintaining realism, then compare your artwork to Figure 4.

12. Set the opacity of your Whiten Eyes layer to 30%.

13. Select the Start and Whiten Eyes layers, click the **Layers palette list arrow**, click **New Group from Layers**, name the new group **Whiten Eyes**, then click **OK**.

14. Save your work.

DESIGNnote

Take a moment to note what's going on here. The Whiten Eyes layer is serving two purposes. It is whitening the eyes, and it is also hiding the red bloodshot lines. The opacity of the Whiten Eyes layer in Figure 4 is 30%—the eyes are whitened dramatically, yet they still look realistic. Many designers get carried away and make the eyes too white, which I think is a bad choice for a realistic image. It flattens the eye and makes the subject look like a cyborg. Note, however, that because the opacity is only 30%, the bloodshot lines are not completely camouflaged. Is that a bad thing? The answer depends on your personal taste. For me, when working on a realistic image, those lines are necessary and should be there, because everybody has bloodshot eyes.

USE THE
Sponge Tool

What You'll Do

The Sponge Tool is very handy as a retouching tool. With it, you can increase or decrease saturation in specific areas of the image. This makes the Sponge Tool very useful for making eyes and lips more vivid.

On the other hand, the desaturation option can be very useful as well. For example, when retouching teeth, you'll find that most have a yellowish color cast. To whiten them, you want to brighten those pixels. But if they're yellowish, brightening them just gives you a brighter yellow. If you desaturate them first and change the yellow color cast to a gray color cast, when you brighten them, you brighten the gray toward white. That puts you in much closer range toward achieving the effect of bright white teeth.

In this lesson, you'll use the Sponge Tool to make the model's eyes more vibrant and—you guessed it—eye-catching.

FIGURE 5

Saturating the left eye

1. Verify that the Whiten Eyes group is targeted.

2. Create a new stamp visible layer, then name it **Saturate**.

3. Click the **Sponge Tool** , click the **Mode list arrow** in the Options bar, then click **Saturate**.

   TIP The Sponge Tool is hidden beneath the **Dodge Tool** .

4. Set the Flow to 75%.

   TIP The Set to enable airbrush capabilities button on the Options bar should not be pressed.

5. Zoom in to 200%, so that you can see both eyes enlarged.

6. Choose the Soft Round 21 pixels brush.

7. In one move, starting at the top left of the iris of the left eye, drag the **Sponge Tool** counterclockwise over the colored areas.

   The Sponge Tool is a "flow tool." It continues to flow as you drag it. In other words, the more you drag it, the more it will saturate the image. This also means that if you drag the tool slowly, it will have more effect on the area than if you drag quickly.

8. Repeat the move, then compare your result to Figure 5.

(continued)

9. Apply the same two moves to the right eye, then compare your artwork to Figure 6.

At 75% flow and executed twice, the impact is dramatic—too dramatic. The eyes no longer appear realistic; they've obviously been manipulated, and the young man looks like he's about to transform into a werewolf. Some designers like to use the Sponge Tool with a low flow and slowly work on an area with many small moves. That is not my preference. I prefer to make dramatic moves to push the effect over its limit, then I use opacity (and a layer mask, if necessary) to bring the effect back to reality.

(continued)

FIGURE 6
Saturating the right eye

FIGURE 7
Reducing opacity of the saturated layer

10. Reduce the opacity of the Saturate layer to 70%.

11. Compare your result to Figure 7.

    At 100% opacity, the light areas become too distinct from the dark areas, and the iris appears to be two colors. With the reduction in opacity, the increased vividness is maintained, and the iris appears to be multifaceted but not two colors. The right iris has more yellow areas than the left eye. On its own, it looks a bit odd, and when viewed as a whole, the young man appears to have different-colored eyes. The 70% opacity setting is good for the left eye, but too high for the right eye.

    (continued)

Lesson 2   Use the Sponge Tool

12. Add a layer mask to the Saturate layer, click the **Brush Tool** ✎, set its opacity to 10%, then change the foreground color to black.

13. Working on the right eye, mask areas until you feel that the two eyes together are realistic, then compare your work to Figure 8.

    I toned down only the yellow areas. I didn't mask the dark hazel areas of the right eye.

14. Click ⬭.

    Next, we want to saturate the lips, but we don't want to do so on this layer. This layer is for the eyes only, and we want a separate layer for the lips. But there's a problem. We can't duplicate the Saturate layer to use for saturating the lips, because the Saturate layer has a 70% opacity. If we did duplicate it, we'd create an identical layer that is also transparent. The result of this would be that the saturation effects on the eyes would double. Duplicating the Saturate layer is not an option. Creating a new empty layer is also not an option, because there would be no pixels on that layer to saturate.

    (continued)

FIGURE 8
Adjusting saturation in the right eye with a layer mask

DESIGNnote

Managing layers effectively is a big part of retouching an image, especially when you're making many moves, as we are doing with this image. So here's a layers question: Let's say you wanted to saturate the lips just a bit, because they appear to be a bit gray. Would you do this on the Saturate layer? The answer is no, it's better that you don't. The Saturate layer has a reduced opacity, a percentage that is good for the eyes, but won't necessarily work with the lips. Also, it's always a bit weird to use a tool at say 75% flow on a layer with an opacity of say 60%. With those percentages, it's kind of hard to know what you are doing. You're better off saturating the lips artwork on its own layer, which gives you the options of manipulating opacity and applying a layer mask.

FIGURE 9
Slightly increasing the saturation in the lips

15. Create a new stamp visible layer named **Saturate Lips**.

    Note that the new layer has an opacity of 100%. It is 100% of the visible image created by all the visible layers beneath it. Now we can saturate the lips and not worry about any transparency on the layer. This is a great example of this important concept and the power of stamping all visible layers when working with transparent layers.

16. Use  to increase the saturation in the lips, so that your results look realistic.

    I used a brush that was big enough to affect both lips simultaneously, so that the move affected both lips equally. I used a flow value of 10%, and made only one move. The move was so slight that you probably won't be able to see it when you compare your result to Figure 9.

17. Select both the Saturate and the Saturate Lips layers, then make a new layer group named **Saturate Local**.

18. Save your work.

INVESTIGATE THE OVERLAY
Blending Mode

What You'll Do

If you get a chance to observe a professional retoucher working, you'll see that the Overlay blending mode plays an important role for enhancing detail. "High-end" retouchers refer to overlay techniques as *overlay detail*. These techniques produce remarkable effects, but it's difficult to appreciate how they are achieved until you understand the basics of how the Overlay blending mode works.

Overlay is one of the most practical and powerful of the blending modes, one you use for retouching, for enhancing an image, and for producing special effects. Although most designers use it and are familiar with the effects it produces, many do not understand— on a technical level—how it works.

Use this chapter as an opportunity to investigate this blending mode. Understanding how a blending mode works increases your Photoshop skills set exponentially.

FIGURE 10

Darkening the image by moving the shadow point

FIGURE 11

Lightening the image by moving the highlight point

Investigate the Overlay blending mode

1. Make the Highlight/Shadow layer visible, target it, select the entire right half of the image, then hide the selection.

2. Open the Levels dialog box.

3. Drag the **black triangle** to 128, click **OK**, then compare your artwork to Figure 10.

   The pixels in the selection are darkened dramatically. The pixels that were 128–255 are now 0–255. Any pixel that was 127 or lower is now 0, black.

4. Select the inverse, then open the Levels dialog box.

5. Drag the **white triangle** to 128, click **OK**, then compare your artwork to Figure 11.

   The pixels in the selection are lightened dramatically. The pixels that were 0–128 are now 0–255. Any pixel that was 129 or higher is now 255.

(continued)

6. Deselect all.

7. Hide the Highlight/Shadow layer, then make the Overlay White Black layer visible.

8. Change the blending mode on the Overlay White Black layer to Overlay, then compare your screen to Figure 12.

   The effect is identical to the levels moves. Overlaying black is the same as moving the shadow point to 128. Overlaying white is the same as moving the highlight point to 128.

9. Hide the Overlay White Black layer, then make the Overlay White Gray Black layer visible.

10. Change the blending mode on the Overlay White Gray Black layer to Overlay, then compare your screen to Figure 13.

    With the Overlay blending mode, neutral gray (grayscale value 128) becomes transparent. The fact that gray becomes transparent is one of the key components of the Overlay blending mode.

    (continued)

FIGURE 12
Overlaying white and black

FIGURE 13
Overlaying gray

FIGURE 14
Overlaying a gradient

11. Hide the Overlay White Gray Black layer, then make the Overlay Gradient layer visible.

12. Change the blending mode on the Overlay Gradient layer to Overlay, then compare your screen to Figure 14.

    Overlaying the gradient showcases the true nature (and power) of the Overlay blending mode. It's not just black, white, and gray. Black and white are the extremes—black overlayed produces the darkest effect; white overlayed produces the lightest effect. Gray is neutral. The range between gray and black gradually darkens the image, while conversely, the range between gray and white gradually lightens the image.

13. Hide and show the Overlay Gradient layer to see the effect before and after.

14. Hide the Overlay Gradient layer, then save your work.

DESIGN*note*

Note that black overlay has a more dramatic effect on darker areas. For example, on the right cheek, note that the redness has become much darker, while the effect on the adjacent flesh tones is not so dramatic. Note too—this is very important—that the black areas of the gradient have only a minimal effect on the white background. On the opposite side of the gradient, note that the light areas under the right eye become almost white with the white overlay. However, the effect on the dark areas in the beard and eyebrows is minimal.

OVERLAY
Detail

What You'll Do

Overlay detail is a term retouchers use for a technique that sharpens and enhances detail in an image. When you paint on a layer set to the Overlay blending mode, painting with white or black either lightens or darkens the pixels below, respectively.

This is very different from painting with white or black in Normal mode, and it's important that you understand the distinction. When you paint with white or black in Normal mode, you change the targeted pixels to white or black. Even with reduced opacity, the ultimate expression of the move is to push the pixels toward white or black.

With the overlay detail technique, you change the color of the targeted pixels, but not by introducing white or black "paint." In Overlay mode, you use white and black "paint" to lighten or darken the original pixel information. The ultimate expression of the move is not a white or black pixel. Instead, it is a much lighter or much darker version of the original, but never all white or all black.

With the Overlay blending mode, you are quite literally painting with light.

FIGURE 15

Darkening the edge of the left iris

Overlay detail

1. Click the **Brush Tool** ✐, select a small soft brush, then set the opacity of the tool to 10%.

2. Press **[D]**, then press **[X]** to access a white foreground color.

3. Target the **Saturate Local group**, then create a new layer above it.

4. Name the new layer **Overlay Detail**, then set the blending mode to Overlay.

5. Zoom in on the eyes, then paint over both eyes, lightening the hazel parts of the iris to a point that you think looks good but is still realistic.

    TIP Paint *inside* the iris—don't lighten the edge of the iris, where it meets the whites of the eyes.

6. Press **[X]** to access a black foreground color, then reduce your brush size to 2 pixels.

7. Darken the edge of the left iris—literally paint a dark line around it—then compare your result to Figure 15.

    The effect is stunning yet remarkably realistic. This is a standard retouching technique: lighten the iris, darken the edge of the iris.

    TIP You don't necessarily need to paint the edge in one move. Your paint brush is at only 10% opacity and it does not flow, so the change will be subtle. You will need to paint over the edge a few times to achieve the effect shown in the figure.

    (continued)

8. Darken the edge of the right iris, hide and show the Overlay Detail layer to see a before-and-after view of the effect, then compare your result to Figure 16.

(continued)

FIGURE 16
Darkening the edge of the right iris

DESIGN*note*

It's important that you remember that you are *not* painting with white or black. Because the layer's blending mode is set to Overlay, you are painting with light and dark, either lightening the pixels or darkening the pixels.

FIGURE 17
Identifying areas to be enhanced

FIGURE 18
Enhancing eye areas

9. Note the areas of the eye identified in Figure 17.

   These are the edges of the eyelids. Note that, even without retouching, they already have a highlight.

10. Switch your foreground color to white, then lighten these areas to a point that you feel enhances the eyes but maintains realism.

11. Compare your result to Figure 18.

   We human beings like to see distinct features, even exaggerated. In the movies, we like our leading men and women with square jaws (think Jim Carrey), prominent cheekbones (think Tom Cruise), long necks (think Gwyneth Paltrow) and defined lips (think Angelina Jolie). We look for this detail especially in the eyes. This move exaggerates that definition, and it makes the eyes more interesting. However, this move needs to be very slight and subtle; if you lighten too much, it is noticeably retouched and looks bizarre.

12. Lighten the highlight on the top lip slightly.

   (continued)

13. Switch your foreground color to black, then darken the dark area of the top lip beneath the ridge, identified in Figure 19.

14. Zoom in on the eyes, then darken the top eyelashes on each eye.

15. Change your brush to Hard Round 1 pixel, increase the brush opacity to 18%, darken each of the eyelashes, one at a time, at the bottom of both eyes, and add eyelashes where they're missing.

Did you just groan? This is easier than it sounds. Remember, you are not painting with black, you're painting with dark. Therefore, you can't paint "out of the lines." If you miss an eyelash, all you'll do is darken the skin behind it, and it will be almost unnoticeable.

16. Compare your results to Figure 20.

(continued)

FIGURE 19
Identifying an area to be darkened

FIGURE 20
Darkening and adding eyelashes

FIGURE 21
Darkening eyebrows

FIGURE 22
Darkening the neck and jacket

17. Choose a larger soft brush, then darken the eyebrows.

18. Compare your results to Figure 21.

19. Choose a big soft brush (I used Soft Round 100 pixels), then darken the jacket, the neck, and the line where the jaw meets the neck.

20. Compare your results to Figure 22.

Darkening the jacket and neck serves two important purposes. First, it brings the entire head forward in the image: that which is lighter we interpret as closer; that which is darker we interpret as recessed. Second, darkening the neck but not the jaw makes the jaw line appear stronger and more distinct.

21. Hide and show the Overlay Detail layer to see the image with and without the detail, then save your work.

USE A CHANNEL
as a Mask

What You'll Do

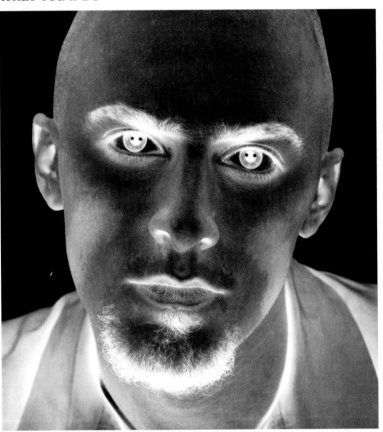

Over the years, the Channels palette has come to occupy some sort of twilight zone in the Photoshop world. Basic technique books give them scant coverage, and it's often limited to saving a selection as a channel.

Manipulating channels offers many useful and powerful options for manipulating an image and for creating special effects, but you'll find that it's usually the advanced users who work with channels, who have an understanding of what they are, and toward what end they can be manipulated. This is so much the case that the ability to work with channels is often the line that separates intermediate users from advanced users or "power" users.

In this chapter, we are going to take the time to investigate the RGB channels to understand what they are and how they contribute to the final image. We're also going to highlight the difference between color channels such as RGB and channels that are used to save selections. Finally, we're going to use a channel to perform a delicate color move on a nonspecific area of an image.

FIGURE 23
Viewing the Red channel

1. Verify that the Info palette is visible, then verify that RGB is displayed on at least one side of the Info palette.

2. Display the Channels palette, click the **Red channel**, then compare your screen to Figure 23.

    TIP If your channel is in red as opposed to black and white as shown in the figure, you need to change your preferences. Go to the Display & Cursors Preferences dialog box, then verify that the Color Channels in Color check box is not checked.

    (continued)

3. Click the **Green channel**, then compare your screen to Figure 24.

(continued)

FIGURE 24
Viewing the Green channel

FIGURE 25
Viewing the Blue channel

The three channels represent the red, green,
and blue components of each pixel in the
image. Think of the three channels as light.
You know that your computer monitor is a
light-emitting device and that the pixels that
make up the image on your monitor are
pixels of light. Therefore the RGB channels
are the red light, the green light, and the
blue light components of each pixel.

5. Click the **Eyedropper Tool** , position the
   pointer in the upper-right corner, then note
   the reading in the Info palette.

The Info palette shows a value only for the
Blue channel. The values next to R, G, and B
are all blue values because the blue channel
is selected. This area of the image has a
high grayscale value in the Blue channel,
somewhere in the 245 range.

6. Sample the upper-right corner of each of the
   Red and Green channels.

The upper-right corner of each channel has a
high grayscale value in the 240s or 250s.

7. Click the **RGB channel**.

The RGB channel is the composite of the
three channels. Mimicking natural light,
the RGB channels combine to produce
other colors.

8. Sample pixels in the red cheeks.

As you would expect, the red component has
a higher grayscale value than the other two
channels—there's more red in this area.

(continued)

9. Zoom in on the left eye, then sample the brightest yellow pixel you can find.

   Regardless of the pixel you sample, if it has a yellow hue, its red and green values must both be significantly higher than its blue value. This is because in the real world red and green light combine to make yellow light, and in the Photoshop world, red and green pixels combine to make yellow pixels. A "pure" yellow pixel would have the RGB value of 255R/255G/0B.

10. Sample an area of the jacket.

    Because the jacket is a neutral color, the RGB values will all be in the same general range.

    TIP Whenever all three channels have similar grayscale values, the result is a relatively neutral tone. When the three colors have identical values, the result is a gray tone. Gray, as in no color. The higher the three identical values, the lighter the gray. The lower the three identical values, the darker the gray.

11. Sample a dark area of the beard.

    The grayscale value for each of the three channels will be low—close to if not zero.

    TIP The number zero in grayscale does not mean black. It means zero light. Nothing. When the grayscale value in each of the three channels is 0, it means that there is zero light from all three channels. Zero light is the absence of light, and the absence of light is black.

    (continued)

DESIGNnote

It's a challenging concept, and an important one: Photoshop identifies each of the three channels as a grayscale image. In each channel, each pixel can be one of 256 shades, from 0–255. When we worked with an image in grayscale mode (in Chapter 3), we discussed grayscale in terms of black and white: 0 represented black, and 255 represented white. In an RGB image, you need to toss out the concept of black and white, and instead think of the range as all or nothing. For example, in the Red channel, a pixel with a grayscale value of 0 means no red. A pixel with a grayscale value of 255 means all of red, or the *most* red.

FIGURE 26
Green channel

12. Sample the white area in the background.

    The grayscale value for each of the three channels will be high—close to if not 255.

    | TIP 255R/255G/255B produces white.

Reduce reds in flesh tones

1. Verify that the Overlay Detail layer is targeted, then create a new stamp visible layer named **Reduce Red Cheeks**.

   TIP The high degree of redness on the young man's cheeks is unusual, but you will find that with most fair-skinned models you will encounter "hot spots" in the flesh tones.

2. Click through the Red, Green, and Blue channels.

   We're looking for the channel in which the red cheeks are most distinct from the adjacent flesh tones. As shown in Figure 26, the Green channel best meets this criterion.

   (continued)

DESIGN*note*

The goal of this lesson is to reduce the distinct red flesh tones in the cheeks, the ears, and the nostrils. The question is, how would you select those areas to reduce the reds? Instead of using the Pen Tool or the Selection Tools or layer masks, which would all be time consuming to create, we're going to use one of the RGB channels as a ready-made layer mask.

3. Drag the **Green channel** to the Create new channel button 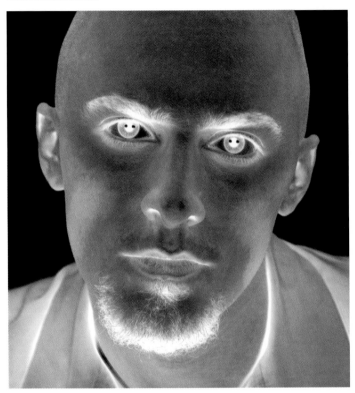 on the Channels palette.

   The Green channel is duplicated and the canvas now shows only the image in the new channel.

4. Name the new channel **First Selection**, then assess it as a selection mask for the red flesh tones.

   As a selection mask, the cheeks are darker than the adjacent flesh tones. If you loaded this channel as a selection, the cheeks would be less selected than the adjacent flesh tones.

5. Click **Image** on the menu bar, point to **Adjustments**, click **Invert**, then compare your channel to Figure 27.

   With the channel inverted, the cheeks are now lighter than the surrounding areas, meaning they will be more selected. However, they are very close in tone to those surrounding areas—not very distinct at all.

   (continued)

FIGURE 27
Selection mask inversed

DESIGN*note*

When you are working with any channel other than the three R, G, and B channels, it's best to think of them as selection masks, which is their essential function. Like any other standard selection mask, the white areas represent that which is selected and the black areas represent that which is not selected. Gray areas represent that which is partially selected.

FIGURE 28

Overlaying an image over itself

6. Click the **RGB channel** to return to the composite image.

7. Change the blending mode of the Reduce Red Cheeks layer to Overlay, then compare your screen to Figure 28.

(continued)

DESIGN*note*

Overlaying duplicate images produces an interesting result. The Reduce Red Cheeks layer was a stamp visible layer—it's a duplicate of the result of all the visible layers beneath it. This means that we have overlaid one image over its duplicate. Remember what we learned about Overlay: dark areas of the top layer dramatically darken dark areas on the below. Light areas on the top layer have more effect lightening light areas on the layer below. With this image, the dark red cheeks get darker while the adjacent flesh tones, which are much lighter, are dramatically lightened.

8. Return to the Channels palette, duplicate the Green channel, name it **Second Selection**, then compare it to Figure 29.

   The channels always reflect the image in its current state. Therefore, the cheeks are dramatically darker than the adjacent flesh tones.

9. Invert the channel, then compare it to Figure 30.

   | **TIP** Use quick keys to invert the channel: [Ctrl][I] (Win) or ⌘[I] (Mac).

   (continued)

FIGURE 29
New selection mask

FIGURE 30
Selection mask inverted

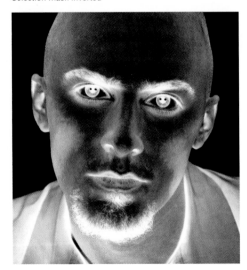

FIGURE 31
Selection mask adjusted

10. Open the Levels dialog box, type **24** in the first Input text box, type **.90** in the second Input text box, type **199** in the third Input text box, click **OK**, then compare your result to Figure 31.

11. Click the **Brush Tool** ✎ , set the opacity to 100%, choose a big soft brush, then paint black so that your selection mask resembles Figure 32.

We've blackened out the eyes, mouth, facial hair, and jacket so that they won't be affected by the following steps.

(continued)

FIGURE 32
"Masking out" areas of the mask

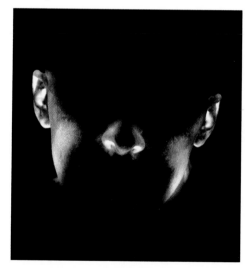

DESIGN*note*

You have all the same options to manipulate a channel as you do the composite image. We drastically improved our selection mask, making our whites whiter (more selected) and our darks darker.

12. Switch the foreground color to white, change the opacity to 50%, then paint the right cheek and the left cheek to lighten them so that your mask resembles Figure 33.

> **TIP** Use a soft brush and choose the right size brush for the job, one that's big enough to paint the area of each cheek with just one click.

13. Click the **RGB channel**, return to the Layers palette, then set the blending mode for the Reduce Red Cheeks layer to Normal.

14. Duplicate the Reduce Red Cheeks layer, then name the new layer **Red-Yellow Hue Swap**.

15. Click **Select** on the menu bar, click **Load Selection**, click the **Channel list arrow**, click **Second Selection**, click **OK,** then compare your selection marquee to Figure 34.

> **TIP** A faster way to load a selection is to [Ctrl] (Win) or ⌘-click the channel.

16. Apply a 4-pixel feather to the selection, then hide the selection marquee.

(continued)

FIGURE 33
Whitening the cheeks

FIGURE 34
Loading the selection mask

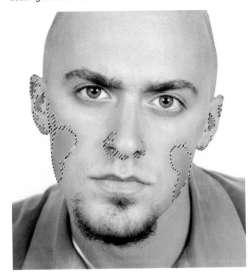

FIGURE 35
Adjusting hue and lightness

17. Open the Hue/Saturation dialog box, drag the **Hue slider** to +14, drag the **Lightness slider** to +12, click **OK**, then compare your result to Figure 35.

18. Deselect all.

19. Select the Whiten Eyes group, the Saturate Local group, the Overlay Detail layer, the Reduce Red Cheeks layer, and the Red-Yellow Hue Swap layer, then make them into a new layer group named **Retouched**.

(continued)

DESIGN*note*

Though all of the adjustments we made were subtle, the overall improvement of the image is stunning, especially the reduction of red in the cheeks, ears, and nostrils and the enhancement of the eyes. Take a moment to appreciate that the image does not look doctored or fake—it just looks like a good photograph.

20. Hide and show the Retouched layer to see the image with and without the retouching, then compare your artwork to Figure 36.

Though we adjusted levels at the very beginning of the project, now that we have achieved a final look, we need to reassess the image. At this stage, I almost always adjust curves or levels, and the adjustment is usually a contrast bump.

21. Expand the Retouched layer, target the **Red-Yellow Hue Swap layer**, then add a new curves adjustment layer named **Contrast Bump**.

22. Add a point anywhere on the curve, change its input value to 75, then change its output value to 65.

(continued)

FIGURE 36
Image before and after retouching

23. Add a second point, change its input value to 188, change its output value to 198, then click **OK**.

24. Hide and show the Retouched group, then compare your artwork to Figure 37.

25. Save your work, then close Bright Eyes.

FIGURE 37
Final image

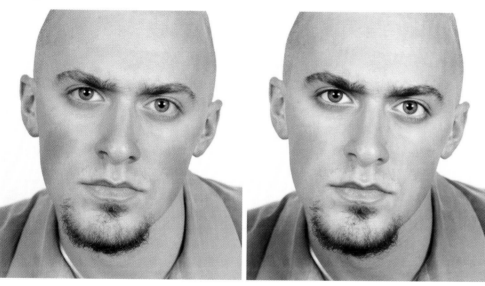

Lesson 5   Use a Channel as a Mask

USE THE
Cloning Tools

What You'll Do

Everybody loves the Clone Stamp Tool. Really, is there any tool in Photoshop that is more fun? Whenever Photoshop is being demonstrated, you can be sure that a substantial amount of time will be given to wowing the crowd with the tricks of the Clone Stamp Tool: cloning in an extra eye, replacing the head of the dog with the head of the horse, cloning the picture of the cat onto the surface of the planet Mars— you know the routine. The Clone Stamp Tool is a blast, and it doesn't take long for any novice user to find it and start playing with it. Mastering it is a whole different game because, along with being the most fun tool, it's also one of the trickiest to use effectively. *Effectively* means achieving the goal you want to achieve. "I want to remove the cow from this picture so that the field is just green grass and pink flowers," is an example. Using the Clone Stamp Tool effectively means choosing the right brush, sampling from the right area, and cloning with the best technique to remove the cow and replace it with green grass and pink flowers that look real. That's the challenge. For many versions, the Clone Stamp Tool was the only cloning tool in Photoshop. Then the Patch Tool and the Healing Brush Tool were introduced to provide options that the Clone Stamp Tool just couldn't. In this lesson, you'll work with all three.

FIGURE 38
First area to retouch

FIGURE 39
Positioning the brush

Use the Clone Stamp Tool

1. Open AP 6-2.psd, then save it as **Smooth Lines**.

2. Hide and show the Eyes Retouched layer group to see the retouching work that I've already done on the eyes.

   | TIP I also adjusted the levels of the image.

3. Verify that the Eyes Retouched layer is showing and targeted, then create a new stamp visible layer named **Smooth**.

4. Figure 38 identifies the first area that we want to retouch.

5. Click the **Clone Stamp Tool** 🔖 , verify that its mode is set to Normal and that its Opacity and Flow are both set to 100%.

6. Create a Soft Round 70 pixels brush, then position it over the area shown in Figure 39.

   We will use this area as the sample. It is very close in color and tone to the area we want to fix, and it is also smooth, with no wrinkles or indents.

(continued)

DESIGN*note*

Let's agree that the goal of this exercise is to retouch this image so that it can be used in a medical advertisement in a magazine targeted toward senior citizens. The advertisement is for a daily vitamin that seniors can take to keep them peppy and zippy. The client has instructed you that the model should represent a vibrant older woman—a portrait of healthy aging. The client also told you something interesting about retouching the image: It's not so much that they want the model to appear younger; instead, they want you to "reduce the harsher signs of aging."

7. Press and hold **[Alt]** (Win) or **[option]** (Mac) then click to sample the area.

   For this lesson, I will presume that you know the basics of how to use the Clone Stamp Tool to clone areas of an image. From this point on, I will simply tell you to sample an area.

8. Position the pointer over the area to be fixed, click once, then compare your result to Figure 40.

9. Using the same method, but with a smaller brush size, clone out the blemish shown in Figure 41.

(continued)

FIGURE 40
Result of clicking Clone Stamp Tool

FIGURE 41
Cloning out the blemish

DESIGN*note*

This would be a best-case scenario for cloning. We found a smooth sample area nearby, and we were able to replace the unwanted pixels with just one click. Note that we used a very large brush for exactly that reason—when you can, it's usually best to replace an area with just one click rather than multiple clicks.

FIGURE 42
Next area to be fixed

FIGURE 43
Result of cloning using smooth area of cheek

10. See Figure 42 for the next area to be fixed.

   This area is usually problematic, whether the model is younger or older. In this image, the area is dotted with small highlights. Possibly, the model's makeup was clumpy or flaky in this area, or maybe the skin itself had large pores or small pock marks. In any case, it's distracting and can be fixed easily.

11. Change the brush size back to 70 pixels, sample a smooth area from the left cheek, then clone out the area completely, so that your image resembles Figure 43.

   TIP I clicked two times to completely cover the area.

   (continued)

12. Reduce your brush size to 27 pixels, then see Figure 44.

13. Sample the area indicated by the black circle, then clone out the entire cheek line by clicking in the area indicated by the green circle and dragging to the area indicated by the red circle.

14. Compare your result to Figure 45.

Yes, this looks fake. Reality is not our goal at this stage of retouching. Our goal is to cover lines with similar flesh tones. Later, we will bring back some of the detail using opacity.

(continued)

FIGURE 44
Third area to be fixed

FIGURE 45
Result of cloning out the cheek line

FIGURE 46
Smooth light area

FIGURE 47
Result of cloning out wrinkles

15. Sampling from the smooth light area at the top of the left cheek, identified in Figure 46, clone out all of the wrinkles under the left eye, then compare your results to Figure 47.

(continued)

16. Sampling from the same area, but with a smaller brush, clone out the line in the forehead to the upper left of the left eyebrow, then compare your result to Figure 48.

17. See Figure 49.

This area is perhaps the most problematic in the image. The flesh tone is bright, making the wrinkles that much more noticeable. The eyes are the first thing everybody looks at, so improving this area is important. The problem with fixing this area is that there's very little area to sample. We have no choice but to clone from another area of the image.

(continued)

FIGURE 48
Cloning out line in the forehead

FIGURE 49
Assessing a problematic area

FIGURE 50
Cloning over the eye

FIGURE 51
Identifying lines on the neck

18. Sample from the middle of the left cheek, then clone over the eye as shown in Figure 50.
19. Save your work.

Use the Healing Brush

1. Note the lines on the neck identified in Figure 51.

    The Clone Stamp Tool is not very effective for cloning out these lines simply because there's no place to sample—there's no other area of the image that has a smooth flesh tone that is as dark as this area.

(continued)

2. Set your brush size to 27 pixels, then sample the area shown in Figure 52.

3. Clone out the lower heavy wrinkle so that your artwork resembles Figure 53.

   The sample area is too light for the area being replaced.

4. Undo the last step.

5. Click the **Healing Brush Tool** , then verify that the Mode is set to Normal, that the Sampled option button is selected, and that the Aligned check box is checked in the Options bar.

   | **TIP** The Healing Brush Tool is hidden behind the Patch Tool .

   (continued)

FIGURE 52
Area to be sampled

FIGURE 53
Result is too light

FIGURE 54
Result using the Healing Brush Tool

FIGURE 55
Cloning upper wrinkle

6. Repeat Steps 2 and 3, then compare your result to Figure 54.

   The Healing Brush Tool clones just like the Clone Stamp Tool. The big difference is that the Healing Brush Tool automatically adjusts the color of the clone to match its new surroundings as closely as possible.

7. Using the same method and sampling from the same location, clone out the upper wrinkle in the same area, then compare your screen to Figure 55.

   (continued)

8. Increase the brush size to 32 pixels, then see Figure 56.

9. Sample the area indicated by the black circle, click the area indicated by the green circle, **[Shift]**-click the area indicated by the red circle, then compare your result to Figure 57.

(continued)

FIGURE 56
Sampling an area

FIGURE 57
Results of Healing Brush Tool

FIGURE 58

Using the Healing Brush Tool on the neck

FIGURE 59

Selecting an area

10. Practice with the Healing Brush Tool on the neck only so that your work resembles Figure 58.

11. Save your work.

Use the Patch Tool

1. Click the **Patch Tool** ◇ , then select the area shown in Figure 59.

(continued)

Lesson 6   Use the Cloning Tools

2. Drag the selection up to a smooth area of the left cheek, as shown in Figure 60, then release the mouse button.

3. Deselect, then compare your result to Figure 61.

The Patch Tool works like the Healing Brush Tool, but it is more powerful. First, you select the area that you want to replace. Then, you drag the selection to an area that has a texture that you want to use. As you drag, you get a dynamic preview of the clone before the color adjustment. When you release the mouse button, the Patch Tool clones the area where you deselect, "patches" it into the original selection, then color corrects it to match the tonal range of the original selection. The Patch Tool is often very successful in matching the clone to the tonal range of the original, and because you can work with large selections, the Patch Tool is very effective for getting a lot of retouching done quickly.

(continued)

FIGURE 60
Dragging selection to smooth area of left cheek

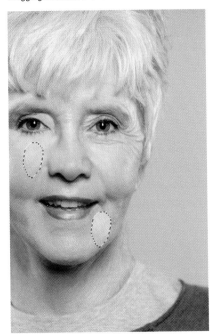

FIGURE 61
Result of using the Patch Tool

FIGURE 62
Selecting an area to patch

FIGURE 63
Result of using the Patch Tool

4. Select the area shown in Figure 62, hide the selection edges, drag the selection to the smooth area under the left eye, release the mouse button, then deselect.

5. Compare your result to Figure 63.

(continued)

Lesson 6   Use the Cloning Tools

6. Select the area shown in Figure 64, clone from the smooth cheek above, deselect, then compare your result to Figure 65.

(continued)

FIGURE 64

Selecting an area to patch

FIGURE 65

Result of using the Patch Tool

FIGURE 66
Selecting the eyelid

7. Select the area shown in Figure 66, then clone from the light area under the left eye.

8. Compare your result to Figure 67.

   Note how much better (and faster and easier) the Patch Tool worked on this eye than the Clone Stamp Tool did on the left eye.

   (continued)

FIGURE 67
Result of using the Patch Tool on eyelid

9. Remove the deep wrinkles to the right of the right eye and the scar on the lower right cheek.

> **TIP** You don't necessarily need to select an entire area. For example, with the wrinkles near the eye, it would be better to clone three or four smaller selections than one large selection.

10. Compare your work to Figure 68.

(continued)

FIGURE 68
Result of removing wrinkles and scar

FIGURE 69

Before and after results

11. Add a layer mask to the Smooth layer, click **Edit** on the menu bar, then click **Fill**.

12. Click the **Use list arrow**, choose 50% gray, verify that the blending mode is set to Normal and the opacity is set to 100%, then click **OK**.

    Rather than set the Smooth layer to 50% opacity, we have used a mask with 50% gray to achieve the effect. This leaves us the option of painting in the layer mask to intensify or lessen the retouching in local areas. Remember this trick; it's always best to leave yourself with options.

13. Select both the Smooth layer and the Eyes Retouched layer group, then make a new layer group named **Retouching**.

14. Hide and show the Retouching layer to see the before-and-after results, then compare your screen to Figure 69.

15. Save your work, then close Smooth Lines.

DESIGN*note*

In my experience, this is the most effective method for retouching wrinkles. We have not removed a single wrinkle. We've only reduced them. Allowing 50% of the original image to show through grounds the image in reality; there's no visible blurring, cloning, or awkward textures. The retouching is invisible.

RETOUCH
Teeth

What You'll Do

If you liked whitening eyes and reducing wrinkles, you're going to love working with teeth. Teeth are usually the greatest challenge to the retoucher. They almost always need work—a little whitening here, a little straightening there. What's really tough about retouching teeth is that it usually requires making precise selections and many small moves with the retouching and paint tools. And the margin of error is small—make that, the margin of reality is small. It's very tricky to retouch teeth in a way that is not noticeable, to fool the eye into believing that the retouched teeth—the color, the shape, and the texture—are the real thing.

In this lesson, instead of retouching the teeth yourselves, you're going to click through the layers to see the retouching that I applied. As I was working, I didn't know if the techniques I was using would ultimately work. They did, and the goal of this chapter is to have you retrace my steps to see the objectives that I identified, the techniques I used to achieve them, and the choices I made along the way.

FIGURE 70
Assessing the model's teeth

Fix teeth

1. Open AP 6-3.psd, then save it as **Fix Teeth**.
2. Regard Figure 70 to assess the model's teeth.
3. Expand the Teeth layer to view the layers within.

(continued)

DESIGN*note*

Teeth almost always need retouching. Sometimes, it's light retouching, such as a slight whitening. Other times . . . let's just say it's extensive. You might be surprised to find that when doing close-ups of celebrities for posters and magazine covers, retouchers sometimes paste in stock photographs of perfect teeth! To be kind, let's just say that the subject of this photo does not have perfect teeth. Note though, that the left side is much worse than the right side. On the left side, one yellow tooth overlaps another, her lip is hooked on one of the bottom teeth, and a silver or gold filling is visible. On the right side, the teeth are a bit chipped, and one bottom tooth is bent behind the others. Other than that, the right side isn't so bad, and we're going to use that to our advantage. One more note: did you notice that whoever did the makeup for this model didn't do a very good job? The application of the lipstick is uneven—note her bottom lip. Also, the edges are soft, making the line of her lips indistinct.

4. Make the Square Off Teeth layer visible.

   As shown in Figure 71, I squared off the three teeth on the right side of the mouth. To do so, I made a clipping path in the shape that I wanted the teeth to be, used the path as a selection, then cloned to make the teeth larger and more square.

5. Make the Fix Bottom Row layer visible.

   The bottom row was more of a challenge because one tooth is bent all the way back. As shown in Figure 72, I cloned out the bent tooth. I then cloned the tooth to the right to replace the old tooth. Then came the challenge: The teeth weren't lining up. The line between the two top front teeth was still to the left of the left edge of the clone. I enlarged the clone slightly, then stretched it to the left.

   (continued)

FIGURE 71
Three teeth squared off

FIGURE 72
Lining up the teeth in the bottom row

FIGURE 73
Darkened lipstick

FIGURE 74
Sharper lipstick line

6. Make the Darken Lipstick layer visible.

   As shown in Figure 73, I darkened the lips to make the lipstick darker, more distinct, and more consistent in tone throughout. I used the overlay detail technique, which worked well, but it was not without its challenges. With red, the color shifts quickly and dramatically. Parts of the lips had lipstick, and parts were bare, and I wanted everything darker. Trying to match the two areas was tricky.

7. Make the Improve Edge layer visible.

   As shown in Figure 74, I created a sharper line for the lipstick to cover the indistinct line beneath it. First, I created a path to use as a selection. When I made the path, I drew the path above the top lip a bit to increase its size, then cloned red into the new area. I did the same to strengthen the edge of the bottom lip.

(continued)

8. See Figure 75.

   I selected the right half of the mouth as shown, copied it, then pasted it on its own layer. Note the left edge of the selection marquee. I positioned that left edge very carefully. I zoomed in to be sure that the pixels that made up the left edge of my selection were the pixels that drew the line between the top two teeth.

9. Make the Flip Horizontal layer visible.

   As shown in Figure 76, I flipped the "good side" of the mouth, then positioned it over the "bad" left side. Up to this point, I wasn't certain that my idea would work. The flipped artwork looked pretty good, but pretty good doesn't cut it when retouching. It needed to be unnoticeable. It needed to hide in plain sight.

   (continued)

FIGURE 75
Selecting right side of the mouth

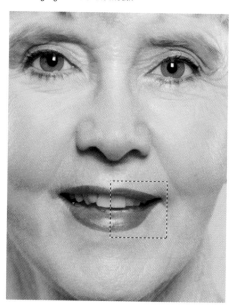

FIGURE 76
Right side of mouth flipped to left side

FIGURE 77

Distorting mouth to create natural look

10. Make the Distort layer visible.

As shown in Figure 77, I distorted the mouth so that the two sides weren't perfect mirror images of one another. The mouth is stretched wider on the left side and is rotated clockwise. It is a subtle move, but it needs to be there. The two sides can't be perfect mirrors. However, the adjustment is too subtle to completely solve the problem, and the horizontal flip is still evident.

11. Hide the Flip Horizontal layer.

The Distort layer artwork replaces the Flip Horizontal artwork, so we no longer want the Flip Horizontal artwork to be visible.

(continued)

12. Press and hold **[Shift]**, then click the **Layer mask thumbnail** on the Distort layer to activate it.

As shown in Figure 78, the layer mask sells it. Hide and show the layer mask to see the change. I used the mask to allow some of the original left sides of the lips to show through. That small but important move solved the problem.

The eye is quick to pick up a mirror image. However, it's just as quick to stop scanning when it picks up asymmetrical detail. It doesn't take much: note the bump on the upper lip, the darker edge at the left side of the bottom lip, and the softer highlight on the bottom lip. They are enough to convince the eye to move on without questioning it.

13. Collapse the Teeth layer, create a new layer group using the Teeth and Retouching layers, then name it **Final Retouch**.

14. Hide and show the Final Retouch layer to assess the final effect.

15. Save your work, then close Fix Teeth.

DESIGN*note*

Overall, the retouching achieved its objective. The improvement in the eyes and the reduced wrinkles dramatically decrease the model's age. However, if you hide the retouching, and take a moment to note how much of the model's character and personality is lost in the retouching.

The final question I always ask myself when retouching is "Did I leave enough personality?" If this were a photo that the model was going to give to her family, I would say I removed too much of her character, especially in her eyes. And I would have not cloned out an entire half of her mouth and changed her smile!

But that wasn't the job. The retouched photo could legitimately be used as part of a medical advertisement in a magazine for seniors. The reduction in wrinkles is just right for the age we want the model to appear to be, and the softer wrinkles actually flatter her. The clear eyes and perfect smile make her an appealing example of healthy aging, and the slight vacantness in those same eyes and smile actually work to our advantage: they make her a bit of a generic everywoman, and that's exactly who the client wants to sell medicine to: every woman.

FIGURE 78

Results of layer mask

1. Open AP 6-4.psd, then save it as **Red Boy**.
2. Whiten the eyes and increase the saturation on the irises.
3. Use the overlay detail method to add detail to the irises.
4. Reduce the harsh lines and bluish tones under the boy's eyes.
5. Create a new stamp visible layer, then name it **Reduce Reds**.
6. Overlay the new layer so that the red cheeks, ears, and chin get darker and redder.
7. Duplicate the Green channel, then name it **Hot Spots**.
8. Invert the channel.
9. Open the Levels dialog box, then make the whites whiter, the blacks blacker, and the midtones darker.
10. Blacken out the areas that you don't want to be affected. (*Hint*: Figure 79 shows one example of the selection mask.)
11. Click the RGB layer, then set the blending mode on the Reduce Reds layer to Normal.
12. Load the Hot Spots selection, apply a 4-pixel feather, then hide the selection.
13. Open the Hue/Saturation dialog box, click the Edit list arrow, then choose Reds. (*Hint*: For this image, we are going to modify specifically the red hues in the selection.)
14. Drag the Hue slider to +14, then click OK.
15. Open the Curves dialog box, increase the contrast to a degree that you feel improves the image, then click OK.
16. Compare your results to Figure 80.
17. Save your work, then close Red Boy.

FIGURE 79
Selection mask

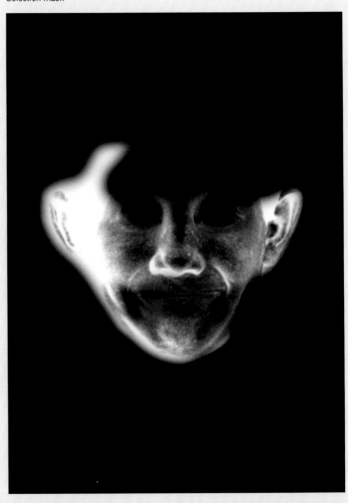

FIGURE 80
Completed Project Builder 1

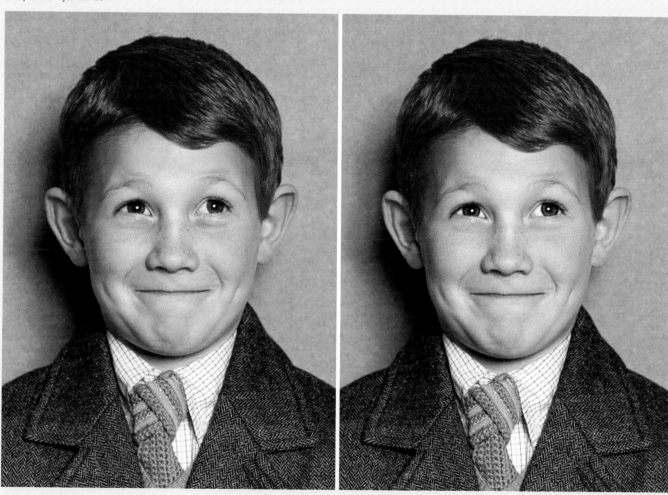

PROJECT BUILDER 1

1. Open AP 6-5.psd, then save it as **Teeth Project**.
2. Click the Rectangular Marquee Tool then make a square marquee that selects the entire mouth.
3. Click Edit on the menu bar, then click Copy Merged.
4. Paste, then name the new layer **Square Off Teeth**.
5. Zoom in, click the Pen Tool, then draw a path that represents the shape of the top right row of teeth as you would want them to be. (*Hint*: Figure 81 shows one example of the path.)
6. Convert the path to a selection with no feather, then use the Clone Stamp Tool to clone the original teeth into the new shape.
7. Use the Clone Stamp Tool, the Pencil Tool, the Sponge Tool (set to Desaturate) or a combination of the three to remove the yellow stains between the teeth. (*Hint*: Be sure you don't remove the lines between the teeth.)
8. Paint out or clone out the bent bottom tooth where it breaks the line between the top row of teeth and the bottom row of teeth.
9. Click the Pen Tool, then draw a path around the tooth to the right of the original bent tooth. (*Hint*: Figure 82 shows an example of the path.)
10. Convert the path to a selection with no feather, copy, paste a new layer, then name the new layer **Fix Bottom Row**.
11. Scale the new tooth slightly, then stretch it horizontally so that its left edge aligns with the line between the top two front teeth.
12. Use a layer mask, if necessary, to hide any of the unwanted areas of the copy.
13. Create a new layer, name it **Darken Lipstick**, then set the layer to the Overlay blending mode.
14. Paint with the overlay detail technique to darken the lipstick over the entire mouth and to make it all more consistent in color.
15. Click the Pen Tool, then draw a path around the lips.
16. Tweak the path to improve the shape of the top lip. (*Hint*: Figure 83 shows an example of the path.)
17. Convert the path to a selection with no feather, copy, then paste a new layer named **Improve Edge**.
18. Use the Clone Stamp Tool, the Paint Brush Tool, or a combination of both to increase the lips to fill the new selection.
19. Click the Rectangular Marquee Tool, then select the right half of the mouth.
20. Click Edit on the menu bar, then click Copy Merged.
21. Paste the selection, then name the new layer **Flip Horizontal**.
22. Click Edit on the menu bar, point to Transform, then click Flip Horizontal.
23. Reposition the artwork to create the left side of the mouth.
24. Duplicate the Flip Horizontal layer, name the new layer **Distort**, then hide the Flip Horizontal layer.
25. Target the Distort layer, then distort or rotate or scale (or any combination of the three transformations) the artwork so that it is no longer a perfect mirror image of the right side of the mouth.
26. Add a layer mask, then mask out the lipstick on the Distort layer to show as much of the original lipstick as you can while maintaining realism.
27. Compare your results to Figure 84.
28. Save your work, then close Teeth Project.

FIGURE 81
Clipping path for top row

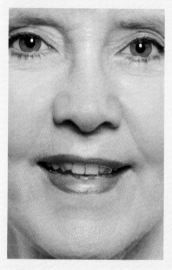

FIGURE 82
Clipping path for bottom tooth

FIGURE 83
Clipping path for lips

FIGURE 84
Completed Project Builder 2

PROJECT BUILDER 2

chapter

7

WORKING WITH TYPE,
Shape Layers,
and Filters

1. Design chiseled type.

2. Design plastic type.

3. Design recessed type.

4. Design eroded type.

5. Mask images with type.

DESIGN CHISELED
Type

What You'll Do

Photoshop has a number of settings and styles that allow you to make gorgeous chiseled type, which is a very good thing because chiseled type is a commonly used type style. Chiseling type has many applications: it can be used for metallic textures, stone textures, and wood textures. It can be shiny or dull, dark or bright. Chiseled text is timeless. Of course, it's the first thing you think of when you think of ancient writing, Roman numerals, and mythology. Yet it is just as appropriate to use it in modern contexts. It connotes hardness, yet it also connotes elegance. In this lesson, you'll explore the many options Photoshop makes available for working with this essential and versatile style.

FIGURE 1
Filling the text with gray

1. Open AP 7-1.psd, then save it as **Chisel Text**.

2. Set the foreground color to **128R/128G/128B**, fill the text on the Text layer with the foreground color, then deselect so that your canvas resembles Figure 1.

   When designing text, it's usually a good idea to start with gray text using 128/128/128, because this gives you the full upper half of the grayscale to create highlights and the full lower half of the grayscale to create shadows.

3. Click **Layer** on the menu bar, point to **Layer Style**, then click **Bevel and Emboss**.

   TIP Position the dialog box so that you can see the changes to the image as you work.

4. Verify that the Style is set to Inner Bevel, click the **Technique list arrow**, then click **Chisel Hard**.

5. Drag the **Depth slider** back and forth to see its effect.

   All bevel and emboss effects are created by making one side of a graphic darker and the other side brighter. The Depth slider controls the darkness of the shadows and brightness of the highlights. Increasing the Depth value increases the contrast between the shadows and highlights.

   (continued)

6. Drag the **Depth slider** to 151.

7. Slowly drag the **Size slider** to the right to increase the chisel effect.

8. Drag the **Size slider** to 42, then compare your canvas to Figure 2.

9. Click the **Gloss Contour list arrow**, click through each setting in the list, then click **Cone – Inverted**, the third contour in the top row.

10. Verify that the Anti-aliased check box is not checked, click **OK**, then compare your result to Figure 3.

FIGURE 2
Setting the Chisel Hard technique in the Layer Style dialog box

FIGURE 3
Chisel effect

DESIGN*note*

Of the many looks available in the Bevel and Emboss layer style category, the chisel effect in Figure 3 is my personal favorite. I really like the way it raises the center of the letterform to a sharp point that is defined by the dark gray line. However, from a design perspective, this is in no way original art. Though the artwork is pleasing, it's a "canned solution," meaning anybody could recreate it simply by dragging the same sliders and inputting the same values. The challenge when working with layer styles is to create a unique effect. Therefore, it's a good idea to think of the art at this stage as the base effect to which you can add your own techniques and create an original piece of artwork.

1. Click **Layer** on the menu bar, point to **New Fill Layer**, then click **Solid Color**.

2. Type **Orange** in the Name text box, click the **Use Previous Layer to Create Clipping Mask check box**, then click **OK**.

3. Type **205R/111G/0B** in the Color Picker, click **OK**, then compare your screen to Figure 4.

   Because the Orange layer is clipped by the Text layer, it takes on the layer style of the Text layer.

FIGURE 4
Overlaying the fill color layer

Create selection masks from artwork

1. Press and hold **[Shift][Ctrl][Alt]** (Win) or **[Shift] [option]** Ⓗ (Mac), press **[N]**, then press **[E]**.

   For the remainder of this chapter, I will refer to this move as "Create a new stamp visible layer."

   Name the new layer **Stamp Visible**.

2. Click the **Magic Wand Tool** ✎, set the Tolerance value to **4**, then verify that the Anti-alias and Contiguous check boxes are both checked.

3. Select the tops and bottoms of the letters *L* and *I* so that your canvas resembles Figure 5.

4. Click **Select** on the menu bar, point to **Modify**, then click **Expand**.

5. Type **1** in the Expand By text box, then click **OK**.

6. Save the selection as **Tops/Bottoms**, then deselect.

7. In the Channels palette, click the **Channel thumbnail** for the Tops/Bottoms channel to see the selection mask.

8. Click the **Channel thumbnails** for the **Red, Green**, and **Blue channels** to see what's on each of them.

(continued)

FIGURE 5
Selecting the tops and bottoms

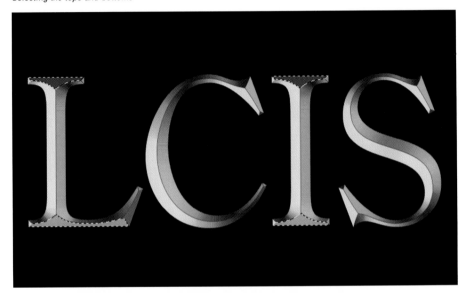

FIGURE 6
Blue channel loaded as a selection

FIGURE 7
Half Round gloss contour

9. Click the **Channel thumbnail** on the RGB channel, press and hold **[Ctrl]** (Win) or ⌘ (Mac), then click the **Channel thumbnail** on the Blue channel.

   TIP   Pressing and holding [Ctrl] (Win) or ⌘ (Mac) when clicking a Channel thumbnail loads the channel as a selection mask.

   Our goal is to create a selection mask for the left side of each letter. As shown in Figure 6, the Blue channel gets us the closest to that goal—but not close enough.

10. Deselect, return to the Layers palette, then delete the Stamp Visible layer.

    We needed the Stamp Visible layer only to select the tops and bottoms.

11. Double-click the **Bevel and Emboss effects layer**, click the **Gloss Contour list arrow**, click **Half Round**, then click **OK**.

    As shown in Figure 7, with the Half Round gloss contour, the chisel effect has very light highlights.

    (continued)

12. In the Channels palette, duplicate the Blue channel, rename it as **Right Side**, then compare it to Figure 8.

13. Open the Levels dialog box, drag the **white triangle** left until the third Input text box reads 182, then click **OK**.

    The right side of the letterforms are now white in the selection mask. However, the tops of the letters are also white, which means they too would be part of any selection made from this mask.

14. Press and hold **[Ctrl]** (Win) or ⌘ (Mac), then click the **Channel thumbnail** for the Tops/Bottoms channel.

    The Tops/Bottoms channel is loaded as a selection in the Right Side channel.

15. Expand the selection by 1 pixel, fill the selection with black, deselect, then compare your selection mask to Figure 9.

    We have now successfully isolated the right side of the letterforms from the left side and from the tops and bottoms of the letterforms. The tops of the C and S letters are white or light gray; they will be selected or partially selected when this mask is loaded. As you'll see, this won't be a problem; keep an eye on these areas as we move forward.

16. Duplicate the Right Side channel, then name the new channel **Left Side**.

    (continued)

FIGURE 8
Duplicated Blue channel

FIGURE 9
Masking out the tops and bottoms

FIGURE 10
Inverted channel

FIGURE 11
Masking out the tops and bottoms

17. Invert the channel.

18. Open the Levels dialog box, drag the **black triangle** right until the first Input text box reads 40, then click **OK**.

    Compare your screen to Figure 10.

19. Load the Tops/Bottoms channel, expand the selection by 1 pixel, fill the selection with black, then deselect so that your Left Side channel resembles Figure 11.

20. Click the **RGB channel**, then return to the Layers palette.

21. Double-click the **Bevel and Emboss effects layer**, click the **Gloss Contour list arrow**, click **Cone – Inverted**, then click **OK**.

22. Save your work.

Create a texture

1. Click **Image** on the menu bar, click **Duplicate**, type **Texture** in the As text box, then click **OK**.

2. Flatten the duplicate file, then fill the canvas with the gray foreground color.

3. Save the file as **Texture.psd**.

4. Click **Filter** on the menu bar, point to **Noise**, then click **Add Noise**.

(continued)

5. Type **124** in the Amount text box, verify that the Uniform option button is selected, then verify that the Monochromatic check box is checked.

   Your Add Noise dialog box should resemble Figure 12.

6. Click **OK**, duplicate the Background layer, then name the new layer **Left Angle.**

7. Duplicate the Left Angle layer, name the new layer **Top**, then hide the Top layer.

8. Target the **Left Angle layer**, click **Filter** on the menu bar, point to **Blur**, then click **Motion Blur.**

9. Drag the **Distance slider** to 32, set the Angle to 45, compare your Motion Blur dialog box to Figure 13, then click **OK**.

10. Show and target the **Top layer**, click **Filter** on the menu bar, point to **Blur**, then click **Motion Blur.**

(continued)

(continued)

FIGURE 12
Add Noise dialog box

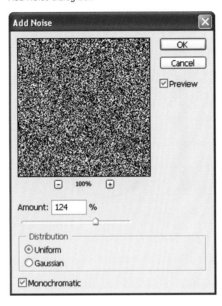

FIGURE 13
Motion Blur dialog box

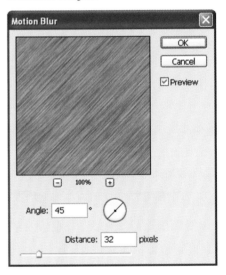

DESIGNnote

When applying filters, it's a good idea to write down the specifications you use because, unlike layer styles or adjustment layers, filters cannot be modified once they are applied. The next time you return to the filter's dialog box—in this case, the Add Noise dialog box—it will show the previous settings that you used. However, that's the only record you have of the move you made. It's best that you write the information down somewhere because if you come back to this illustration three weeks or three years from now, you'll have no idea which settings you used.

Working with Type, Shape Layers, and Filters   Chapter 7

FIGURE 14
Motion Blur dialog box

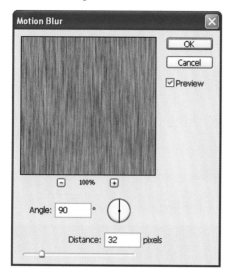

FIGURE 15
Pasting the left-side texture

11. Verify that the Distance slider is set to 32, set the Angle to 90, compare your Motion Blur dialog box to Figure 14, then click **OK** to close the dialog box.

12. Hide the Top layer, target the **Left Angle layer**, select all, then copy.

13. Return to the Chisel Text document, then target the **Orange layer**.

Apply textures

1. Verify that the Orange layer is targeted, then load the **Left Side** selection.

2. Click **Edit** on the menu bar, click **Paste Into**, then compare your canvas to Figure 15.

(continued)

3. Name the new layer **Left**, set its blending mode to Multiply, set its Opacity to **40%**, then compare your canvas to Figure 16.

4. Load the **Right Side** selection, click **Edit** on the menu bar, click **Paste Into**, then compare your canvas to Figure 17.

    The same Left Angle artwork is pasted into the Right Side selection.

5. Click **Edit** on the menu bar, point to **Transform**, then click **Flip Horizontal**.

    As shown in Figure 18, the texture on the right side of the letterforms is now angled in the opposite direction.

(continued)

FIGURE 16
Left side with texture

FIGURE 17
Pasting the left-side artwork into the right side

FIGURE 18
Flipping the artwork

FIGURE 19
Right side with texture

FIGURE 20
Pasting into the tops and bottoms

FIGURE 21
Tops and bottoms with texture

6. Name the new layer **Right**, change its blending mode to Overlay, then compare your canvas to Figure 19.

7. Load the **Tops/Bottoms** selection.

8. Switch to the Texture document, show and target the **Top layer**, select all, (if necessary), copy, then return to the Chisel Text document.

9. Click **Edit** on the menu bar, click **Paste Into**, then compare your canvas to Figure 20.

10. Name the new layer **Top/Bottom**, set the blending mode to Overlay, then compare your artwork to Figure 21.

11. Save your work.

Modify blending modes to modify effects

1. Duplicate the Left layer.
2. Change the blending mode to Overlay, then change the opacity to 100%.

   As shown in Figure 22, the move made the texture more distinct and detailed without darkening highlights.
3. Duplicate the Right layer.

   As shown in Figure 23, duplicating the Right layer intensifies the color and texture on the right side of the letterforms.

   (continued)

FIGURE 22
Duplicating the left side

FIGURE 23
Duplicating the right side

FIGURE 24
Final artwork

4. Target the **Top/Bottom layer**, then change its blending mode to Multiply.

   As shown in Figure 24, the Multiply blending mode darkens both the tops and bottoms of the letterforms, allowing the right sides of the letterforms to be the brightest and most saturated areas of the illustration. The effect is that a gold light source is shining on the letters from the right.

5. Save your work, close Chisel Text, then save and close Texture.

DESIGN PLASTIC
Type

What You'll Do

Plastic type, unlike chiseled text, is unusual and not regularly seen, which makes it a great technique for you to have in your skills set. One of the great things about working with type is that it allows you to use some of the more extreme filters—ones that would have little or no application for a realistic image. The Plastic Wrap filter is one of those filters—a very cool effect, but one that is rarely used with images, except maybe for dramatic special effects. When you learn how to use it with text, it opens the door for a number of practical applications: its fun, it's playful and it is an eye-catcher. The important features to note in this lesson are the soft and round Bevel and Emboss layer style that works so well with the Plastic Wrap filter and the blending modes that produce various examples of the unmistakable and uniquely modern material that is plastic.

FIGURE 25
Applying the Round Corners filter to Illustrator text

PLASTIC

FIGURE 26
Pasting text as a shape layer

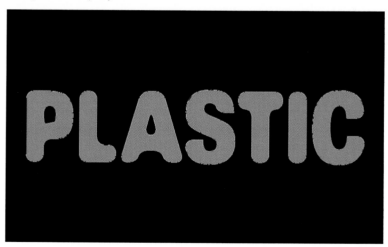

1. Open AP 7-2.ai in Adobe Illustrator, then save it as **Round Corners**.

2. Select all, click **View** on the menu bar, then click **Hide Edges**.

3. Click **Filter** on the menu bar, point to the first **Stylize** command, then click **Round Corners**.

4. Type **.1** in the Radius text box, click **OK**, then compare your artwork to Figure 25.

5. Click **Edit** on the menu bar, click **Copy**, then save your work.

6. Switch to Photoshop, open AP 7-3.psd, then save it as **Plastic.psd**.

7. Set the foreground color to **128R/128G/128B**, then paste.

8. In the Paste dialog box, click **Shape Layer**, click **OK**, then compare your canvas to Figure 26.

   The artwork is pasted on its own layer as a vector graphic and uses the current foreground color as its fill. The path that defines the letterforms is a vector graphic, like any path in Photoshop or Illustrator. As a vector graphic, the path—and therefore the letterforms—can be scaled, rotated, and otherwise transformed without any loss in quality.

(continued)

9. Show the Paths palette.

   When you create a shape layer, the path on the layer is automatically listed in the Paths palette as a vector mask. The vector graphic on the shape layer is no different than creating a path in Photoshop using the Pen Tool.

10. Double-click **Shape 1 Vector Mask** in the Paths palette.

11. Type **Text Path** in the Name text box of the Save Path dialog box, then click **OK**.

    The path on the shape layer is added to the Paths palette as a path.

12. Switch to the Layers palette, click the **Vector mask thumbnail** on the Shape 1 layer to make the path invisible, then compare your canvas to Figure 27.

13. Save your work.

FIGURE 27
"Base text" in Photoshop

FIGURE 28
Applying the Pillow Emboss

Emboss for a plastic effect

1. Click **Layer** on the menu bar, point to **Layer Style**, then click **Bevel and Emboss**.

2. Set the Style to **Pillow Emboss**, then verify that the Technique is set to Smooth.

3. Drag the **Depth slider** to 101, drag the **Size slider** to 98, then drag the **Soften slider** to 7.

4. Click **OK**, then compare your canvas to Figure 28.

   The pillow emboss gave us the texture we want for the letterforms; it also gave us the white shadows behind the letterforms, which we don't want.

5. Press and hold **[Ctrl]** (Win) or ⌘ (Mac), then click the **Layer thumbnail** on the Shape 1 layer to load it as a selection.

6. Click **Edit** on the menu bar, then click **Copy Merged**.

   Copy Merged is an important and extremely useful command. When you apply the Copy Merged command to layered artwork, it copies the selected artwork as though all the layers were merged and the image was flattened. To put it in other terms, the Copy Merged command copies selected artwork as it *appears*, regardless of how many different layers are involved in creating the artwork.

(continued)

7. Click **Edit** on the menu bar, click **Paste**, and name the new layer **Plastic Text**.

8. Hide the Shape 1 layer, then compare your canvas to Figure 29.

9. Save your work.

Apply color for a plastic effect

1. Click **Layer** on the menu bar, point to **New Fill Layer**, then click **Solid Color**.

1. Type **Gold** in the Name text box, click the **Use Previous Layer to Create Clipping Mask check box**, then click **OK**.

3. Type **255R/234G/94B** in the Color Picker, then click **OK**.

(continued)

FIGURE 29
Letterforms alone

DESIGNnote

Plastic objects are created by pouring a liquid into a mold and then allowing it to solidify. My goal with the pillow emboss was to make the text appear rounded, with soft shadows and soft highlights as though it were created from a mold. The round corners that were created in Illustrator bring a roundness to the edge of the letterforms that complements the interior roundness created by the pillow emboss.

FIGURE 30
Applying the Soft Light blending mode

FIGURE 31
Increasing saturation

4. Set the blending mode on the Gold layer to Soft Light, then compare your result to Figure 30.

5. Click the **Create new fill or adjustment layer button** ⬤ on the Layers palette, then click **Hue/Saturation**.

   TIP When you use this method to create an adjustment layer it is, by default, created as an overall adjustment and not one that is clipped into the previous layer.

6. Drag the **Saturation slider** to +50, click **OK**, then compare your result to Figure 31.

   The combination of the Soft Light blending mode and the increased saturation creates an effect that mimics the vibrant color and muted sheen of plastic. Note that the overall texture is smooth and round because the shadows are not too deep. Though the highlights are distinct, they are not harsh or glaring.

7. Save your work.

Apply the Plastic Wrap filter

1. Verify that the Hue/Saturation adjustment layer is targeted, select all, click **Edit** on the menu bar, then click **Copy Merged**.

2. Click **Edit** on the menu bar, click **Paste**, then name the new layer **Plastic Wrap**.

   TIP The Select All – Copy Merged – Paste sequence yields the same result as the Stamp Visible sequence.

3. Click the **Rectangular Marquee Tool** ⬚, then select the left side of the canvas as shown in Figure 32.

4. Hide the selection edges, click **Filter** on the menu bar, point to **Artistic**, then click **Plastic Wrap**.

5. Drag the **Highlight Strength slider** to 15, drag the **Detail slider** to 8, then drag the **Smoothness slider** to 9.

6. Click **OK**, then compare your result to Figure 33.

   The Plastic Wrap filter has different effects on different selections. For example, if we had selected the entire image, the filter would have yielded a different result. We selected only the first four letters because, after experimenting, this was my favorite result for the *P*, the *L*, and the *A*.

7. Click **Edit** on the menu bar, then click **Fade Plastic Wrap**.

(continued)

FIGURE 32
Selecting the first four letters

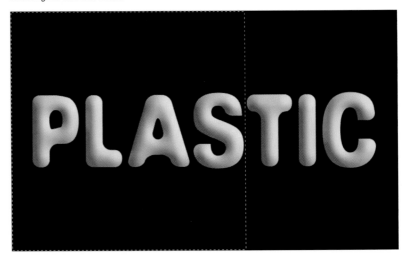

FIGURE 33
Applying the Plastic Wrap filter to the selection

FIGURE 34
Applying the Plastic Wrap filter to the remainder

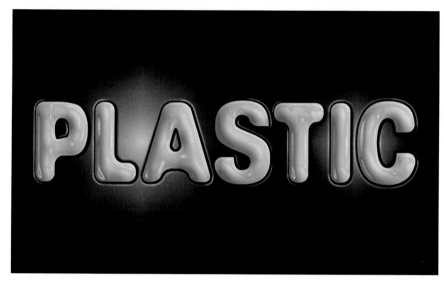

8. Verify that Preview is checked, drag the **Opacity slider** to 75%, click the Mode list arrow, click **Hard Light**, and keep the Fade dialog box open.

   The Fade dialog box is something of a secret when it comes to working with filters. It offers a onetime chance to apply an opacity setting and/or a blending mode to a filter. I think of it as a secret because who would think to check the Edit menu to modify a filter? We're not going to execute this Fade Plastic Wrap command. Because we are applying the filter to a merged layer, we can apply an opacity setting and/or a blending mode to the layer itself. What's better about that method is that, if we want to, we'll be able to modify the opacity and/or blending mode whenever we want to.

9. Click **Cancel**.

10. Click **Select** on the menu bar, then click **Inverse**.

11. Hide the selection, click **Filter** on the menu bar, click **Plastic Wrap** at the very top of the Filter menu, then compare your result to Figure 34.

   TIP The Filter menu lists the last filter used (with the settings last used) at the top of the menu.

12. Save your work.

Using blending modes to modify a filter effect

1. Verify that the Plastic Wrap layer is targeted, press and hold **[Ctrl]** (Win) or ⌘ (Mac), then click the **Layer thumbnail** on the hidden Shape 1 layer to load a selection of the shape.

2. Click **Select** on the menu bar, click **Inverse**, fill the selection with black, deselect, then compare your result to Figure 35.

   On its own, with no blending mode, this effect could be used for a number of real-world applications, especially for graphic projects like a comic book, a graphic novel, or as cover art for a video game. In terms of looking like plastic, however, without a blending mode, the result looks a bit more like wax than it does plastic.

3. Change the blending mode to Hard Light, then compare your result to Figure 36.

   The Hard Light blending mode saturates the yellow overall. It removes the midrange effects from the filter while maintaining the extreme highlights. The result is a very dramatic effect that does indeed look like plastic.

   (continued)

FIGURE 35
Plastic Wrap filter applied

FIGURE 36
Applying the Hard Light blending mode

FIGURE 37

Applying the Lighten blending mode

FIGURE 38

Applying the Luminosity blending mode

4. Change the blending mode to Lighten, then compare your result to Figure 37.

   With the Lighten blending mode, only the areas of the top layer that are lighter than those of the image below it remain visible. With this artwork, this means that the grayish, midrange "plastic" from the filter becomes invisible, because it is darker than the image below. Only the white highlights from the filter remain visible, because they are so much lighter than the image below.

5. Change the blending mode to Luminosity, then compare your result to Figure 38.

   Luminosity is just another word for brightness. The Luminosity blending mode applies the brightness information of the image on the targeted layer to the image below. It doesn't alter the hue or the saturation of the pixels below, only the brightness. For this artwork, I found Luminosity to be the most interesting choice. As with the Hard Light and Lighten blending modes, it maintains the highlights from the filter. Unlike the Hard Light and Lighten blending modes, Luminosity allows the midrange plastic wrap effects from the filter to show through.

6. Save your work, then close the Plastic document.

Lesson 2   Design Plastic Type

DESIGN RECESSED
Type

What You'll Do

Recessed type is one of those effects that always looks good. As a designer, I often find myself working to *build up*—to make my artwork three-dimensional, to make it jump off of the canvas. Let's just say that I use the Bevel and Emboss layer style quite often. This lesson is designed to remind you to look the other way and to remember that dimensionality can also be created by pushing things back, pushing them in, and pushing them away. This is a complex, in-depth exploration into one of my favorite techniques for creating dramatic recessed type effects. It's also a great example of a great challenge: how to make multiple layer styles work together to produce a single effect.

FIGURE 39

Inner Shadow dialog box

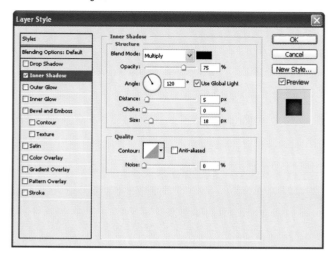

1. Open AP 7-4.psd, then save it as **Inner Shadow.psd**.

2. Target **Layer 1**, click the **Add a layer style button** 🟢. on the Layers palette, then click **Inner Shadow**.

3. Set the **Angle** to 120, then drag the **Size slider** to 18 so that your dialog box resembles Figure 39.

4. Click **OK**, then compare your artwork to Figure 40.

   This is the most basic effect from the Inner Shadow layer style.

5. Save your work, then close Inner Shadow.

FIGURE 40

Inner Shadow effect

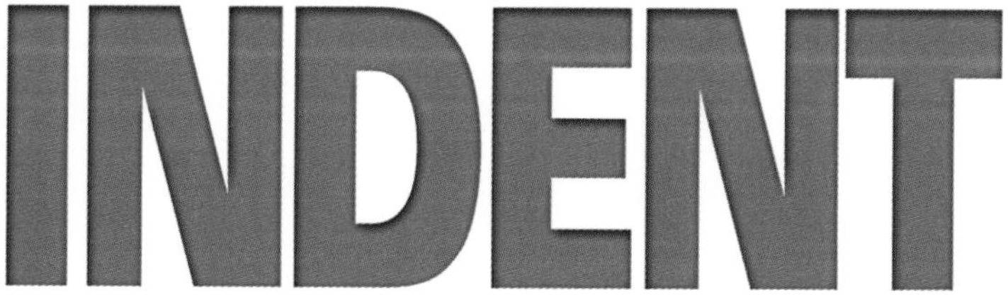

INDENT

Use the Inner Shadow layer style in conjunction with a drop shadow

1. Open AP 7-5.ai in Adobe Illustrator.

   In this Illustrator file, I used the Offset Path command to create the larger black type behind the red type.

2. Close AP 7-5.ai, switch to Photoshop, open AP 7-6.psd, then save it as **Indent**.

   I exported the Illustrator file with its layers as a .psd document, then added the hidden gradient layer when I opened it in Photoshop.

   TIP For an in-depth explanation of exporting layered artwork from Illustrator to Photoshop, see Chapter 1.

3. Target the **Background layer**, then fill it with black.

4. Target the **Offset layer**, fill the black type with white, then compare your result to Figure 41.

5. Click the **Add a layer style button** 🎨. on the Layers palette, then click **Inner Shadow**.

6. Set the **Angle** to 135, verify that the Use Global Light check box is checked, then set the **Opacity** to 85%.

7. Drag the **Distance slider** to 9, drag the **Size slider** to 8, click OK, then compare your artwork to Figure 42.

   The black area is now a foreground element, and it is casting a shadow on the white and red type, which are both on one plane behind the black area.

(continued)

FIGURE 41
Modifying the artwork

FIGURE 42
Applying the Inner Shadow to the white type

FIGURE 43
Applying a drop shadow to the red type

FIGURE 44

Sample letterforms with interesting negative spaces

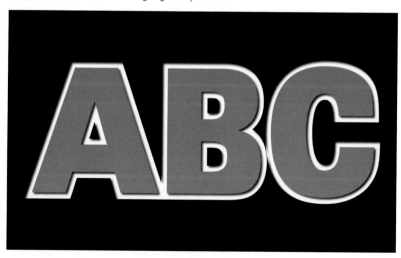

8. Target the **Red Type layer**, click ⓕ. on the Layers palette, then click **Drop Shadow**.

9. Verify that the Angle is set to 135 and that the Use Global Light check box is checked, then set the **Opacity** to 85%.

10. Drag the **Distance slider** to 9, then drag the **Size slider** to 8.

   Since we want the red text and the black areas to appear to be on the same plane, they must cast the same shadow. Therefore, we are inputting the same specifications for the drop shadow as we did for the inner shadow.

11. Click **OK**, then compare your artwork to Figure 43.

12. Note the black at the center of the letter *D* and between the lines of the *E*.

   When working with type, you're always at the mercy of the letters that make up the word. In this case, the word *INDENT* is a bit boring—all straight lines except for the letter *D*.

13. Compare your artwork to Figure 44.

   The letters in Figure 44 are a bit more interesting for this effect—the triangle in the letter *A*, the two half circles in the letter *B*, and the black negative space that defines the letter *C*. For these letters, the black negative spaces add an interesting component to the overall effect. For the word *INDENT*, the black negative spaces are awkward, especially in the letter *E*.

(continued)

14. Target the **Offset layer**, then unlock the transparent pixels.

15. Drag a **rectangular marquee** around the two black rectangles in the letter *E*, as shown in Figure 45.

16. Fill the selection with white, deselect, then compare your artwork to Figure 46.

17. Using the same method, remove the negative space from the center of the letter *D*, then deselect.

18. Target the **Red Type layer**, click **Filter** on the menu bar, point to **Noise**, then click **Add Noise**.

19. Type **15** in the Amount text box, verify that the Uniform option button is selected and that the Monochromatic check box is checked, then click **OK**.

20. Click **Edit** on the menu bar, click **Fade Add Noise**, set the blending mode to Multiply, click **OK**, then compare your results to Figure 47.

(continued)

FIGURE 45
Selecting negative spaces in the white text

FIGURE 46
Removing the black rectangles

FIGURE 47
Applying the Add Noise filter

Working with Type, Shape Layers, and Filters   Chapter 7

FIGURE 48
Multiplying the gradient layer

When working with type only, say for a logo or a headline, adding noise is a favorite technique of mine for adding texture to the type and making the artwork more interesting. However, many creative directors don't like to see noise—they love grain, but they tend to not like noise. I suspect that it's because Noise is one of the "obvious" filters. You see it in artwork, and you know immediately that the designer used the Add Noise filter. That doesn't bother me. For me, I think it adds richness to the text and the suggestion of sparkle. You'll have to decide for yourself.

21. Make the Gradient layer visible, set its blending mode to Multiply, then clip it into the Red Type layer.

22. Compare your artwork to Figure 48.

23. Save your work, then close the Indent document

Use the Inner Shadow layer style in conjunction with the Bevel and Emboss layer style

1. Open AP 7-7.psd, save it as **Jazz 2006**, then compare your screen to Figure 49.

   This is artwork that I created in Illustrator. The red type was the original artwork that I set in a Universe bold typeface. I used the Offset Path command to create the three offset outlines, then exported the artwork to Photoshop.

2. Change the foreground color to **128R/128G/128B**.

   | **TIP** From this point on this lesson, we'll refer to this color as "neutral gray."

3. Hide the Red and Orange layers.

4. Fill the Blue layer with neutral gray.

   | **TIP** The Lock transparent pixels option is activated on all four layers.

5. Click the **Add a layer style button** 🖉. on the Layers palette, then click **Bevel and Emboss**.

6. Verify that the Style is set to Inner Bevel, click the **Technique list arrow**, then click **Chisel Hard**.

7. Slowly drag the **Size slider** to 16, and watch the effect on the artwork as you drag.

   As shown in Figure 50, at a 16-pixel size the chiseled edge butts up against the edge of the green artwork.

   (continued)

FIGURE 49
Original artwork

FIGURE 50
Applying the Bevel and Emboss layer style

FIGURE 51
Bevel and Emboss dialog box

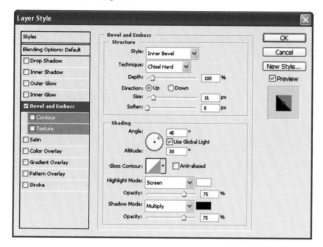

FIGURE 52
Applying the Inner Shadow layer style

8. In the Shading section, set the **Angle** to 45, then compare your dialog box to Figure 51.

 Your settings should match the figure.

9. Click **OK**, then fill the Green layer with neutral gray.

10. Click ⭕. on the Layers palette, then click **Inner Shadow**.

11. Verify that the Blend Mode is set to Multiply, the Opacity is set to 75%, the Angle is set to 45, and that the Use Global Light check box is checked.

12. Drag the **Distance slider** to 11, drag the **Choke slider** to 14, drag the **Size slider** to 16, then compare your artwork to Figure 52.

 The illustration at this point is composed of two pieces of artwork on two different layers. However, it's important that you note that the two layer styles are working in conjunction so that the artwork appears as one object. The bevel and emboss creates the outer edge of the "object." The inner shadow creates indentations to the interior of the "object." Take a moment to analyze the overall effect, because it's a fine example of an important concept. Many designers get caught up in trying to make one layer style carry the whole load, but more often than not, i *many* layer styles working together that create a *single* effect.

(continued)

13. Click the words **Pattern Overlay** on the left side of the dialog box.

    TIP If you clicked the Pattern Overlay check box instead of the words, the pattern overlay would be activated with the current texture. Because you clicked the words, the Pattern Overlay style is activated and its dialog box is visible.

14. Click the **Pattern list arrow**, then click the third pattern in the top row (Woven).

15. Click the **Blend Mode list arrow**, click **Soft Light**, click **OK**, then compare your artwork to Figure 53.

16. Make the Orange layer visible, then fill it with neutral gray.

17. Click the **Add a layer style button** 🔘, on the Layers palette, then click **Bevel and Emboss**.

18. Click the **Technique list arrow**, then click **Chisel Hard**.

19. Drag the **Size slider** to 9.

20. Click the **Gloss Contour list arrow**, then click **Ring**.

21. Click the **Anti-aliased check box**, then compare the settings in your dialog box to Figure 54.

(continued)

FIGURE 53
Applying the Pattern Overlay

FIGURE 54
Bevel and Emboss dialog box

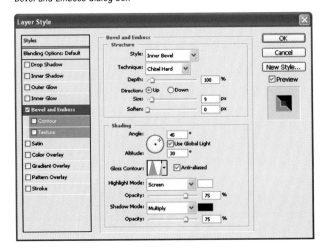

FIGURE 55
The second bevel and emboss effect

FIGURE 56
Inner Shadow dialog box

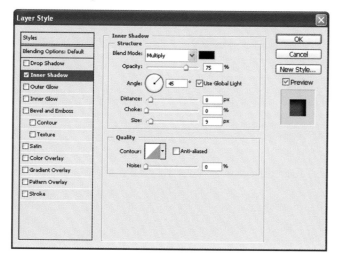

22. Click **OK**, then compare your artwork to Figure 55.
23. Make the Red layer visible, then fill it with neutral gray.
24. Click the 🅕 on the Layers palette, then click **Inner Shadow**.
25. Type the settings shown in Figure 56, then click **OK**.

(continued)

26. Compare your artwork to Figure 57.

27. Click the **Create new fill or adjustment layer button** 🖊. on the Layers palette, then click **Solid Color**.

28. Create a color that is **147R/55G/144B**, then click **OK**.

29. Clip the new fill layer into the Red layer, then compare your artwork to Figure 58.

Now that the text has been filled with purple, the pattern overlay looks too light; there's no contrast between it and the letters above it.

(continued)

FIGURE 57
The second inner shadow effect

FIGURE 58
Applying a fill layer to the artwork

30. Double-click the **Pattern Overlay effects layer** (in the Green layer), change the blending mode to Multiply, change the **Opacity** to 65%, click **OK**, then compare your artwork to Figure 59.

When designing this illustration, at this point, the effect was not working for me. My goal with this illustration was to create the effect of recessed type; I wanted the purple letters to be *indented* into the layer beneath it. I wasn't sure of what was wrong, but I knew the effect wasn't right.

The essential problem for me was that the most notable effect of the illustration was the embossing, which is exactly the opposite of the recessed effect that I was going for. Also, the Inner Shadow effect on the purple letters was not doing the trick.

If you look at the purple letters, you can see the Inner Shadow effect, and they appear to be recessed. But you can look at them another way in which the inner shadow looks like an emboss! This is especially noticeable in the two zeros in 2006. They look embossed, as though they were *above* the silver artwork behind them rather than indented.

Since the word *embossed* kept coming up as the problem for me, I decided that I would make the embossing less shiny and eye-catching, with the hopes that it would no longer dominate the inner shadow effect.

(continued)

FIGURE 59
Changing the blending mode on the Pattern Overlay

31. Double-click the **Bevel and Emboss effects layer** on the Orange layer.

We used the Bevel and Emboss layer style on two layers: the Blue layer and the Orange layer. However, only on the Orange layer did we apply a gloss contour.

32. Click the **Gloss Contour list arrow**, click **Linear**, click **OK**, then compare your result to Figure 60.

This one step solved the entire problem! If you undo and redo the last step, you'll see what a dramatic difference it made. With the gloss contour removed, the embossed artwork is no longer the dominant effect. Instead, the eye goes immediately to the purple letters.

The purple letters themselves are unmistakably recessed—they are inset into the embossed artwork. Even if you try, you can't make your eye see them as embossed, not even the two zeros. The only problem is that, without the gloss contour, the artwork is now a bit boring; it's gray overall and lacks contrast. The solution for that is very straightforward: if the art works, but it lacks contrast, don't change the art, just increase the contrast.

(continued)

FIGURE 60
Removing the gloss contour from the beveled edge

DESIGN*note*

Take a moment to think back to the original artwork. The purple text was taken from the original text that I set in Illustrator. Knowing what I was trying to achieve, I made some specific design decisions when setting the type. The first was the letter *J*. I made it extra large so that it would integrate the two lines of text into one piece of artwork: the *J* is the bridge, so to speak. But even more importantly, I used the hook of the big *J* to get that interesting shape on the left side of the artwork. I knew that it would show off the embossing and the inner shadow effects quite dramatically. I did the same thing with the number *6*. Note how the point at the top extends farther to the right than the *Z* above it. I knew that the *6*, with its point and its round base, would be very interesting once the layer styles were applied.

FIGURE 61
Final artwork with increased contrast

33. Target the **Color Fill 1 layer**, click on the Layers palette, then click **Curves**.

34. Add a point to the curve, then set its Input value to **80** and its Output value to **47**.

35. Add a second point to the curve, set its Input value to **155**, set its Output value to **185**, then click **OK**.

36. Compare your artwork to Figure 61.

Again, one step solved the entire problem. Note that although the increase in contrast is substantial, we did not go too far. The shadows on the embossed artwork are dark gray, not black. The highlights are light gray, not white.

There's an interesting design lesson to be learned here. My initial instinct was to use the gloss contour to add contrast and snap to the artwork. But the gloss contour ended up working against the effect. As it turns out, all I needed to do was add contrast to get contrast.

37. Save your work, then close Jazz 2006.

DESIGN ERODED
Type

What You'll Do

The need for type with rough edges comes up regularly, and the ability to create it is an essential skill every designer must have. It's ironic, really, when you consider that in the early days of desktop publishing the great goal and the great achievement was to produce smooth lines and curves, both for type and for line art. And yet, you will find that smooth lines and curves are exactly what you don't want for a number of types of artwork. The technique you'll use in this lesson is very versatile; it can be used to create many different rough, very rough, and not-so-rough edges that you can use for all kinds of type applications or for line art or even with clip images. Don't get so caught up in the details though that you miss the big picture. You're going to manipulate a layer mask to achieve the effect. That technique is essential, very powerful, and one that has applications far beyond just making rough edges.

FIGURE 62

Artwork on the shape layer

1. Open AP 7-8.psd, save it as **Eroded Text**, then compare your screen to Figure 62.

   The gray artwork was designed in Illustrator and then copied into Photoshop as a shape layer, as shown by the Vector mask thumbnail on the Original Paste layer.

   TIP By default, shape layers appear as gray in the Layers palette so that they are easy to distinguish from layer masks.

2. Press and hold **[Shift]**, then click the **Vector mask thumbnail** in the Original Paste layer to deactivate the shape layer.

   TIP [Shift]-clicking the Vector mask thumbnail in a shape layer toggles it between active and inactive.

(continued)

DESIGN*note*

The design concept for this lesson is a logo for Machine Iron Works, a new gym located near Muscle Beach in Los Angeles. They are all about body building; they have only free weights—a real "no pain, no gain" type of place. They want to build an identity that is tough and serious and targeted to attract the hardcore weight lifter.

---

3. Release **[Shift]**, click the **Vector Mask thumbnail** again to activate its path, then compare your screen to Figure 63.

The Original Paste layer is filled with the gray foreground color. It's important that you understand that the *entire* layer is filled with the gray foreground color. The shape layer uses paths—vector graphics, just like you would create with the Pen Tool—to define what is visible on the layer and what is not visible. With shape layers, anything within the path is visible; anything outside is not.

> **TIP** Single-clicking a Vector mask thumbnail toggles the path between visible and not visible.

4. [Shift]-click the **Layer mask thumbnail** to reactivate it.

5. Click the **Path Selection Tool** .

> **TIP** The Path Selection Tool is located above the Pen Tool.

6. Click the center of the letter *c*, then drag it to another location on the canvas.

Your screen should resemble Figure 64. The paths in a shape layer are all editable. They can be moved. The gray color is visible wherever the path is moved to.

7. Undo your last move, then click anywhere on the black iron background to deactivate the path on the letter *c*.

(continued)

FIGURE 63
Deactivating the shape layer

FIGURE 64
Moving a path with the Path Selection Tool

FIGURE 65
Transforming the path

FIGURE 66
Moving a single anchor point with the Direct Selection Tool

8. Click **Edit** on the menu bar, point to **Transform Path**, click **Rotate 180°**, then compare your artwork to Figure 65.

   Paths used in a shape layer can be transformed just like any other path or any other artwork in Photoshop.

9. Undo your last move.

10. Click the **Direct Selection Tool** ▶, which is located behind the Path Selection Tool.

11. Position your cursor at the edge of the letter *w* in works, then click the path.

   The anchor points on the path become visible. The anchor points all have a hollow center, which indicates that they can be selected individually. That is the difference between the Path Selection Tool and the Direct Selection Tool—with the Direct Selection Tool, you can select individual anchor points on a path.

12. Click and drag any anchor point on the letter *w* to a different location, then compare your result to Figure 66.

   The path is redrawn. More of the layer's gray fill is visible.

13. Delete the Original Paste layer.

   (continued)

14. Target the **M layer**, then make it visible.

    The first design move we are going to make is to add a Bevel and Emboss layer style to the artwork. However, because the letter *M* is so much bigger than the surrounding letters, we need different settings for the two components. Therefore, we will isolate the letter *M* on its own layer.

15. Duplicate the M layer, then name the new layer **Machine**.

16. Hide the M layer.

17. Click , then select and delete the letter *M* and the circle around it.

    Your screen should resemble Figure 67.

18. Hide the Machine layer, target the **M layer**, then show the M layer.

19. Delete the surrounding text and lines so that your artwork resembles Figure 68.

20. Save your work.

FIGURE 67
The Machine layer

FIGURE 68
The M layer

FIGURE 69
Clipping the Rust layer

FIGURE 70
Clipping the New Rust layer

1. Verify that the M layer is targeted and the Machine layer is hidden.

2. If the path on the M layer is showing, click the **Vector mask thumbnail** to hide the path.

3. Make the Rust layer visible, then drag it down so it is immediately above the M layer.

4. Clip the Rust layer into the M layer, then compare your artwork to Figure 69.

   The shape layer defines the perimeter for the clipped artwork.

   TIP The paths will be hidden in the remaining figures in this lesson unless there is a reason for them to be visible.

5. Click the **Move Tool** , then move the Rust image around in the layer mask to find interesting textures and colors.

   From a design perspective, this is an important step and one you should take some time to work on. The rust artwork contains some bright yellow areas that you can use as interesting highlights on the letter M.

6. Duplicate the Rust layer, then name the new layer **New Rust**.

7. Drag the **New Rust layer** above the Machine layer, show the Machine layer, then clip New Rust into the Machine layer.

   Your artwork should resemble Figure 70.

   (continued)

8. Hide the Black Iron layer.

   The Black Iron layer is so dark that it would be difficult to see the subtle changes we're about to make.

9. Target the **M layer**, click the **Add a layer style button** 🔘 on the Layers palette, then click **Bevel and Emboss**.

10. Using Figure 71 as a guide, apply the settings shown in the Structure section, apply the same settings for Angle and Altitude, and leave the Layer Style dialog box open when finished.

   The Chisel Hard edge is an important component to this effect. We want to "erode" the type along its edges, so the visual qualities of the edges play an important role in the final effect. The Chisel Hard style creates a clean, sharp edge that readily shows the pits and dents that create the erosion effect.

11. Click the **Set color for highlight box** (next to Highlight Mode), type **250R/250G/150B**, then click **OK**.

   The yellow highlight works better with the orange rust.

12. In the Styles section on the left, click the words **Drop Shadow**, then enter the settings shown in Figure 72.

(continued)

FIGURE 71
Bevel and Emboss dialog box

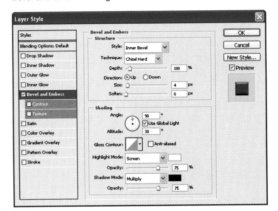

FIGURE 72
Drop Shadow dialog box

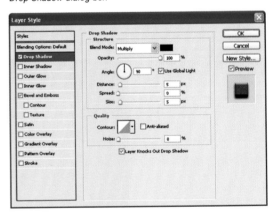

DESIGN*note*

Ultimately, this lesson is about creating eroded text, so take a moment at this stage of the work to look at the logo. It's a cool effect, but notice how the clean straight lines and smooth curves work against the concept of rusted iron. Smooth is the very last word you would think of when you think of rust.

FIGURE 73

Layer styles applied to the M layer

FIGURE 74

Layer styles applied to the Machine layer

13. Click **OK**, then compare your artwork to Figure 73.

14. Copy the layer styles from the M layer to the Machine layer.

15. Double-click the **Bevel and Emboss effect** on the Machine layer, change the Size setting to 3, then click **OK**.

16. Make the Black Iron layer visible, then compare your artwork to Figure 74.

    Ultimately, this lesson is about creating eroded text, so take a moment at this stage of the work to look at the logo. The shadow and the bevel and emboss contribute greatly to the illusion of this logo being raised from an iron background. It's a cool effect, but notice how the clean straight lines and smooth curves work against the concept of rusted iron. Smooth is the last word you would think of when you think of rust.

17. Save your work.

Use the Spatter filter

1. Hide the two rust layers so that you can better see the base artwork.

2. Hide the Machine layer, then target the **M layer**.

3. Press and hold **[Ctrl]** (Win) or ⌘ (Mac), then click the **Vector mask thumbnail** on the M layer to load it as a selection.

(continued)

4. Click the **Add layer mask button** 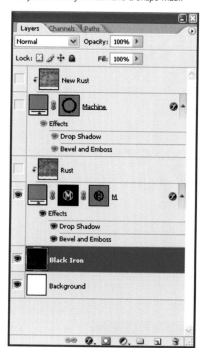 on the Layers palette, then compare your Layers palette to Figure 75.

   A layer mask is added to the layer. Don't be confused when a layer has both a layer mask and a shape layer, because all of the basic rules still apply. The layer mask works like a layer mask, and the shape layer works like a shape layer; nothing changes in terms of how they function.

5. Click the **Path Selection Tool** , select the path, then move the path straight up to the top of the canvas.

   As shown in Figure 76, the artwork is visible *only* where the path overlaps the white areas of the layer mask. The black areas of the layer mask continue to mask the art.

6. Undo your last move.

7. Press and hold **[Alt]** (Win) or **[option]** (Mac), then click the **Layer mask thumbnail** on the M layer.

   The canvas changes to show the contents of the layer mask.

8. Verify that the shape layer's path is not visible.

(continued)

FIGURE 75
A layer with a layer mask and a shape mask

FIGURE 76
Moving the path but not the mask

FIGURE 77
Spatter dialog box

FIGURE 78
Modified layer mask and the path

9. Click **Filter** on the menu bar, point to **Brush Strokes**, then click **Spatter**.

10. Drag the **Spray Radius slider** to 14, drag the **Smoothness slider** to 15, then compare your Spatter dialog box to Figure 77.

11. Click **OK**, click the **Vector mask thumbnail** to make the path visible, then compare your screen to Figure 78.

The path shows the outline of the original artwork. The Spatter filter modified the layer mask in such a way that some of the white areas now extend outside of the original outline, and some of the black areas now extend into the outline, thus creating the rough edge. However, this layer mask does not show the true result of how the filter will affect the artwork, because all of the white areas outside the path will *not* be transparent. The white areas of the layer mask only function as white where they overlap the path. In other words, when a layer has both a layer mask and a shape layer, white areas of the layer mask don't function and are not transparent if they are outside of the path.

(continued)

12. Press and hold [Alt] (Win) or [option] (Mac), click the **Layer thumbnail**, then compare your screen to Figure 79.

    No part of the layer is visible outside of the path, which is *perfect* for this illustration. Our goal is to create eroded type—in this case, rusted type. When metal rusts, its edges chip and fall away, leaving indentations *into* the edge. It doesn't corrode *outside* of its original shape; it doesn't get bigger when it corrodes. So the path masking out the white areas of the layer mask allows the spatter filter to only cut *into* the original artwork.

13. Hide the path, then compare your artwork to Figure 80.

14. Show the Machine layer, load the selection from the shape layer, then create a new layer mask.

    (continued)

FIGURE 79
Eroded edge with the path visible

FIGURE 80
Eroded artwork

Working with Type, Shape Layers, and Filters   Chapter 7

FIGURE 81
Eroded edge with clipped imagery

FIGURE 82
Final artwork

15. Press and hold **[Alt]** (Win) or **[option]** (Mac), click the **Layer mask thumbnail** to view it, click **Filter** on the menu bar, point to **Brush Strokes**, then click **Spatter**.

16. Drag the **Spray Radius slider** to 12, then click **OK**.

17. Press and hold **[Alt]** (Win) or **[option]** (Mac), click the **Layer thumbnail**, then compare your screen to Figure 81.

   | TIP Hide the path if necessary.

18. Show the two Rust layers, then compare your artwork to Figure 82.

19. Save your work, then close the Eroded Text document.

MASK IMAGES
with Type

What You'll Do

always use text as a mask as part of my demonstration, and it always gets a big reaction. In this lesson, you're going to create lots of different effects using type to mask images. The lesson is not designed to show you how to do it—it's designed more to show you how to *think* it: how to choose images that work well with a given style of typography, how to combine blending modes to create an effect, how to duplicate and invert layers to branch off into unexpected directions. When I created this lesson, I really had no final artwork in mind. Instead, I just wrote the steps as I went along. Now you get to take that trip with me. Where you end up is where I ended up. This lesson is designed to show you how I got there, and then you're free to keep going in any direction your imagination leads you.

Masking images with type is easy—you clip the image, or you use a layer mask. It's a technique that you can learn quickly, yet the applications are endless.

There is some sort of fascination that comes with images masked by type, and not just for the designer. Whenever I demonstrate Photoshop to an audience, I

FIGURE 83
Clipping the Wave image

FIGURE 84
Inverting the Wave image

Use chiseled type to mask images

1. Open AP 7-9.psd, then save it as **Chisel Type Images**.
2. Hide the Orange layer, then show and target the **Wave layer**.
3. Clip the Wave layer into the Text layer, then compare your artwork to Figure 83.

   Earlier in this chapter, when we were first designing the chiseled text, we discussed the goal of using layer styles as base art then finding ways to make the artwork unique. With this simple move, clipping the image into the text, we achieved that goal. The image adds an interesting color dynamic that works very well with the silvery layer style and texture overlay.
4. Invert the Wave layer, then compare your artwork to Figure 84.

   Another simple move that yields a dramatic effect. Inverted, the whites of the Wave image overlaying the chiseled text creates a sheen that fades into steel blues—perfect for this illustration.

   (continued)

5. Change the blending mode to Color Burn, then compare your result to Figure 85.

6. Hide the Wave layer, show and target the **Wood layer**, click the **Blending mode list arrow**, click **Overlay**, then compare your artwork to Figure 86.

Though the effect is visually interesting, the shine on the text has too much sheen and is too shiny to appear realistically as a wooden texture. Also, the overlayed texture looks too much like brushed steel to work with the wood artwork.

7. Hide the Texture layer.

(continued)

FIGURE 85
Color Burn mode

FIGURE 86
Wood image overlayed

DESIGNnote

What's great about working with text is that it gives you the freedom to use the blending modes you seldom use with straight images. Color Burn is one of the blending modes that yields dramatic color shifts. With images, generally it is used only when creating special effects. With type illustrations, it can be integrated into the artwork in a way that is still dramatic but also realistic.

FIGURE 87
Wood image overlayed without the gloss contour

FIGURE 88
Duplicating the Wood layer to achieve a richer image

FIGURE 89
Inverting and multiplying the Wood layer

8. Double-click the **Bevel and Emboss** layer style, change the Gloss Contour to **Linear**, click **OK**, then compare your result to Figure 87.

9. Duplicate the Wood layer, then compare your artwork to Figure 88.

10. Invert the Wood Copy layer, change the blending mode to Multiply, then compare your artwork to Figure 89.

(continued)

Lesson 5   Mask Images with Type

11. Change the blending mode to Color, change the Gloss Contour on the **Bevel and Emboss** layer style back to Cone-Inverted, then compare your artwork to Figure 90.

12. Hide the two wood layers, show and target the Granite layer, change its blending mode to Overlay, then compare your artwork to Figure 91.

Unlike the Wood image, the Granite image can overlay the shiny gloss contour and maintain a realistic appearance.

(continued)

FIGURE 90
Color mode

FIGURE 91
Granite image overlayed

FIGURE 92

Granite image multiplied

FIGURE 93

Final artwork

13. Change the blending mode to Multiply, then compare your artwork to Figure 92.

14. Duplicate the Granite layer, then change the blending mode on the copy to Overlay.

15. Make the Wood copy layer visible, then compare your artwork to Figure 93.

   We now have two images and three different blending modes working together to create the final effect.

16. Save your work, then close the file.

Use plastic type to mask images

1. Open AP 7-10.psd, then save it as **Plastic Type Images**.

2. Show and target the **Abstract blue layer**, change its blending mode to Overlay, then compare your artwork to Figure 94.

3. Hide the Abstract blue layer, show and target the **Mountains layer**, change its blending mode to Overlay, then compare your artwork to Figure 95.

(continued)

FIGURE 94
Abstract blue artwork overlayed

FIGURE 95
Mountains artwork overlayed

Working with Type, Shape Layers, and Filters   *Chapter 7*

FIGURE 96
Geometry artwork overlayed

FIGURE 97
Flowers artwork overlayed

4. Hide the Mountains layer, show and target the **Geometry layer**, change its blending mode to Overlay, then compare your artwork to Figure 96.

5. Hide the Geometry layer, show and target the **Flowers layer**, change its blending mode to Overlay, then compare your artwork to Figure 97.

6. Save your work, then close the file.

Use inset type to mask images

1. Open AP 7-11.psd, then save it as **Inset Type Images**.

2. Open AP 7-12.psd, select all, copy, then close the file.

3. Hide the Red, Orange, and Green layers, then target the **Blue layer**.

(continued)

4. Paste, clip the image into the Blue layer, then compare your artwork to Figure 98.

5. Show and target the **Green layer**, paste, then clip the image into the Green layer.

6. Compare your artwork to Figure 99.

7. Show and target the **Orange layer**, paste, then clip the image into the Orange layer.

(continued)

FIGURE 98
Clipping the image into the Blue layer

FIGURE 99
Clipping the image into the Green layer

FIGURE 100
Multiplying the image

FIGURE 101
Final artwork

8. Change the blending mode on the image to Multiply, then compare your result to Figure 100.

9. Show and target the **Red layer**, paste, then clip the image into the Red layer.

10. Compare your artwork to Figure 101.

11. Save your work, then close the file.

Lesson 5   Mask Images with Type

1. Open AP 7-13.psd, then save it as **Carved Wood**.
2. Target the Logo layer, add an Inner Shadow layer style using the settings shown in Figure 102, then keep the Layer Style dialog box open.
3. In the Styles column on the left, click the words Inner Glow.
4. Click Center as the source, then enter the settings shown in Figure 103.
5. Click OK, then set the Logo layer to Multiply.
6. Duplicate the Outer layer, then name the new layer **Inner**.
7. Drag the Inner layer below the Outer layer.
8. Load the selection of the Logo layer.
9. Target the Outer layer, then click the Add layer mask button on the Layers palette.
10. Invert the layer mask.
11. Add a Bevel and Emboss layer style to the Outer layer, input the settings shown in Figure 104, then keep the Layer Style dialog box open.
12. Change the color on both the Highlight and Shadow modes to 250R/250G/140B.
13. Set the Opacity on the Highlight mode to 100%.
14. Change the blending mode on the shadow mode to Screen, change its Opacity setting to 45%, then click OK.
15. Target the Inner layer, then move it 3 pixels to the left.
16. Target the Outer layer, then lock the transparent pixels.
17. Click Edit on the menu bar, then click Fill.
18. Fill the layer with 15% White, click OK, then compare your result to Figure 105.
19. Save your work, then close Carved Wood.

FIGURE 102

Applying the Inner Shadow

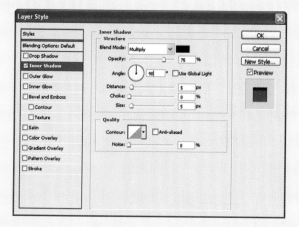

FIGURE 103

Applying the Inner Glow

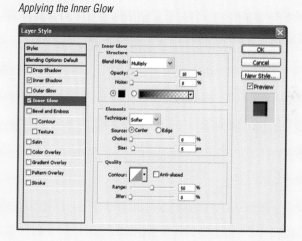

PROJECT BUILDER 1

FIGURE 104
Applying the Bevel and Emboss

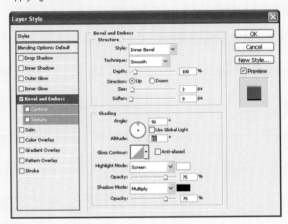

FIGURE 105
Completed Project Builder 1

1. Open AP 7-14.psd, then save it as **White Mischief**. (*Hint*: This is a well-known effect, created with a Drop Shadow layer style. There's a neat variation to this that is less common.)
2. Change the foreground color to **235R/235G/235B**.
3. Fill the Background layer with the new foreground color, then fill the text.
4. Double-click the Drop Shadow effect, then change its size to 6 pixels.
5. Click Bevel and Emboss, then drag the Depth slider all the way to the right.
6. Set the Opacity slider on the Highlight mode to 100%.
7. Drag the Opacity slider on the Shadow mode to 0, then click OK.
8. Compare your artwork to Figure 106. (*Hint*: The effect is similar, but improved by the subtle and elegant white highlight at the top right of the letterforms. You can manipulate the size and distance settings on both the Drop Shadow and Bevel and Emboss layer styles to create many effective variations.)
9. Save your work, then close White Mischief.

FIGURE 106
Completed Project Builder 2

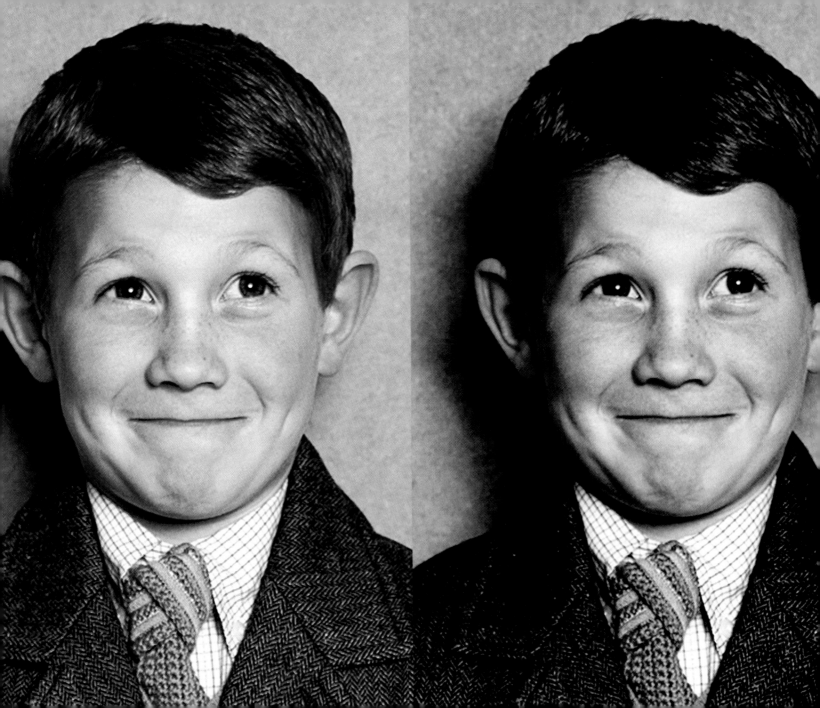

chapter

8

INVESTIGATING PRODUCTION
Tricks and Techniques

1. Verify duplicate images.
2. Use the Lab Color mode to create a grayscale image.
3. Use the Unsharp Mask filter to sharpen edges.
4. Use the High Pass filter to sharpen an image.
5. Apply grain effects.
6. Create monotones and duotones.
7. Automate workflow.

VERIFY DUPLICATE
Images

What You'll Do

In a real-world project, it often happens that files get mixed up. Even with job numbers, version numbers, and round numbers—which all help to keep a project organized and on track—you may find yourself with two seemingly identical images and not know which one you're supposed to use. In this lesson, you'll learn a technique that designers and production artists use to check whether or not two images are truly identical. You can use this technique to check if the color has shifted from one image to another. You can also use this technique if you are trying to align duplicate images, such as when you are replacing a low-resolution piece of art with a high-resolution piece of art.

FIGURE 1

Layers palette

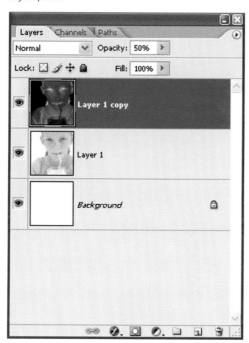

1. Open AP 8-1.psd, then save it as **Verify Duplicates**.

2. Duplicate Layer 1 keeping the default name for the duplicated layer.

3. Click **Image** on the menu bar, point to **Adjustments**, then click **Invert**.

4. Set the opacity on the new layer to 50% so that your Layers palette resembles Figure 1.

   Your canvas should be entirely gray. When a duplicate image is inverted and layered over its duplicate at 50%, the resulting image must be an entirely gray canvas. If you run the numbers it makes sense. If an original pixel has the number 100, that same pixel will have the number 155 when the image is inverted (255 − 100 = 155). When the inverted layer's opacity is set to 50%, the equation becomes [(100 + 155)(.5)], which is 255 × .5, which equals 127.5. In this layered relationship, all the overlayed pixels must add up to 255. At 50%, their result must be 127.5.

(continued)

5. Display the Info palette, then sample the image.

   Every pixel value is almost always 127. If it's not 127, it's 128. You won't find a pixel with another number. Most of the pixels are 127 because Photoshop does not round up the 127.5 average. The reason some pixels will have a 128 value is because they had a 128 value originally. In this layered relationship, 128 does not change $[(128 + 128) (.5)] = 128$.

6. Delete the new layer.

7. Open AP 8-2.psd, select all, copy, then close the file.

8. Paste the copy, invert it, then set the opacity to 50%.

   If you look closely, you will see a ghost of the image, because these two images were not duplicates. Figure 2 shows an exaggerated example of what you should see on your screen. A result like this—in which a ghost of the image appears—signifies that the color of one or both of the images has been modified.

   (continued)

FIGURE 2
Exaggerated example of canvas

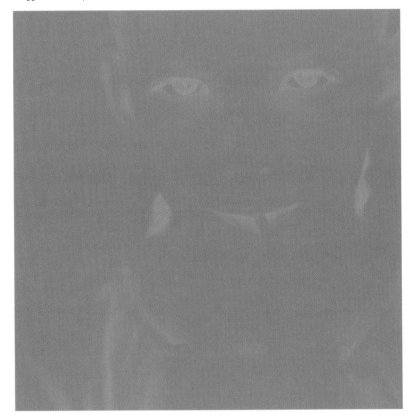

FIGURE 3

Exaggerated example of canvas

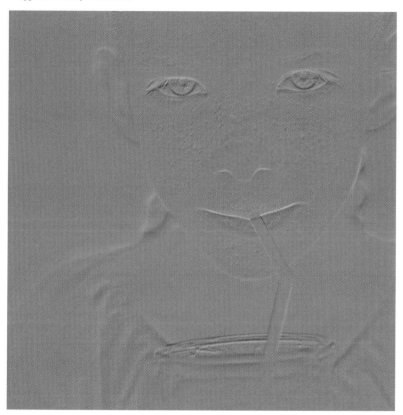

9. Delete Layer 2 then open AP 8-3.psd.

10. Select all, copy, then close the file.

11. Paste the copy, invert it, then set the opacity to 50%.

Your canvas will look as though the image has been embossed slightly. Figure 3 shows an exaggerated example. This result indicates that the images are not aligned pixel for pixel—at least one of the images has been offset.

10. Save and then close the file.

USE THE LAB COLOR MODE
to Create a Grayscale Image

What You'll Do

It's always smart to question single-method solutions. Take creating a black-and-white image, for example. If you have a color image that you want to use as a black-and-white image, the most basic solution is to convert it to Grayscale mode. Photoshop discards the color information, and you are left with a single-channel, black-and-white image.

It's a solution. That's true. To some, it's the only solution. That's false. Photoshop offers many alternative methods for creating a black-and-white version of a color image; you aren't stuck with only the image in Grayscale mode.

In this lesson, you'll use the Lab Color mode to create a variety of grayscale images. The techniques you learn here will provide you with alternative methods for creating grayscale images and, perhaps more importantly, prompt you to experiment with different methods until you find the best grayscale effect for a given image.

FIGURE 4

Result of converting to Grayscale mode

FIGURE 5

Image from the Blue channel

1. Open AP 8-4.psd, then save it as **Simple Grayscale**.

2. Click **Image** on the menu bar, point to **Mode**, click **Grayscale**, then click **Don't Flatten** in the dialog box that follows.

3. Compare your canvas to Figure 4.

4. Open AP 8-5.psd, then save it as **LAB Grayscale**.

5. Display the Channels palette, click the **Channel thumbnail** on the Blue channel, then compare your canvas to Figure 5.

   TIP If your channel is in blue as opposedto gray as shown in the figure, you need to change your preferences. Go to the Display & Cursors Preferences dialog box, then verify that the Color Channels in Color check box is not checked.

(continued)

The Channel thumbnails in the Channels palette often provide interesting versions of grayscale images. In this case, the image on the Blue channel is darker and very interesting. If you were designing for an unconventional look, this image would probably be a better choice. Remember too that you can always modify the image. Figure 6 shows the image from the Blue channel with a simple levels correction, and the result is a stunning black and white.

> **TIP** If you want to use an image in a channel as a file, click the Channel thumbnail, select all and copy, click File on the menu bar, click New to create a new document, then paste the copied channel.

6. Click the **RGB Channel thumbnail** in the Channels palette.

7. Click **Image** on the menu bar, point to **Mode**, then click **Lab Color**.

8. Note the channels in the Channels palette, as shown in Figure 7.

   In Lab Color mode, the image is created by three channels: Lightness, a, and b.

(continued)

FIGURE 6
Image from the Blue channel after Levels correction

FIGURE 7
Channels palette in Lab Color mode

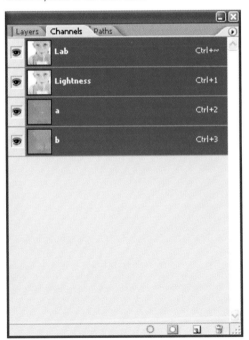

FIGURE 8

Image from Lightness channel

9. Click the **Channel thumbnail** on the Lightness channel, then compare your canvas to Figure 8.

    To paraphrase a well-known saying, Lab Color is like a box of chocolates—you never know what you're gonna get. The Lightness channel is always a black-and-white image, and sometimes it produces an interesting alternative. In the case of this file, the image from the Lightness channel is quite beautiful in the smoothness of its light gray tones. If you were going for a light, wispy effect, this image would make for an interesting choice, one that other designers might not come up with. What this image lacks, however, is detail and definition in the eyes. As you know, there are a number of methods to correct this. When working in Lab Color mode, don't forget that the a and b channels are also there for your use.

10. Duplicate the Lightness channel, select all, copy, then click the **Channel thumbnail** on the Lab channel.

11. Return to the Layers palette, then paste the copy as a new layer.

12. Name the new layer **Lightness Art**, then hide the Lightness Art layer.

13. Duplicate the b channel in the Channels palette, select all, copy, then click the **Channel thumbnail** on the Lab channel.

(continued)

Lesson 2   Use the Lab Color Mode to Create a Grayscale Image

14. Return to the Layers palette, then paste the copy as a new layer so that your canvas resembles Figure 9.

    TIP It was critical that you hid the Lightness Art layer in Step 12. Remember, art in the Channels palette is dynamic; whatever is visible on the canvas is represented in the channels. Had you kept the Lightness Art layer visible, the a and b channels would have been totally gray with no art.

15. Name the new layer **b Art**, then show the Lightness Art layer.

    From this point, there are a number of directions you can experiment with. However, whenever you have a predominantly gray image on a layer, the first move you should try is the Overlay mode, because—as you know from Chapter 6—gray becomes invisible in Overlay mode.

16. Set the blending mode on the b Art layer to Overlay, then compare your canvas to Figure 10.

    TIP Hide and show the b Art layer to see the change.

    The result is not very satisfactory; the eyes are still too light, and the image as a whole is too light. This is an important hint of what to try next. The image as a whole was lightened in Overlay mode—the opposite of what we wanted. This tells us that the image on the b Art layer is too light; we want its opposite.

(continued)

FIGURE 9
Image from b channel pasted as the top layer

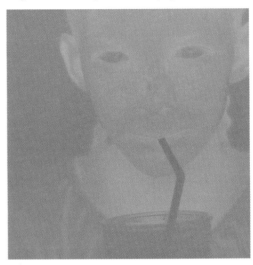

FIGURE 10
Image from b channel in Overlay mode

FIGURE 11

Inverted b channel image in Overlay mode

FIGURE 12

Multiplying the b channel image

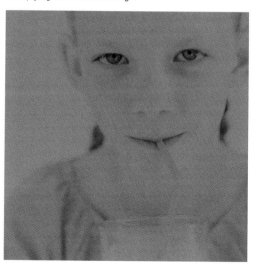

17. Invert the b Art layer, then compare your canvas to Figure 11.

    Now we're moving in the right direction. Inverted, the Channel thumbnail on the b channel is darker in the areas of detail, like the eyes, eyebrows, lips, and so on. The detail has definitely improved, but the image has darkened over all. This means that we've lost those airy, light gray flesh tones from the Lightness channel. We could, of course, use a layer mask and allow only the eyes, lips, and so on from the b Art layer to show, but we're going to go with another method.

18. Undo your last step.

    The image on the b Art layer is no longer inverted.

19. Change the blending mode of the b Art layer to Multiply, then compare your artwork to Figure 12.

    The darkest areas of the b channel art were in the eyes. It follows logically that, if multiplied, the b channel artwork must darken the eyes.

20. Select all, click **Edit** on the menu bar, then click **Copy Merged**.

21. Paste a new layer, name it **Merged**, then hide the b Art layer.

    (continued)

Lesson 2   Use the Lab Color Mode to Create a Grayscale Image

22. Change the blending mode on the merged layer to Overlay, then compare your canvas to Figure 13.

The result is stunning. Overlayed, the merged art has dramatically darker eyes. However, because the other areas of the merged art are close to a neutral gray, they have very little impact when the Overlay mode is applied.

(continued)

FIGURE 13
Overlaying the merged art

Compare this black-and-white image to the black-and-white image in the Simple Grayscale file.

As shown in Figure 14, the two images are dramatically different. The important point to remember is that there is no standard color correction—e.g., curves, levels, and so on—that you could apply to the simple grayscale black and white that would mimic the nuance and depth of the Lab Color black and white.

24. Close the LAB Grayscale and Simple Grayscale documents, saving your work in both of them.

FIGURE 14

Comparing the simple grayscale to the LAB grayscale

USE THE UNSHARP MASK FILTER
to Sharpen Edges

What You'll Do

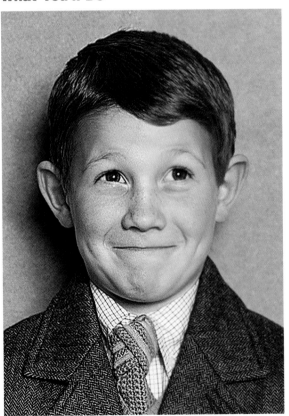

When you scan an image, the resulting scan is, by definition, of lesser quality than the original. That's because it's a second-generation reproduction, and a reproduction is always inferior to an original. When you scale an image—especially when you enlarge an image—you will suffer a loss of quality as well. In both of these examples, the loss of quality will be a blurring of the image—a loss of fine detail.

Unsharp Mask is an important filter that addresses this issue. It's a sophisticated algorithm that creates the effect of sharpening an image. It's only an effect, of course. The filter works by shifting color to create contrast, which the eye perceives as sharpness—an increase in focus and detail.

Because Unsharp Mask is so useful, it's a smart idea for you to take some time to investigate it, to understand its settings, and to get a sense of how it does what it does.

Your ability to apply unsharp masking in a way that is best for a given image can really make the difference in attaining excellent results.

FIGURE 15
Image Size dialog box

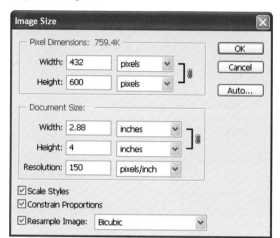

1. Open AP 8-6.psd, then save it as **Unsharp Mask**.

2. Assess the image for contrast.

   The Unsharp Mask filter creates the illusion of sharpness by increasing the contrast at the image's "edges." In Photoshop, *edges* refer to areas of an image where pixels differ noticeably from surrounding pixels. It would be a mistake to use the Unsharp Mask filter to improve contrast overall. That's why it's always a good idea to, when you are about to use the Unsharp Mask filter, first verify that the image's contrast is where you want it to be.

3. Make the Contrast layer visible.

   With the Contrast layer visible, it is clear that the image needs a bit of a contrast bump. Curves are designed to do just that, not the Unsharp Mask filter.

4. Target the **Background layer**, click **Image** on the menu bar, then click **Image Size**.

   As shown in Figure 15, the image is 4" tall at 150 pixels per inch. In other words, if you were to count one column of pixels from bottom to top, you would count a total of 600 pixels, which is what is shown in the top section of the dialog box.

   (continued)

5. Type **7** in the Height text box in the Document Size section so that your Image Size dialog box matches Figure 16.

   By making this move, you are saying you want this image to be resized to the height of 7 inches. Note that the Resample Image check box is checked. This means that at 7 inches tall you still want 150 pixels per inch. From top to bottom, that's a total of 1050 pixels per column. Where will you get 450 extra pixels per column?

6. Click **OK**, then compare your image to Figure 17.

   When enlarging an image, Photoshop creates the additional pixel data based on the existing data, a process referred to as interpolation. This means that the resulting image is composed of data that is not original—data that was neither photographed nor scanned. This process always results in a loss of image quality, and that loss is usually most visible as a blurring of the image and a loss of fine detail.

7. Click the **Rectangular Marquee Tool**, select the left half of the image, then hide the selection marquee.

8. Zoom in so that you are viewing the boy's face at 100%, if necessary.

   (continued)

FIGURE 16
Image Size dialog box

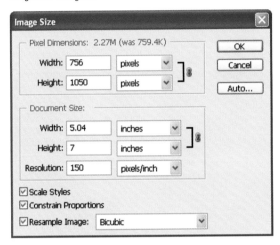

FIGURE 17
Image enlarged with interpolated pixel data

FIGURE 18
Filter applied with a high Amount value

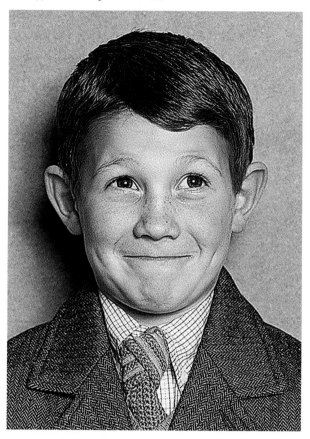

DESIGN*note*

Though the Unsharp Mask dialog box has a preview window, you are much better off moving the box to the side and viewing the effect on the image at 100%. The result of the Unsharp Mask filter is much more noticeable on screen than when printed because of the many factors in play during the offset printing process that blend and blur fine detail.

9. Click **Filter** on the menu bar, point to **Sharpen**, then click **Unsharp Mask**.

The Unsharp Mask filter works by identifying the edges of the image. Remember that edges refer to areas of an image where pixels differ noticeably from surrounding pixels. For example, in this image, the line where the boy's white shirt collar meets the coat's brown collar would be an edge, as would the point where his dark hairline meets his pale forehead. The Unsharp Mask filter increases the contrast in these areas—it makes the light edges lighter and the darker edges darker—to create the effect of focus and sharpness.

10. Type **150** in the Amount text box.

For high-resolution images—images that are 300 pixels per inch or more—an amount of 150–200% is typically recommended. Though this image is not high resolution, we have entered a high Amount value so that the effect will be dramatic and noticeable. The higher the Amount value, the more pronounced the effect. For example, Figure 18 shows the image sharpened drastically with a high Amount value. Note the sharpness especially in the hair and the tweed coat. The effect is most visible in these areas because they include so many dark pixels that abut light pixels.

(continued)

11. Drag the **Radius slider** to 2.0 pixels.

The Radius value determines the number of pixels surrounding the edge pixels that are included in the calculation that produces the sharpening. That's not a calculation that you need to keep in your head. Instead, remember that the higher the Radius value, the wider and more visible the sharpened edges will be. For high-resolution images, set the Radius value to 1 or 2. Figure 19 shows an example of the Radius value set at 24.

12. Set the Threshold value to 0, if necessary.

The Threshold value offers significant control of how this filter is applied—it determines what Photoshop defines as an edge. For example, if the Threshold were set to 10 pixels, that would mean that pixels surrounding a given pixel would need to be at least 10 grayscale values higher or lower than that given pixel to be considered an edge and therefore sharpened. When the Threshold value is higher, fewer areas of the image are sharpened. Zero is the default Threshold value meaning that, by default, all areas of the image will be sharpened to some degree.

(continued)

FIGURE 19
Filter applied with a high Radius value

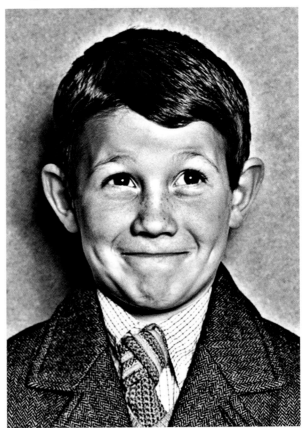

FIGURE 20

Image with left side sharpened

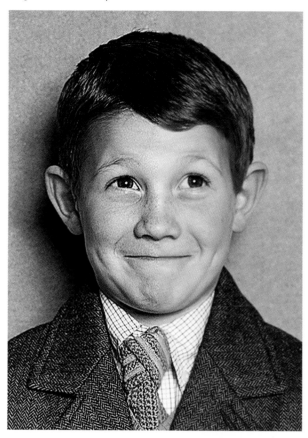

13. Click **OK**, then compare your result to Figure 20.

    On screen especially, the effect is substantial. If you undo and redo your last step, you'll see that it is most noticeable in the hair, the tie, and the tweed coat. If you zoom in on the tweed coat, then undo and redo again, you'll get a vivid example of how the filter lightens the lights and darkens the darks. Viewed at 100%, note the more subtle sharpening in the areas with less contrast, such as on the boy's cheeks and even in the texture on the wall behind him.

14. Save and then close the file.

DESIGNnote

The Unsharp Mask filter doesn't necessarily need to be used for practical, realistic image improvement. When applied at high values, it also produces an interesting special effect, one that can be used especially when you want to exaggerate the lines within an image, such as for cartooning purposes.

USE THE HIGH PASS FILTER
to Sharpen an Image

What You'll Do

Earlier in the chapter, we discussed that one should not be satisfied with single solutions; that you should at least try to find alternate ways to achieve a similar result. In doing so, you learn more about the application, and you provide yourself with alternate methods that can make dramatic or subtle differences. In the previous lesson, you worked with the Unsharp Mask filter. Though there are other Sharpen filters, Unsharp Mask has been, up to this version of Photoshop, the only sharpening filter that provided controls to emphasize sharpening in specific areas of an image. With CS2, Adobe has added the Smart Unsharp Mask filter. You should check it out; it's pretty cool. But it's really the Unsharp Mask filter on steroids, offering additional controls that let you get really specific about how you want to sharpen, where you want to sharpen, and how much you want to sharpen. For an alternate solution, in this lesson you'll use the High Pass filter in conjunction with the Overlay blending mode to learn a really neat way to sharpen an image. This is one of those super-secret techniques that those "in the know" seldom share.

Investigating Production Tricks and Techniques   Chapter 8

FIGURE 21
High Pass dialog box

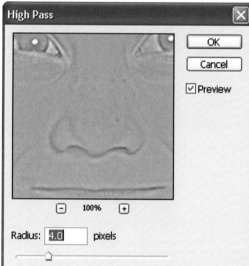

1. Open AP 8-7.psd, then save it as **High Pass**.

2. Duplicate the Background layer, then name the new layer **High Pass**.

3. Click **Filter** on the menu bar, point to **Other**, then click **High Pass**.

4. Drag the **Radius slider** all the way left to 0.1.

   At a zero radius, the High Pass filter makes the image entirely neutral gray.

5. Drag the **Radius slider** to 4.0 pixels, compare your High Pass dialog box to Figure 21, then keep the dialog box open.

   (continued)

6. Compare your canvas to Figure 22.

   The High Pass filter, like the Unsharp Mask filter, finds edges in an image. With a zero Radius value, the filter makes the image totally gray. As you increase the Radius value, the filter allows the pixel data of edge areas to become visible through the gray.

7. Click **OK**.

(continued)

FIGURE 22
High Pass filter result

FIGURE 23

Image sharpened with High Pass filter

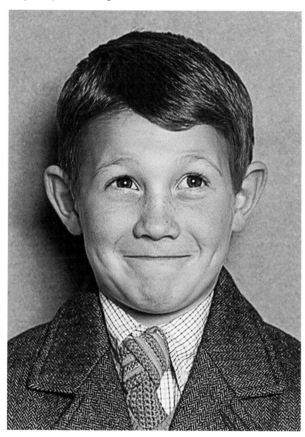

8. Change the blending mode on the High Pass layer to Overlay, then compare your canvas to Figure 23.

   If you hide and show the High Pass layer, you will see that it has sharpened the image. This makes sense, given the rules of Overlay mode. With the High Pass filter, much of the image is grayed out, but edge areas and detail are allowed to show through the gray. In Overlay mode, the gray areas disappear. Only the visible edge detail affects the image on the layer beneath. When an image is overlayed over itself, the light areas get lighter and the dark areas get darker. In this case, that is happening only in the edge areas, thus creating a sharpening effect overall.

9. Duplicate the High Pass layer, and accept the default name.

   The sharpening effect is increased.

10. Save your work, then close High Pass.

   If you compare using the High Pass filter with the Unsharp Mask filter forsharpening an image you'll find what's neat about the High Pass method isthat it gives you a visual representation of what areas of the image are beingsharpened. Duplicating the filtered layer and using layer masks and layer opacityoffer you the ability to choose which parts of the image you want sharpened andwhich you want less sharpened, or not sharpened at all.

APPLY GRAIN
Effects

What You'll Do

Adding grain to an image is a very popular design technique, one that most designers use very often. Grain adds texture and nuance to an image. Applying grain across multiple images from different sources is useful for making them all appear to be more consistent in tone and texture. Photoshop offers a number of options for creating and simulating grain. The techniques you'll learn in this lesson offer the ability to apply grain and the flexibility to determine where and how the grain affects the image.

FIGURE 24
Grain dialog box

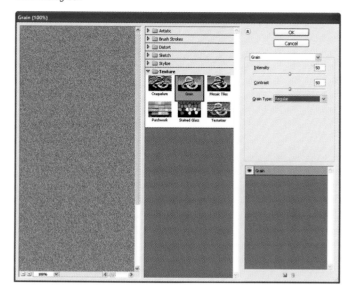

FIGURE 25
Multicolored grain

Apply a basic grain effect

1. Open AP 8-8.psd, then save it as **Grain**.

2. Zoom in so that you are viewing the image at 100%, then center the girl's face in the window.

    TIP   When working with fine detail such as grain, you must view the image at 100% to get a realistic representation of the effect.

3. Create a new layer, name it **Regular Grain**, then fill it with 128R/128G/128B.

4. Click **Filter** on the menu bar, point to **Texture**, then click **Grain**.

    The Grain dialog box opens.

5. Click the **Grain Type list arrow**, view the list of grain types, then click **Regular**.

6. Set the Intensity and Contrast values to 50 so that your Grain dialog box resembles Figure 24, then click **OK**.

7. Change the blending mode on the Regular Grain layer to Overlay, then compare your artwork to Figure 25.

(continued)

8. Use the Hue/Saturation dialog box to completely desaturate the Regular Grain layer, then compare your results to Figure 26.

   Undo and redo your last step to see the change between the colored grain effect and the desaturated grain.

9. Duplicate the Regular Grain layer, name the new layer **Black Grain**, then compare your artwork to Figure 27.

10. Save your work.

FIGURE 26
Desaturated grain

FIGURE 27
Grain effect doubled

FIGURE 28

Image with black grain effect

FIGURE 29

Overlaying the Black Grain layer

Apply black grain and white grain

1. Hide the Regular Grain layer.

2. Set the blending mode of the Black Grain layer to Normal, then fill it with white.

3. Click **Filter** on the menu bar, point to **Noise**, then click **Add Noise**.

4. Type **30** in the Amount text box, click the **Gaussian option button**, then click the **Monochromatic check box** to select it.

5. Click **OK**.

6. Set the layer's blending mode to Multiply, then compare your artwork to Figure 28.

   | **TIP**   When multiplied, white pixels become transparent.

7. Change the blending mode to Overlay, set the opacity to 50%, then compare your screen to Figure 29.

   This effect is a nice alternate to a basic grain overlay. It's not for every image, and not for every type of project, but as an effect, it's an interesting and rather unusual method for adding grain.

(continued)

8. Hide the Black Grain layer, create a new layer named **White Grain**, then fill it with black.

9. Click **Filter** on the menu bar, point to **Noise**, then click **Add Noise**.

10. Set the Amount value to 40%, then click **OK**.

11. Set the layer's blending mode to Screen, then compare your artwork to Figure 30.

    | **TIP**   When screened, black pixels become transparent.

12. Click **Filter** on the menu bar, point to **Blur**, then click **Motion Blur**.

13. Set the Angle to -45 degrees, set the Distance to 5 pixels, then click **OK**.

(continued)

FIGURE 30
Image with white grain effect

FIGURE 31

White grain artwork in Color Dodge mode

FIGURE 32

Using two grain layers and two grain effects

14. Set the blending mode to Color Dodge, then compare your result to Figure 31.

Dodge is synonymous with light; the Color Dodge blending mode lightens the image using information on the blended layer as brightening information for the layers beneath. With the Color Dodge blending mode, black has no effect, which makes sense as this mode is all about lightening. Light pixels lighten areas of the image, with white pixels having the most extreme brightening effect.

15. Set the blending mode back to Screen, make the Black Grain layer visible, then compare your canvas to Figure 32.

16. Save your work, then close the file.

CREATE MONOTONES
and Duotones

What You'll Do

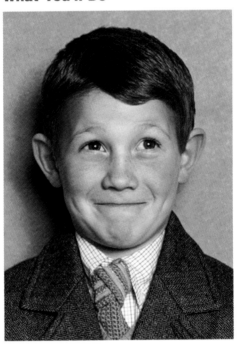

With blending modes and color overlays, the Layers palette offers a number of options for creating effects that look like colorized black-and-white images. As a result, over the last decade or so, many designers have steadily moved away from creating monotones and duotones. It's not so much that they've fallen out of fashion as that everybody's sort of forgotten about them. Don't let that be you. Monotones, duotones (and tritones) are very practical and important components in a designer's bag of tricks. From a design point of view, if you are laying out a page that has a number of color images, you can use duotones to "push back" or "mute" some images—which allows you to emphasize the full-color images. Duotones also offer variety and a relief from just resorting to a black-and-white image when color won't do. And they're a great challenge for your understanding of curves.

When you are working on a two-color job, usually Black and a PMS color, that's when duotones really come into play. In Duotone mode, you can apply the PMS color to the images in the piece, which can be very effective. I can't tell you how many times I see two-color jobs in which the designer uses the PMS color only in the type elements and runs black-and-white images. That's a designer that has forgotten about Duotone mode. One more thing: if you get a chance to do a three-color job (Black and 2 PMS inks), then take some time to experiment with tritones (in Duotone mode). With three colors, you can create some really cool color effects.

FIGURE 33

Duotone Options dialog box

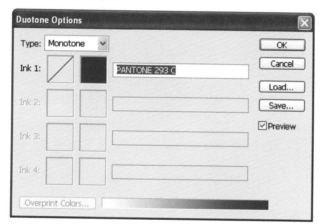

1. Open AP 8-9.psd, then save it as **Monotone**.

    To access the Monotone, Duotone, or Tritone modes, you must first convert an image to Grayscale mode.

2. Click **Image** on the menu bar, point to **Mode**, then click **Duotone**.

3. Click the **Type list arrow**, then click **Monotone**.

4. Click the **black square** next to Ink 1 in the Duotone dialog box, then click **Color Libraries** in the Color Picker dialog box.

5. Click the **Book list arrow**, then click **PANTONE® solid coated**.

6. Use the triangles to scroll to Pantone 293 C, click **Pantone 293 C**, then click **OK**.

    Your Duotone Options dialog box should resemble Figure 33. Photoshop automatically names the ink with the standard PANTONE naming convention.

(continued)

7. Click **OK**, then compare your canvas to Figure 34.

   A monotone image is the same thing as a grayscale image. Both refer to a single-channel image that will be printed with a single ink, and both have 256 colors available per pixel. The term *monotone* is used to distinguish an image that prints with an ink other than black, usually a PANTONE ink.

8. Save and then close the file.

Create a duotone

1. Open AP 8-10.psd, then save it as **Duotone**.

2. Click **Image** on the menu bar, point to **Mode**, then click **Duotone**.

3. In the Duotone Options dialog box, click the **Type list arrow**, then click **Duotone**.

   PANTONE 293 C is automatically set as the first color if you did the previous lesson before doing this lesson.

4. Click the white square next to Ink 2, then click **Picker** in the Color Libraries dialog box.

(continued)

FIGURE 34
Monotone image

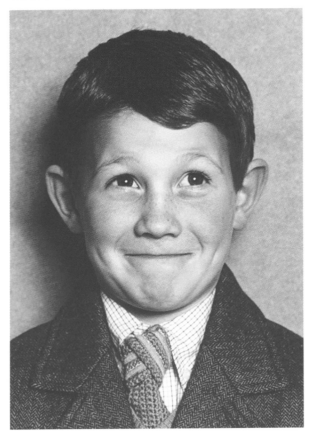

FIGURE 35
Duotone Options dialog box

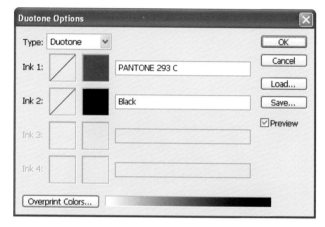

FIGURE 36
Duotone image, Black and PANTONE 293 C

5. Choose Black—0R/0G/0B—then click **OK**.

   Notice that "Black" is automatically supplied next to Ink 2. Your Duotone Options dialog box should resemble Figure 35.

   TIP When typing the name of an ink, it is standard to capitalize the first letter of the four process inks.

6. Click **OK**, then compare your duotone to Figure 36.

   In a layout application such as InDesign, this image would be separated onto two inking "plates"—the Black process ink plate and a plate for PANTONE 293 C. When printed, the image is printed using those two inks only. This is why duotones are often referred to as *two-color images*.

7. Save your work.

Edit a duotone

1. Click **Image** on the menu bar, point to **Mode**, then click **Duotone**.

   To edit a duotone, you must do so in the Duotone Options dialog box.

2. Click the blue PANTONE 293 C color box.

3. Scroll to and click **PANTONE 485 C**, then click **OK**.

4. Click **OK** again, then compare your canvas to Figure 37.

   In addition to changing the colors in a duotone, you can also manipulate the relationships between the two inks and control how each is distributed across the grayscale.

5. Click **Image** on the menu bar, point to **Mode**, then click **Duotone**.

6. Click the diagonal line in the box next to the PANTONE 485 C ink to open the Duotone Curve dialog box.

   At this point, the distribution of the two inks across the grayscale is identical. Wherever you would find a certain value of black ink, you'd also find the same value of PANTONE 485 C ink.

   (continued)

FIGURE 37
Duotone, Black and PANTONE 485 C

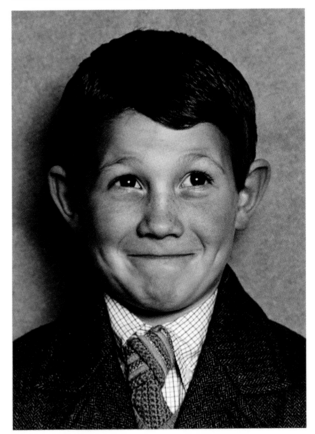

FIGURE 38
Duotone Curve dialog box

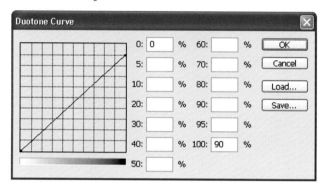

7. Type **90** in the 100% text box, then compare your Duotone Curve dialog box to Figure 38.

The Duotone Curve dialog box is specified in ink printing percentages. 0% ink is no ink and represents the highlight areas of an image. 100% ink is full ink coverage and represents the shadow areas of an image.

Note the gradient at the bottom of the grid; it moves from highlight to shadow, left to right. This means that the lower-left corner represents the highlight areas of the image, and the upper-right corner represents the shadows. Lowering the value for any point on the curve means the point prints with less ink.

For example, because we typed 90 in the 100% text box, this means that a 90% dot of PANTONE 485 C will be used to print in the shadow areas. Because we haven't changed the curve on the Black ink, a 100% dot of black will print in this same area.

(continued)

8. Type **20** in the 50% text box, click **OK**, click **OK** to close the Duotone Options dialog box, then compare your artwork to Figure 39.

9. Display the Info palette, click the **Tracks actual color values button** (eyedropper) in the Info palette, then click **Actual Color**.

10. Sample different areas of the image to see the distribution of PANTONE 485 C throughout the image and in relation to Black.

    At these settings, PANTONE 485 C will print heavily in the shadow areas only. If you sample the shadow areas, such as the boy's hair or coat, you will see a high percentage of PANTONE 485 C (identified as *1* in the Info palette) along with Black (*2*). If you sample light areas, such as the face, you will see that the PANTONE 485 C values are drastically lower than the Black values in the same area.

11. Click **Image** on the menu bar, point to **Mode**, then click **Duotone**.

12. Click the **duotone curve** beside PANTONE 485 C.

(continued)

FIGURE 39
Duotone, Black and PANTONE 485 C

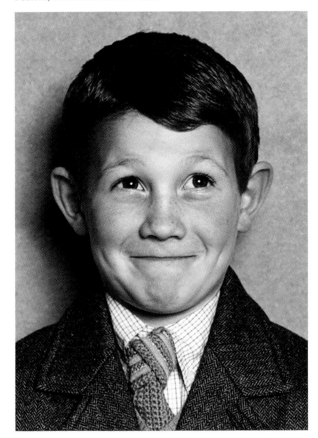

FIGURE 40
Duotone, Black and PANTONE 485 C

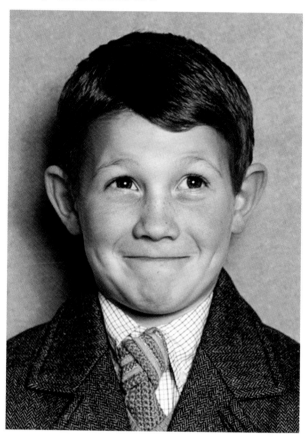

13. Type **50** in the 50% text box, then click **OK**.

14. Click the **duotone curve** beside the Black ink.

15. Type **20** in the 40% text box, type **60** in the 80% text box, then click **OK**.

16. Click **OK** to close the Duotone Options dialog box, then compare your artwork to Figure 40.

   If you sample the image, you will see that the Black ink values in the face are reduced and the PANTONE 485 C inks are increased.

17. Save the file, then close Duotone.

AUTOMATE
Workflow

What You'll Do

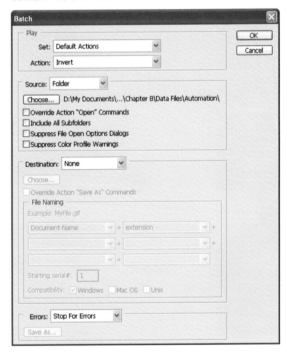

The title says it all: Automate workflow. As designers, we like to focus on the big projects: the magazine covers, the posters, the billboards, the CD covers. But in the real world, it's not only the big projects that come across the desk, is it? No, it's often the small stuff that you've got to handle as well. And often, the small stuff requires repetition. For example, here are twenty-five RGB files. Please convert them to CMYK, and resize them so that they're all seven inches wide. Or, here's a folder full of PSD files. Please open them all, convert to Grayscale, then save them as 72-dpi JPEG files that we can use on our Web site. Sound like fun?

Fortunately, Adobe has made an enormous commitment to automation, especially since the advent of the Internet and the enormous amount of image processing that creating and maintaining a Web site demands.

You might have played with the Actions palette before, but in this lesson, you're going to take a more rigorous and in-depth tour, and you're going to play with more advanced features like batch processing and modal controls. Also, you're going to use Photoshop's new Image Processor, which is a file conversion dream come true. Then, you can move on to that billboard. And that magazine cover. And that poster . . .

FIGURE 41

Image Processor dialog box

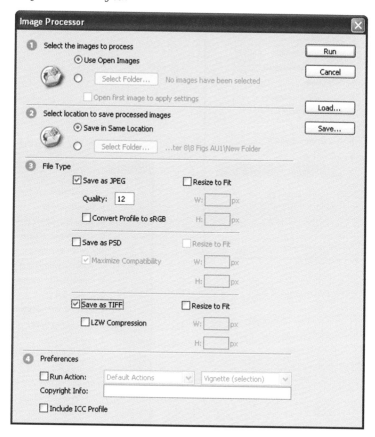

1. Open the seven files in the Automation folder located in the Chapter 8 Data Files folder.

   The files are all Photoshop.psd files. The goal of this lesson is to create one TIFF and one JPEG copy of each of the seven files.

2. Click **File** on the menu bar, point to **Scripts**, then click **Image Processor**.

3. In Section 1, click the **Use Open Images option button**.

4. In Section 2, click the **Save in Same Location option button**.

5. In Section 3, click the **Save as JPEG check box**, then type **12** in the Quality text box.

6. In Section 3, check the **Save as TIFF check box**.

7. Verify that nothing is checked in Section 4, then compare your Image Processor dialog box to Figure 41.

8. Click **Run**.

   The seven PSD files remain open after the Image Processor is done.

9. Navigate to the Automation folder, then open the Automation folder.

   The Automation folder contains the seven original PSD files. It also contains a folder named JPEG and a folder named TIFF. These two folders contain the JPEG and TIFF copies generated by the Image Processor.

10. Return to Photoshop.

Create and run an action in the Actions palette

1. Click **Window** on the menu bar, then click **Flowers.psd**.

2. Click **Window** on the menu bar, then click **Actions**.

3. Click the **Actions palette list arrow**, then remove the check mark next to Button Mode to deactivate Button Mode, if necessary.

4. Click the **Actions palette list arrow**, then click **New Action**.

5. Type **Invert** in the Name text box, click **Record**, then compare your Actions palette to Figure 42.

   A new action named Invert appears in the list and is highlighted. The red Begin recording button is activated on the Actions palette.

   > **TIP** The other actions listed in your Actions palette may vary.

6. Click **Image** on the menu bar, point to **Adjustments**, then click **Invert**.

   The Flowers.psd image is inverted.

7. Click **File** on the menu bar, then click **Save**.

8. Click **File** on the menu bar, then click **Close**.

9. Compare your Actions palette to Figure 43.

   The three commands that you executed—Invert, Save, and Close—are listed as commands under the Invert action.

10. Click the **Stop playing/recording button** on the Actions palette.

(continued)

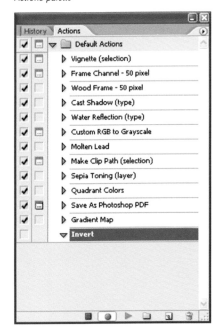

FIGURE 42
Actions palette

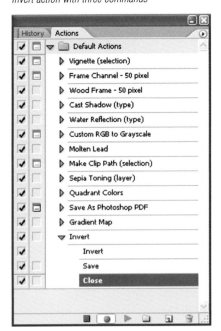

FIGURE 43
Invert action with three commands

FIGURE 44

Invert action targeted in Actions palette

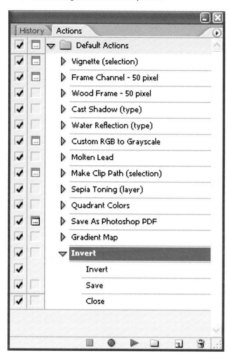

11. Click **Window** on the menu bar, then click **Marble.psd**.

12. Click **Invert** in the Actions palette list so that it is highlighted as shown in Figure 44.

 TIP When running actions, this is an easy step to miss—you must target the action itself before you can apply it.

13. Click the **Play selection button** ▶ in the Actions palette.

 You will see nothing happen other than the image closing. This is because Close is the final command of the action.

14. Repeat Step 12 to apply the Invert action to the remaining open images.

15. Open all seven PSD files in the Automation folder.

 All seven images have been inverted.

16. Close all seven PSD files.

Batch process an action

1. Click **File** on the menu bar, point to **Automate**, then click **Batch**.

2. In the Play section, click the **Action list arrow** to see all the actions available, then click **Invert**.

 All of the actions in the Actions palette are listed.

3. In the Source section, verify that Folder is chosen, then click **Choose**.

4. Navigate to and select the Automation folder, then click **OK** (Win) or **Choose** (Mac).

(continued)

5. Verify that none of the four check boxes in the Source section are checked.

   Remember, because of the work we did with the Image Processor in the first lesson of this chapter, the Automation folder now contains two subfolders—JPEG and TIFF. We do not want to apply the action to the contents of those folders.

6. In the Destination section, verify that None is chosen.

   No destination means that we want to affect the targeted images in the folder and for those images to be saved with the change. If we wanted to affect them and save the affected images as *copies*, then we'd need to specify a destination for the copies.

7. In the Errors section, verify that Stop for Errors is chosen, then compare your Batch dialog box to Figure 45.

8. Click **OK**.

   The seven images open, are affected by the action, then closed.

9. Open all seven PSD files from the Automation folder.

   All seven have been inverted and now appear as they did originally.

Create a complex action

1. Click **Window** on the menu bar, then click **Flowers.psd**.

2. Click the **Actions palette list arrow**, then click **New Action**.

   (continued)

FIGURE 45
Batch dialog box

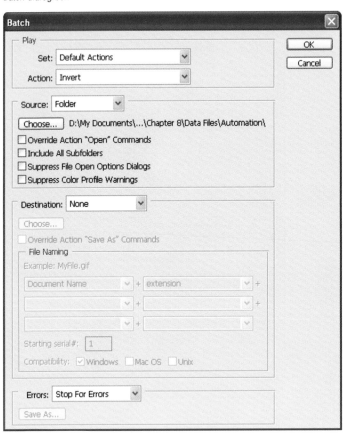

FIGURE 46
Image Size dialog box

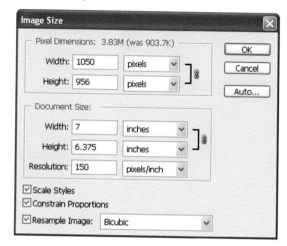

FIGURE 47
Unsharp Mask dialog box

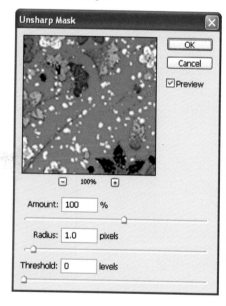

FIGURE 48
Curves bump

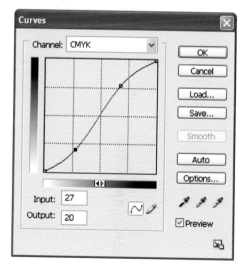

3. Type **Processed Textures**, then click **Record**.

4. Click **Image** on the menu bar, point to **Mode**, then click **CMYK Color**.

5. Click **Image** on the menu bar, then click **Image Size**.

6. Type **150** in the Resolution text box, then verify that all three check boxes in the Image Size dialog box are checked so that your dialog box resembles Figure 46.

7. Click **OK**.

8. Click **Filter** on the menu bar, point to **Sharpen**, then click **Unsharp Mask**.

9. Enter the settings shown in Figure 47, then click **OK**.

10. Click the **Create new fill or adjustment layer button** ⬤, on the Layers palette, then click **Curves**.

11. Create a contrast bump similar to the one shown in Figure 48, then click **OK**.

12. Click **File** on the menu bar, then click **Save As**.

13. Navigate to the Automation folder, then create a new folder named **Processed Textures**.

14. Save the file as a .PSD in the Processed Textures folder.

   Note that we did not enter a new name for the file.

15. Click the **Stop playing/recording button** ◼ in the Actions palette.

(continued)

16. Click the triangle next to Make adjustment layer in the Actions palette to expand the action, then compare your palette to Figure 49.

The specific settings that you used when creating the contrast bump in the curves adjustment layer are recorded with the command. (Your settings will differ slightly based on the specific curve that you made.)

17. Expand the Save action in the Actions palette.

The file format and the destination folder are recorded with the command.

18. Collapse the Make adjustment layer and Save commands.

19. Click **Window** on the menu bar, click **Wood.psd**, then target the **Processed Textures action** in the Actions palette.

20. Click the **Play selection button** 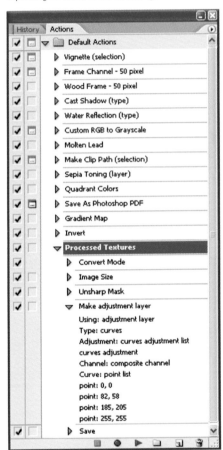 in the Actions palette.

All of the commands are applied to the Wood.psd file and it is saved to the new folder as a .PSD file. It is important that you understand that all of the commands were applied with the exact settings that you entered when creating the action.

Apply modal controls to an action

1. Click **Window** on the menu bar, then click **Water.psd**.

(continued)

FIGURE 49
Expanding an action to see its settings

FIGURE 50

Modal controls activated for two actions

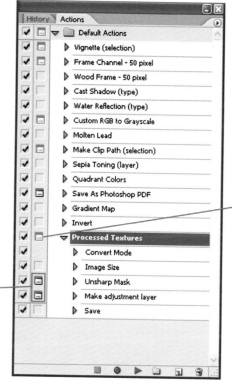

The two boxes you clicked are named Toggle Dialog on/off. When running an action, they do exactly that: toggle a dialog box on or off. When showing, they are set to toggle on the dialog boxes for these two commands. These two icons are also called modal controls.

The red modal control icon beside the Processed Textures action indicates that the action contains some commands that are modal.

2. Click the **Toggle dialog on/off button** FPO next to the Unsharp Mask command and the Make adjustment layer command so that your Actions palette resembles Figure 50.

3. Target the **Processed Textures action** in the Actions palette.

4. Click the **Play selection button** ▶.

   The Processed Textures action is run as before; however, this time, when it comes to the Unsharp Mask command, it opens the dialog box and awaits your input.

5. Change the Amount value to 75%, then click **OK**.

   The command is executed, then the New Layer dialog box is opened to create the Curves adjustment layer.

6. Type **Water Curve** in the Name text box, then click **OK**.

   The Curves dialog box opens showing the exact curve that was originally created for this command.

7. Tweak the contrast bump to increase the contrast even more, then click **OK**.

   The remaining commands run through to completion.

8. Apply the Processed Textures action to the remaining four PSD files, entering whatever settings you like in the dialog boxes.

9. Close all open files.

1. Open AP 8-11.psd, then save it as **Project Builder 1**.
2. Click Image on the menu bar, point to Mode, then click Lab Color.
3. In the Channels palette, click the Channel thumbnail on the Lightness channel.
4. Duplicate the Lightness channel, select all, copy, then click the Lab Channel thumbnail in the Channels palette.
5. Return to the Layers palette, then paste the copy as a new layer.
6. Name the new layer **Lightness Art**, then be sure to hide it.
7. Duplicate the b channel, select all, copy, then click the Lab Channel thumbnail in the Channels palette.
8. Return to the Layers palette, then paste the copy as a new layer named **B**.
9. Show the Lightness Art layer.
10. Set the blending mode of the B layer to Multiply.
11. Select all, click Edit on the menu bar, then click Copy Merged.
12. Paste a new layer, name it **Merged**, then hide the B layer.
13. Change the blending mode on the Merged layer to Overlay.
14. Set the opacity of the Merged layer to 40%, then compare your result to Figure 51.
15. Save your work, then close Project Builder 1.

FIGURE 51
Completed Project Builder 1

1. Open AP 8-12.psd, then save it as **Project Builder 2**.
2. Convert to RGB mode, then click Don't Flatten when you are prompted.
3. Create a new empty layer at the top of the Layers palette, then name it **Grain**.
4. Fill the Grain layer with 128R/128G/128B.
5. Click Filter on the menu bar, point to Texture, then click Grain.
6. Accept all the default settings and click OK.
7. Set the blending mode on the Grain layer to Overlay.
8. Convert the file to Grayscale, then click Flatten when you are prompted.
9. Convert the file to Duotone mode.
10. Change the Ink 1 color to PANTONE 290 C.
11. Open the Duotone Curve dialog box for Ink 1, type **0** in the 0% text box, type **70** in the 50% text box, type **100** in the 100% text box, then verify that all the other text boxes are empty.
12. Click OK.
13. Open the Duotone Curve dialog box for Ink 2, type **0** in the 0% text box, type **20** in the 50% text box, type **100** in the 100% text box, then verify that all the other text boxes are empty.
14. Click OK, then click OK to close the Duotone Options dialog box.
15. Compare your duotone to Figure 52.
16. Save your work, then close Project Builder 2.

FIGURE 52
Completed Project Builder 2

chapter

9

CREATING SPECIAL
Effects

1. Create a solarize effect.

2. Create mezzotint and halftone effects.

3. Create neon effects.

4. Create a ripped effect.

CREATE A
Solarize Effect

What You'll Do

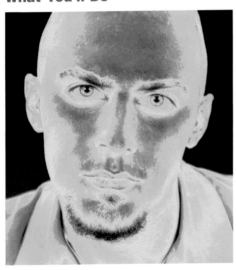

Solarize is a filter that has been available since the first release of Photoshop. It mimics a long-established effect in photography: mixing both the positive areas with negative areas. What's really interesting is that you can use the Curves dialog box to reproduce the Solarize filter's effect or to create your own solarize effect. Solarize is a special effect; in no way does it mimic a realistic image. It may not be practical for a conventional project, but it's a great effect to employ when you have the creative freedom to take a detour from the norm. With the right image and the right curve, you can produce an effect that is stunning and otherworldly. It's great for any type of progressive magazine illustrations, poster work, or cover art for a book or a musical CD. Best of all, because most designers only know how to use the basic Solarize filter, it's a seldom-used effect. The Solarize filter does not offer a dialog box with settings that you can adjust. It simply executes an algorithm and you are stuck with the results. However, the solarize effect can be reproduced—and manipulated with curves. When you know how to customize a solarize effect the best way for a given image, it gives you the power to be not only effective, but unusual as well.

FIGURE 1
Image inverted

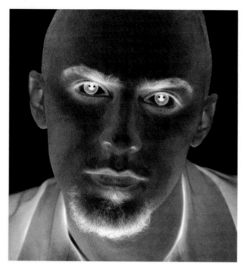

FIGURE 2
Image with the Solarize filter applied

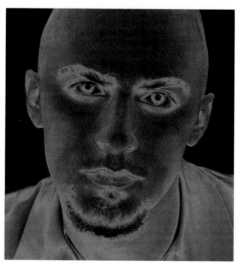

Solarize an image

1. Open AP 9-1.psd, then save it as **Solarize**.
2. Convert to Grayscale mode, then convert back to RGB Color mode.

   This is a standard method for working with a black-and-white image in a color mode.
3. Invert the image, then compare your result to Figure 1.

   Note especially the dark areas that have become white, such as his beard and eyebrows.
4. Undo your last step.
5. Click **Filter** on the menu bar, point to **Stylize**, click **Solarize**, then compare your result to Figure 2.

   With the Solarize filter, the light areas of the image are inverted, while the dark areas are not affected. If you compare this to the fully inverted image in Figure 1, you can see the difference. Note how the dark areas of the beard and the black pupils in his eyes remained black.
6. Undo your last step to remove the filter.
7. Duplicate the Background layer, then name the new layer **Solarize**.

(continued)

8. Click the **Create new fill or adjustment layer button** 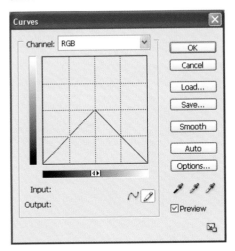 on the Layers palette, then click **Curves**.

9. Click the **pencil icon** in the Curves dialog box, then click the lower-left corner of the grid.

10. [Shift]-click the center point of the grid, then [Shift]-click the lower-right corner of the grid so that your Curves dialog box resembles Figure 3.

    This curve is easy to "read." From 0–128, nothing has changed. From 129–255, everything has been inverted—the curve moves downward instead of upward, meaning the pixels move back toward black rather than toward white.

11. Click **OK**, then compare your canvas to Figure 4.

    The result is identical to Figure 2, because this is the exact curve used when the Solarize filter is applied. Using the Curves dialog box to solarize opens up many options for manipulating the effect.

    (continued)

FIGURE 3
Standard solarize curve

FIGURE 4
Image solarized

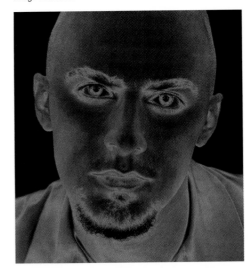

FIGURE 5
Darkening the solarize effect

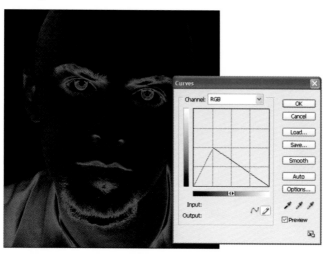

FIGURE 6
Lightening the solarize effect

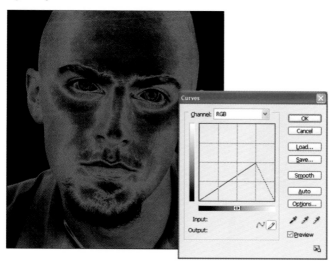

12. Reopen the Curves adjustment layer then, starting at the lower-left corner, redraw the curve so that it resembles Figure 5.

The shadow half of the curve is shortened by this move, and the dark areas of the image are therefore darkened. With a solarize effect, the goal is usually to create a "silver" person or image, which involves brightening, not darkening the image. This is not a curve that is typically used to solarize.

13. Using the same method, redraw the curve so that it resembles Figure 6.

This move is more in the right direction to achieve the silver effect.

(continued)

Lesson 1   Create a Solarize Effect

14. Redraw the curve to match Figure 7, then click **OK**.

15. Click the **Create new fill or adjustment layer button** 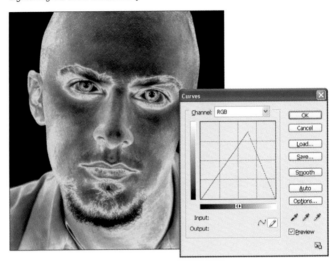, on the Layers palette, then click **Solid Color**.

16. Type **255R/216G/0B**, click **OK**, set the new layer's blending mode to Overlay, then compare your artwork to Figure 8.

17. Click the **Brush Tool**, set the Opacity to 50%, then set the foreground color to black.

(continued)

FIGURE 7
Lightening the effect substantially

FIGURE 8
Applying a color fill

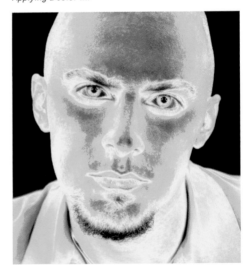

FIGURE 9

Masking the effect from the eyes

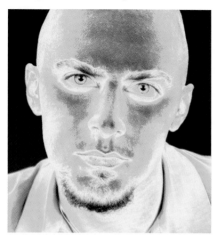

FIGURE 11

Final effect

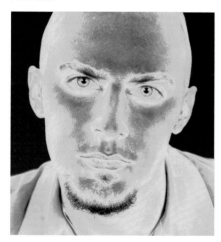

FIGURE 10

Reducing the effect in the highlights

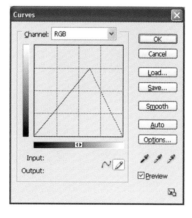

18. Using the layer mask beside the curves adjustment layer, reduce the solarization effect over the eyes so that your artwork resembles Figure 9.

Since the solarize effect at this point is very extreme, we can always reduce the contrast by adjusting the curve.

19. Double-click the **Curves adjustment layer thumbnail**, then redraw the curve as shown in Figure 10.

20. Click **OK**, then compare your result to Figure 11.

21. Save your work, then close the file.

CREATE MEZZOTINT AND
Halftone Effects

What You'll Do

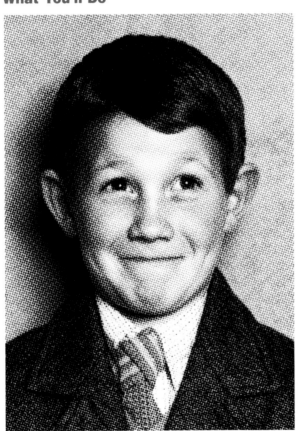

Mezzotints and halftoning are long-established procedures in the world of printing and prepress. In one sense, they're practical: they're used as part of the process to reproduce an image on a printing press. In another sense, they're a special effect, because they make an image look pretty cool. Of the two, you are certainly most familiar with halftoning. A continuous-tone image is reproduced with dots of ink that are various sizes. In prepress and printing, a mezzotint is a screening technique that you can use as an alternative to a conventional halftone. As an effect, it's a sweet alternative to applying a conventional grain overlay. Speaking of *overlay*, it's good for you to know that in the early versions of Photoshop, it required more complex procedures to apply the halftone and mezzotint filters as components in an overall effect. Photoshop's relatively new blending modes—like Overlay and Soft Light—have made it much quicker and easier to apply these filters in a way that *integrates* the effect with the base image.

FIGURE 12
Mezzotint filter

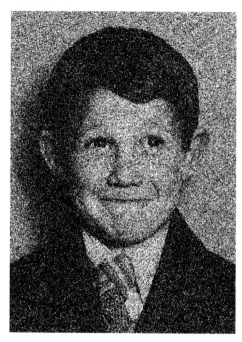

FIGURE 13
Mezzotint filter in Overlay mode

Create a mezzotint effect

1. Open AP 9-2.psd, then save it as **Mezzotint**.

2. Duplicate the Background layer, then name the new layer **Mezzotint**.

3. Click **Filter** on the menu, point to **Pixelate**, then click **Mezzotint**.

4. Verify that the Type is set to Fine Dots, click **OK**, then compare your result to Figure 12.

5. Zoom in on the effect so that you can see the pixels.

   The effect produced by the Mezzotint filter is often called a "bitmap effect" because it renders the image with only black or white pixels. Though this file is in Grayscale mode—256 shades of gray available per pixel—there are no gray pixels that make up the filtered image.

6. Zoom out so that you are viewing the image at 50%.

7. Set the blending mode on the Mezzotint layer to Overlay, then compare your result to Figure 13.

   Overlayed, the mezzotint effect produces a grainy, high-contrast image with white whites, dark blacks, and very few midtones.

(continued)

8. Change the blending mode to Soft Light, then compare your result to Figure 14.

   The Soft Light blending mode produces a much softer grain effect with less contrast and more detail in the midtones.

9. Save your work, then close Mezzotint.

Create a halftone effect

1. Open AP 9-3.psd, then save it as **Halftone**.

2. Duplicate the Background layer, then name the new layer **Halftone**.

3. Click **Filter** on the menu bar, point to **Pixelate**, then click **Color Halftone**.

4. Type **4** in the Max. Radius text box, click **OK**, then compare your result to Figure 15.

5. Convert the file to RGB Color mode, then click **Don't Flatten** in the dialog box that follows.

   TIP Throughout this book, always click Don't Flatten when prompted.

6. Zoom in on the image so that you can see the pixels.

   Unlike with the Mezzotint filter, the Color Halftone filter produces both black and gray pixels to create the effect.

   (continued)

FIGURE 14
Mezzotint filter in Soft Light mode

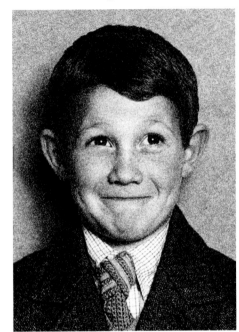

FIGURE 15
Color Halftone filter

FIGURE 16

The Blue, Red, Yellow gradient

7. Click the **Magic Wand Tool** , type **8** in the Tolerance text box, then verify that the Anti-alias and Contiguous check boxes are not checked.

8. Click a white pixel.

   All of the white pixels in the image are selected.

9. Click **Select** on the menu bar, then click **Inverse**.

   All of the non-white pixels that make up the filtered image are selected.

10. Zoom out so that you are viewing the image at 50%.

11. Copy, paste a new layer, then name the new layer **Halftone Transparent**.

   With this step, you have isolated the filtered image on a transparent layer—the pixels that were originally white are now transparent.

12. Delete the Halftone layer, then create a new layer named **BRY Gradient** above the Halftone Transparent layer.

13. Click the **Gradient Tool** , click the **Gradient picker list arrow** on the Options bar, then click the **Blue, Red, Yellow gradient**.

14. Drag the **Gradient Tool pointer** from the upper-left corner to the bottom-right corner of the canvas so that your result resembles Figure 16.

(continued)

Lesson 2   Create Mezzotint and Halftone Effects

15. Clip the BRY Gradient layer into the Halftone Transparent layer so that your canvas resembles Figure 17.

16. Select both the Halftone Transparent and the BRY Gradient layers in the Layers palette, click the **Layers palette list arrow**, then click **Merge Layers**.

17. Change the blending mode on the new merged layer to Overlay.

18. Compare your result to Figure 18.

19. Save your work, then close the Halftone document.

FIGURE 17
Clipping the gradient into the filtered artwork

FIGURE 18
Overlaying the merged artwork

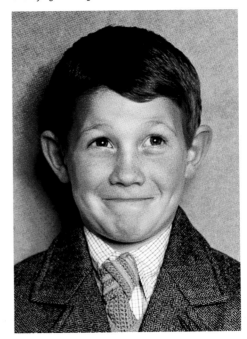

FIGURE 19
Final variation

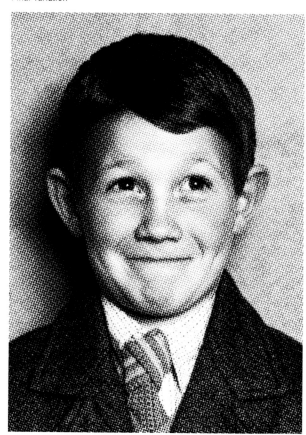

1. Open AP 9-3.psd, then save it as **Halftone Variation**.

2. Duplicate the Background layer, then name the new layer **Halftone**.

3. Click **Filter** on the menu bar, point to **Pixelate**, then click **Color Halftone**.

4. Type **4** in the Max. Radius text box, then click **OK**.

5. Convert the file to RGB Color mode.

6. Create a new layer named **BRY Gradient** above the Halftone layer.

7. Click the **Gradient Tool** , click the **Gradient picker list arrow** in the Options bar, then click the **Blue, Red, Yellow gradient**.

8. Drag the **Gradient Tool pointer** from the upper-left corner to the bottom-right corner of the canvas.

9. Change the blending mode on the BRY Gradient layer to Overlay.

10. Merge the BRY Gradient and the Halftone layers, then set the blending mode on the merged layer to Overlay.

11. Compare your result to Figure 19.

12. Save your work, then close the Halftone Variation document.

CREATE NEON
Effects

What You'll Do

Neon effects are another Photoshop staple, one that you've been able to do one way or another since the first release. They make for stunning special effects, and they're practical enough because they work so well with type. Neon is effective and it's a classic: it can be used as a title treatment for many different types of projects, both conventional and progressive.

Many books and manuals supply tips and tricks for creating simple neon effects—and that's the problem. They usually stop at the simple, which usually involves stroking a path or using the Inner Glow or Outer Glow layer styles. But if you spend some time driving around and noticing the many types of neon effects just sitting out there in the real world, you'll see soon enough that you can get a lot more creative than simply stroking a single path.

That's what this lesson is about—creating a complex neon effect. You'll do it the old-fashioned way, with paths rather than layer styles. You'll learn some great techniques for reproducing a neon effect, but you'll also explore more complex design concepts that will lead you to a multilayered effect that shines and fades and glows hot.

FIGURE 20
Path 2 stroked with Top Blue

1. Open AP 9-4.psd, then save it as **Neon**.
2. Display the Paths palette, then click **Path 2** to activate it.
3. Create a new foreground color that is **0R/127G/254B**, then save it in the Swatches palette as **Top Blue**.

   TIP To add a color to the Swatches palette, click the Swatches palette list arrow, then click New Swatch, enter a name in the Color Swatch Name dialog box, then click OK, or click the Paint Bucket Tool and then click an empty section in the Swatches palette. The foreground color on the toolbox is the color that will be added to the Swatches palette.

4. Click the **Brush Tool**, then set its size to Soft Round 28 pixels.

   Throughout this chapter, verify that your Brush Tool is set to 100% Opacity and 100% Flow.

5. Create a new layer named **Top Blue 28px**.
6. Click the **Paths palette list arrow**, then click **Stroke Path**.
7. Click the **Tool list arrow** in the Stroke Path dialog box, click **Brush**, then click **OK**.
8. Deactivate Path 2, then compare your result to Figure 20.

   The Stroke Path command strokes the path with the tool you select. It uses the tool's current settings for size, hardness, opacity, and so on, when creating the stroke.

(continued)

TIP For all the figures in this lesson, the path is deactivated so that you can better see the artwork. To avoid repetition, we won't continue to instruct you to deactivate your path when comparing it to a figure, though you can feel free to.

9. Create a new layer named **Top Border**.

10. Click **Path 1** to activate it, then click the **Stroke path with brush button** ⬭ on the Paths palette.

Like the Stroke Path command in the palette menu, the **Stroke path with brush button** strokes the path with the Brush Tool using its current settings.

11. Compare your canvas to Figure 21.

Had the two paths been combined as one path, we could have created this artwork with one stroke instead of two. However, it is necessary for the final artwork that we are able to access these two paths independently from one another.

12. Create a Hue/Saturation adjustment layer named **Colorize** for the Top Border layer only.

13. Click the **Use Previous Layer to Create Clipping Mask check box**, then click **OK**.

14. In the Hue/Saturation dialog box, click the **Colorize check box**.

15. Set the Hue value to 0, the Saturation value to 25, the Lightness value to 0, click **OK**, then compare your result to Figure 22.

(continued)

FIGURE 21
Path 1 stroked with Top Blue

FIGURE 22
Path 1 colorized

FIGURE 23

Paths 1 and 2 stroked with White 19 pixels

16. Change the diameter on the Brush Tool to 19 pixels, then change the foreground color to white.

17. Create a new layer named **White 19px**.

18. Click **Path 1**, then click the **Stroke path with brush button** ◯ in the Paths palette.

19. Click **Path 2**, click the **Stroke path with brush button** ◯, then compare your artwork to Figure 23.

20. Create a new layer group of the artwork named **Tubes**.

> **TIP** Don't include the Background layer in the group.

21. Save your work.

DESIGN*note*

This is the point at which most books on Photoshop stop, with the neon "tubes" against a black background. It's a cool effect, but there's so much more you can do to enhance the effect by creating a reflection of the neon graphics, which is what we'll do in the next lesson.

Design a drop shadow for neon effects

1. Create a new foreground color that is 129R/156G/182B, then save it in the Swatches palette as **Drop Blue**.

2. Increase the Brush Tool diameter to 50 pixels.

3. Hide the Tubes layer group.

4. Target the **Background layer**, then create a new layer named **Drop Blue 1 (50px)**.

5. Verify that Path 2 is active, click the **Path Selection Tool** , click the letter **O**, then [Shift]-click the letter **P** so that your selection resembles Figure 24.

6. Click the **Paths palette list arrow**, then click **Stroke Subpaths**.

7. Click **OK**, then compare your result to Figure 25.

(continued)

FIGURE 24
Selecting only the O *and* P *paths*

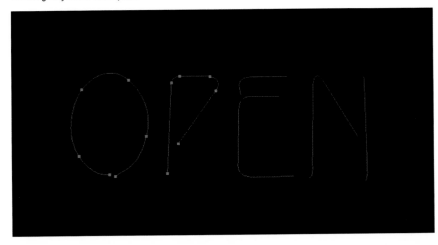

FIGURE 25
Stroking the subpaths

FIGURE 26
Selecting only the E *and* N *paths*

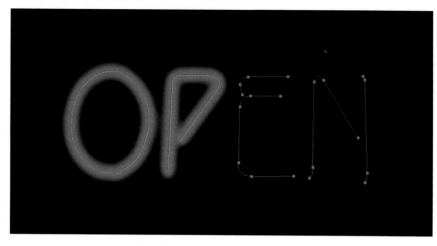

FIGURE 27
Stroking the subpaths

8. Select the paths for the letter **E** and **N** so that your selection resembles Figure 26.

9. Create a new layer in the Layers palette, then name it **Drop Blue 2**.

10. Stroke the subpaths, then compare your results to Figure 27.

    The first two and the last two letters are on different layers.

11. Show the Tubes layer group, then target the **Drop Blue 1 (50px) layer**.

12. Click **Filter** on the menu bar, point to **Other**, then click **Offset**.

13. Type **13** in the Horizontal text box, type **8** in the Vertical text box, then click **OK**.

14. Target the **Drop Blue 2 layer**, then return to the Offset dialog box.

15. Type **-13** in the Horizontal text box, type **8** in the Vertical text box, then click **OK**.

(continued)

16. Change the opacity for both the Drop Blue layers to 50%, then compare your artwork to Figure 28.

17. Target the **Background layer**, then create a new layer named **Drop Red 64px**.

18. Create a new foreground color that is 178R/39G/27B, then save it in the Swatches palette as **Drop Red**.

19. Increase the Brush Tool diameter to 64 pixels, click **Path 1**, then stroke the path.

20. Set the layer's opacity to 50%, then compare your results to Figure 29.

21. Save your work.

FIGURE 28
Final drop shadow effect

FIGURE 29
Adding the red drop shadow

DESIGN*note*

If you compare Figure 29 to Figure 23, you'll see that the drop shadow behind the text and the glow behind the border goes a long way in enhancing the effect, mostly by creating a sense of depth. However, you must ask yourself, what is the neon shining against? What is the background that is reflecting that drop shadow? It's a key question when creating a neon effect, because you can use a background as a reflective surface to really make the neon glow.

FIGURE 30
Fill Path dialog box

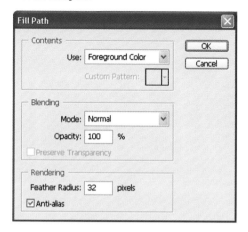

FIGURE 31
Adding the reflective background surface

1. Target the **Background layer**, then create a new layer named **Top Blue Fill**.

2. Change the foreground color to Top Blue, then click **Path 4** to activate it.

3. Click the **Paths palette list arrow**, then click **Fill Path**.

4. Enter the settings shown in Figure 30, then click **OK**.

5. Deactivate the path, change the opacity on the layer to 25%, then compare your artwork to Figure 31.

   Some neon signs are set within a metal box, and the neon light reflects off that surface. The fill that we added in Figure 31 represents that surface, and it is very effective in creating context for the drop shadow behind the neon text. The drop shadow now has a background to reflect off, and that gives us the opportunity to reflect even more dramatic colors off that surface.

(continued)

6. Create a new layer above the Top Blue Fill layer, then name the new layer **Drop Red 150px**.

7. Change the foreground color to Drop Red, then increase the Brush Tool's diameter to 150 pixels.

8. Stroke Path 1, change the layer's opacity to 33%, then compare your result to Figure 32.

9. Create a new layer above Drop Red 150px, then name the new layer **Top Blue 150px**.

10. Change the foreground color to Top Blue, click **Path 2** to activate it, then stroke the path.

(continued)

FIGURE 32
Adding the large glow behind the neon border

DESIGNnote

The deep blue artwork on the Top Blue 150px layer has enormous impact on the illustration, and there are many interesting insights to be gained by analyzing its role. If you turn the layer on and off, you see that the deep blue artwork actually makes the neon tubes appear to glow more intensely. That's because your eye reads the glow as the reflection of the neon tubes against the background surface, and any light that creates such a large and intense reflection must itself be very intense. The deep blue glow also enhances the role of the drop shadow behind the letters; it now appears to reflect *through* the blue glow. Toggle the blending mode between Normal and Hard Light; this effect is a great example of how Hard Light is one of the few blending modes that works well against a dark or even black background, which is important to remember. In Normal mode, the glow still works, but in Hard Light mode it takes on the quality of a deep, dark midnight blue that contrasts so well with the pale, "hot" blue of the neon tubes.

FIGURE 33

Adding the large glow behind the neon text

11. Set the opacity on the layer to 55%, change the blending mode to Hard Light, then compare your results to Figure 33.

12. Save your work.

Finish the illustration

1. Merge the Drop Blue 1 (50px) and Drop Blue 2 layers.

2. Rename the merged layer **Drop Blue (50px)**, then click the **Add layer mask button** on the Layers palette.

3. Set the foreground color to black.

4. Expand the Tubes group layer, then load the selection of the Top Blue 28px layer (the blue neon type).

5. Click **Select** on the menu bar, point to **Modify**, then click **Expand**.

6. Type **2** in the Expand By text box, then click **OK**.

(continued)

7. Feather the selection 4 pixels.

   Your canvas should resemble Figure 34.

8. Click the **Layer mask thumbnail** on the Drop Blue (50px) layer, then fill the selection with black.

9. Deselect, then compare your artwork to Figure 35.

   If you undo, redo the move, you'll see that this move is both subtle and important. Prior to this move, the shadow appeared to be emanating from the tubes themselves. With the move, the drop shadow no longer abuts the neon tubes, and by creating this separation, the neon tubes are now clearly *in front* of the drop shadow, and the drop shadow itself is now a reflection *against the back surface*.

10. Collapse the Tubes layer group, target the **Tubes layer**, then create a new layer named **Black Tubes**.

11. Change the diameter on the Brush Tool to 18 pixels, then change the Hardness value to 80%.

(continued)

FIGURE 34
Selecting the neon text

FIGURE 35
Masking pixels behind the tubes

FIGURE 36

Stroking the path to create the "black" tubes

FIGURE 37

Adding a highlight

12. Display the Color palette, click the **Color palette list arrow**, click **Grayscale Slider**, then specify a foreground color that is 94% Black.

13. Click **Path 3** to activate it, stroke the path, then compare your canvas to Figure 36.

14. Change the foreground color to 88% Black.

15. Change the diameter on the Brush Tool to 10 pixels, then change the Hardness value to 0%.

16. Stroke Path 3 again, deactivate the path, then compare your artwork to Figure 37.

    The second stroke plays the role of a subtle highlight; we used a 0% Hardness value so that its edge would be soft, like a highlight. Note that when we created the first black stroke, we used a high hardness value. The neon effect is created by using very soft edges of color; the soft edges create the effect that they glow. Because we want these black tubes to *not* glow, we used a harder edge.

17. Drag the **Black Tubes layer** below the Tubes layer group in the Layers palette.

(continued)

Lesson 3   Create Neon Effects

18. Reduce the opacity on the Black Tubes layer to 35%, then compare your artwork to Figure 38.

The black tubes add what I call a "recognizable reality" to the artwork. I especially like the tubes above the letter N, *behind* the N, and between the P and E. However, there's a problem that I saw immediately when I first designed this. Note the relationship between the black tubes and the type's drop shadow. Because the black tubes artwork is at 35% opacity, we see the drop shadow behind it. The effect is that there's a highlight on the black tubes, as though the drop shadow is emanating from the neon text and shining on the black tubes. That's the problem. As noted above, we want the drop shadow to be a reflection off the back surface. This means that the drop shadow must be behind the neon tubes. I call this a "visual logic" problem. Visually, it doesn't make sense. Don't make the mistake of thinking that it's so subtle it's not important or that I'm just being overly picky. Visual logic problems, even when subtle, can do great damage to an illustration. We've discussed this in earlier chapters: if the eye says "No, something's wrong," it can ruin an illustration.

(continued)

FIGURE 38
Viewing the black tubes art

FIGURE 39
Final artwork

19. Undo your last move so that the Black Tubes artwork is at 100% opacity, then [Ctrl]-click (Win) or ⌘-click (Mac) the **Layer thumbnail** to load a selection.

20. Click the **Layer mask thumbnail** on the Drop Blue (50px) layer, fill the selection with black, then deselect.

21. Change the opacity on the Black Tubes layer back to 35%, then compare your final artwork to Figure 39.

    If you look at the black tube between the *O* and the *P*, you can really see how important it is to the overall effect that the black tube is in front of the neon drop shadow.

22. Save your work, then close the Neon document.

DESIGN*note*

From a design perspective, the black tubes are what I call "extra mile" artwork. The illustration looked great without them, but going the extra mile to add them really pays off. They add complexity to the illustration because their texture is completely different from every other element in the illustration. By contrast, the black tubes' dullness and hardness only serve to make the neon that much more vibrant and glowing. As a designer, I always keep an eye out for these extra elements or extra details that I can use to enrich an illustration.

CREATE A
Ripped Effect

What You'll Do

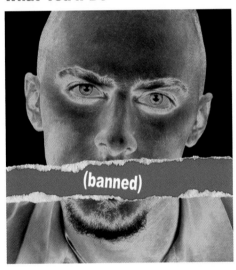

(banned)

Rips are your friend; rips are your buddy. Rip effects—as though an image has been torn, leaving a rough edge—are an old standby when creating a concept. That's because they are so versatile. For any kind of conflict—war, homicide, law and order, love triangle—a ripped effect gets the message across. But rips can also be fun. They can be used for a cool before-and-after effect. For example, if you had a picture of your house in summer and another in winter when the house is covered with snow, you could put the two together side by side, then mask around the ripped edge so that the summer view on the left half "rips" to show the winter view on the right.

In this lesson, we're going to design the most complex type of ripped edge: one with texture in the ripped edge. It involves some foresight when scanning the original, and some tricky layer mask moves. One last word on ripped effects though: they're a bit overused, and because of that, they can be a bit cliché. Just be aware of that, but don't be put off. For the right concept and with the right artwork, a ripped effect can be just the right trick to make the whole thing work.

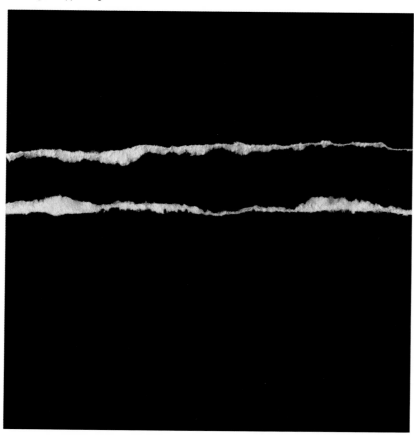

FIGURE 40
Isolating the ripped edges

Prepare a layer mask for a ripped effect

1. Open AP 9-5.psd, then save it as **Ripped Original**.

   This file is a scan of a manila folder that has been torn in half. Using a magic marker, I first filled in the length of the folder with black ink. I then tore the folder down the middle of the black ink, creating two torn edges. I then scanned each half against a black background, which produced the file at hand.

2. Click **Image** on the menu bar, point to **Rotate Canvas**, then click **90° CCW**.

3. Open the Levels dialog box, drag the **black triangle** to the right until the first Input Value text box reads 60, then click **OK**.

4. Paint the manila folder surface with black isolating the ripped edges, so that your artwork resembles Figure 40.

   TIP Paint carefully when you get close to the ripped edges. You want to maintain as much of the original rip detail from the scan as possible.

5. Open the Levels dialog box, drag the **black triangle** to the right until the first Input Value text box reads 16, drag the **gray midtone triangle** left until the middle Input text box reads 1.40, then click **OK**.

(continued)

6. Click **Filter** on the menu bar, point to **Sharpen**, then click **Smart Sharpen**.

The Smart Sharpen dialog box is a new feature in Photoshop CS2. It is an upgrade of the Unsharp Mask dialog box. In addition to providing a large preview window, it offers the ability to control how specific areas of the image (such as highlights, shadows, and so on) are sharpened and the ability to choose different algorithms for sharpening the image.

7. Note that the Remove setting is set to Gaussian Blur.

The Remove option determines which algorithm will be used to sharpen the image. You can choose between three: Gaussian Blur is the same algorithm that the Unsharp Mask filter uses; Lens Blur is designed to sharpen fine detail; Motion Blur is designed to sharpen areas of an image that are blurry because the subject moved or was moving when the image was captured.

8. Click the **Remove list arrow**, then click **Lens Blur**.

We want to sharpen the fine detail in the grains of paper in the ripped edge.

9. Set the Amount value to 120, then verify that the Radius value is set to 1.0.

10. Click the **More Accurate check box**, if necessary, so that your Smart Sharpen dialog box resembles Figure 41.

11. Click OK.

(continued)

FIGURE 41
Smart Sharpen dialog box

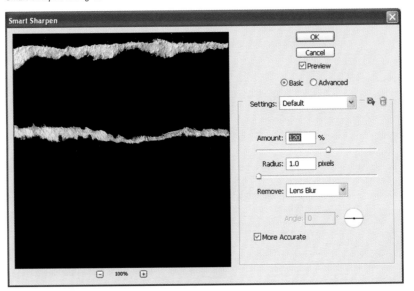

FIGURE 42

Applying a Hue/Saturation adjustment layer

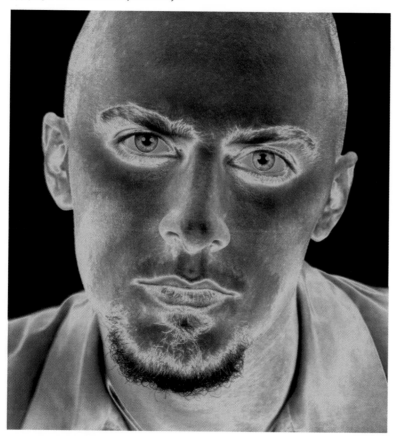

12. Click **Select** on the menu bar, click **Load Selection**, click the **Channel list arrow**, click **Top Rip**, then click **OK**.

Top Rip is a selection that I made with the Magic Wand Tool by clicking the black areas then inverting the selection. I then spent about 10 minutes tweaking the selection to exclude stray black pixels.

13. Click **Edit** on the menu bar, then click **Copy**.

14. Open AP 9-6.psd, then save it as **Ripped**.

15. Duplicate the Background layer, rename it **Solarize**, then drag it to the top of the Layers palette.

16. Click **Layer** on the menu bar, point to **New Adjustment Layer**, then click **Hue/Saturation**.

17. Type **Blue** in the Name text box, click the **Use Previous Layer to Create Clipping Mask check box**, then click **OK**.

18. Click the **Colorize check box**, drag the **Hue slider** to 200, drag the **Saturation slider** to 35, click **OK**, then compare your artwork to Figure 42.

On the comedy circuit, if an act is risque or uses foul language, the comic is said to "work blue" or to use "blue material." Sometime, the act itself is called "a blue act." Because this illustration is about an artist whose work is controversial, the Hue/Saturation move is a nice metaphor.

(continued)

19. Click **Edit** on the menu bar, click **Paste**, then position the top rip as shown in Figure 43.

20. Return to the Ripped Original document, load the selection called Bottom Rip, copy it, then paste it in the Ripped document as shown in Figure 44.

21. Merge the two ripped layers, then name the new layer **Rips**.

22. Click the **Magic Wand Tool** ✎ , set the Tolerance value to 4, then verify that the Anti-alias check box is not checked and that the Contiguous check box is checked.

23. Click the canvas in the area above the top rip, then [Shift]-click the area below the bottom rip.

(continued)

FIGURE 43
Positioning the top rip

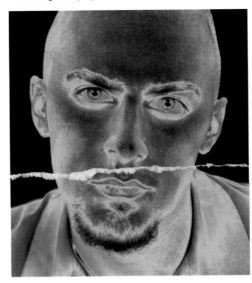

FIGURE 44
Positioning the bottom rip

FIGURE 45
Selecting with the Magic Wand Tool

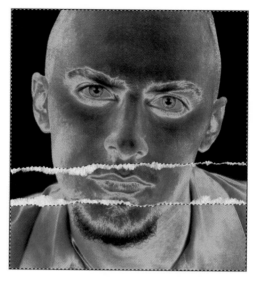

FIGURE 46
Adding a layer mask to the Solarize layer

24. Expand the selection by 1 pixel, then compare your selection to Figure 45.

25. Target the **Solarize layer**, click the **Add layer mask button** on the Layers palette, then compare your result to Figure 46.

26. Paint white in the Solarize layer mask to hide any red pixels that are showing through the ripped texture.

27. Target the **Rips layer**, open the Hue/Saturation dialog box, drag the **Saturation slider** to 0, then click **OK**.

    Photos are printed on white paper. We don't want the yellowish cast to suggest that we used a manila folder to create the rip.

28. [Ctrl]-click (Win) or ⌘-click (Mac) the **Rips Layer thumbnail** to load it as a selection.

(continued)

29. Expand the selection by 1 pixel, then feather the selection by 1 pixel.

30. [Ctrl]-click (Win) or ⌘-click (Mac) the **Create new layer button**  on the Layers palette.

   A new layer is added *below* the Rips layer.

31. Name the new layer **Rips Shadow**, fill the selection with black, then deselect all.

32. Add a layer mask to the Rips Shadow layer, then completely mask out the shadow along the top edge of the top rip and along the bottom edge of the bottom rip.

33. Reduce the opacity of the Rips Shadow layer to 50%, then compare your results to Figure 47.

34. Save your work, close the Ripped document, save the Ripped Original document, then close it as well.

FIGURE 47
Completed artwork

(banned)

DESIGN_note_

A key factor in this artwork is the texture of the rip. You will often see this effect done with the quickie method of having a hard edge with no texture or with a white-filled ripped edge. The paper texture within the ripped edge is very satisfying and a fine example of how some effects just demand scanned artwork. The Smart Sharpen filter played an important role in exaggerating the ripped paper detail. Remember that a sharpening filter is always more noticeable on your monitor screen than it is when printed. Our use of hard-edged selections (not anti-aliased) was important for maintaining the hard edge of the rip. Of course, you see this where the rip meets the red, but take a moment to notice the effect where the rip meets the image—it's very realistic. Remember to keep a copy of these two rips in your collection of artwork—you can use them over and over again. Finally—and this has nothing to do with rips—think back to Chapter 6 when you retouched this artwork. You've done so many extreme modifications to the artwork with the high-contrast solarize effect and the blue hue move, but don't make the mistake of thinking that the retouching was all for naught. Note the clarity in the whites of the eyes, the dark rim around the irises, the white highlights surrounding the eyes, and the dark intensity of the eyebrows and beard. Those are just some of the payoffs from the retouching, and they are important to the final image.

1. Open AP 9-7.psd, then save it as **Color Mezzotint**.
2. Target the Silo Layer, then apply the Mezzotint filter with fine dots.
3. Zoom in on an area of the silo so that you can see white pixels easily.
4. Click the Magic Wand Tool, set its Tolerance value to 4, verify that neither the Anti-alias nor the Contiguous check boxes are checked, then click a white area to select all the white pixels on the layer.
5. Inverse the selection to select all the black pixels on the layer, copy then paste.
6. Name the new layer **Black Only**, then zoom out to view the entire face.
7. Set the Silo layer's blending mode to Overlay.
8. Show the Gradient layer at the top of the Layers palette, then target it.
9. Clip the Gradient layer into the Black Only layer.
10. With the Gradient layer still targeted, click the Layers palette list arrow then click Merge Down.
11. Zoom in so that you are viewing the face at 100%
12. Change the blending mode to Overlay.
13. Change the blending mode to Soft Light.
14. Change the blending mode to Hard Light.
15. Change the blending mode to Vivid Light.
16. Change the blending mode to Linear Light.
17. Change the blending mode to Pin Light.
18. Change the blending mode to Hard Mix, change the zoom level to 50% to see the entire face then compare your result to Figure 48.

FIGURE 48
Completed Project Builder 1

1. Open AP 9-8.psd, then save it as **Single Rip**.
   (*Hint*: A single rip effect is very different from the rip effect created in Lesson 4 of this chapter. In that project, the photo had two ripped edges, as though a strip had been torn from the image. With a single rip, the image is ripped along a single edge.)

2. Load the Rip layer as a selection, then save the selection as **Rip Right**.

3. Deselect, then click the Rip Right channel to view it.

4. Make everything to the right of the rip white, so that the entire right half of the channel is completely white.

5. Click the RGB channel, then click the Background layer.

6. Click Image on the menu bar, then click Canvas Size.

7. Change the width measurement to 7.52 inches, click the square to the left of the center square, then click OK.

8. Target the Rip layer, load the Rip Right selection, click Edit on the menu bar, then click Copy Merged.

9. Click Paste, then name the new merged layer **Right Half**.

10. Load the Rip Right selection again, target the Solarize layer, then click the Add layer mask button on the Layers palette.

11. Invert the layer mask.

12. Drag the Rip layer below the Solarize layer, then hide the Rip layer.

13. Click the Move Tool, then drag the artwork on the Right Half layer all the way to the right edge of the canvas.

14. Target the Rip layer, make it visible, then load it as a selection.

15. Contract the selection by 2 pixels.

16. Press and hold [Alt] (Win) or [option] (Mac), then click the Add layer mask button [O].
    (*Hint*: With this keyboard command, the layer mask is added with the selected pixels being masked.)

17. Click the Brush Tool, then use a hard brush to mask out the remaining right edge of the rip.

18. Click the Pencil Tool, then set the diameter to 3 pixels.

19. Painting in the layer mask, hide additional areas of the white edge and also show more of the white edge so that it is not so even down the left half.

20. Add a Drop Shadow layer style to the Right Half layer, then compare your artwork to Figure 49.

21. Save your work, then close the Single Rip document.

FIGURE 49
Completed Project Builder 2

FAST
COMPANY

they drive by night

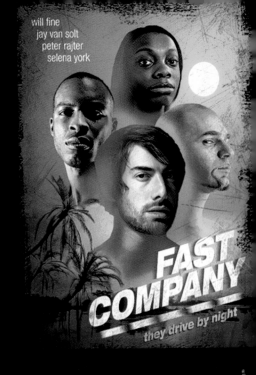

FAST
COMPANY

they drive by night

FAST
COMPANY

they drive by night

FAST
COMPANY

they drive by night

FAST
COMPANY

they drive by night

chapter

10

WORKING WITH
Blending Modes

1. Color balance a photo montage.
2. Add depth and dimension to a photo montage.
3. Use the Hard Light blending mode.
4. Use blending modes in calculations.
5. Use the Overlay and Screen blending modes.
6. Use the Multiply, Color, and Soft Light blending modes.
7. Combine blending modes with color fills.
8. Work with textures.

COLOR BALANCE A
Photo Montage

What You'll Do

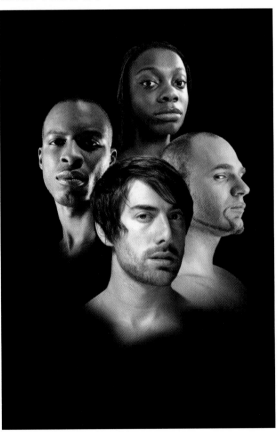

Whenever you are creating a montage with different images, color becomes an important consideration, especially if the images are from different sources and different photographers. Even if all the component images are themselves color balanced and color corrected, when juxtaposed in a montage, variations in tonal range and color cast are evident immediately. If your goal is to create a montage with all the images having consistent color, then you'll need to adjust levels and color balance to achieve that goal.

In this lesson, you'll do just that. You'll be supplied with four images from an online stock photography service. Each is from a different studio and a different photographer. You'll be surprised at how very different they are in terms of color and tone, and you'll be pleasantly surprised at how effective you can be in making that color and tone consistent between the four.

FIGURE 1
Comparing four component images

Compare images in a
montage for lighting
and color

1. Open the following four files: North.psd, South.psd, East.psd and West.psd.

   The four images will be used together as a composite image. Each was found on an online stock photography Web site, and each was taken by a different photographer. I did some minor retouching on all four (removed blemishes, whitened eyes, and so on), but I did not manipulate levels, curves, or color balance in any way.

2. Close the four images.

3. Open AP 10-1.psd, then save it as **Fast Company Composite**.

   Throughout this chapter, I will refer to each image as North, South, East, and West.

4. Compare your screen to Figure 1.

   When the images are juxtaposed, it becomes clear immediately how different they are on so many visual levels. The goal of this lesson is to manipulate the images so that they can be used together as composite art for a poster. In design circles, this is referred to as "making them look like they are in the same room." In other words, we want the four images to appear consistent, as though the four models were photographed together. Presently, they appear to be anything but consistent.

   (continued)

5. Identify the direction of the light source on each of the four images.

In terms of light source, this montage isn't perfect by any means, but it's not so bad either. North and West share the same source, from the right. The intensity of the light is similar for both, but definitely more intense on North. East is interesting; he's very well lit from the right, but you can see the intense highlight coming from the left and shining above where his ear would be if it were visible. This makes East consistent with South, as the light source for South clearly comes from a left angle. Overall, the composite works well with its two light sources, one from the left, the other from the right. The eye accepts the lighting as realistic, which is the most important test.

6. Compare the four images in terms of color.

This is where all four diverge from one another. If you compare North and West, North's flesh tone appears to incorporate "warm" reds, and yellows, whereas West's is cold, dark, and blue. South is cold too, but in a different way. Whereas West is dark, South is bright—but not warm. The brightness has a blue cast—like an ice blue. Comparing North to South, North looks like she's in some cozy living room with a lamp and a fire for light. South looks like he's in a hospital under fluorescent light. And then there's East, whose color is completely different from the other three.

DESIGNnote

Light source is a critical component when creating a montage. If the models in a montage were in the same room, then they'd be subject to the same lighting conditions. As a designer, however, when compositing with "found imagery" consider yourself lucky if all the images share a consistent light source. It's not usually the case. This is why most professional studios will schedule a special photo shoot with all the models literally in the same room to be photographed. If you can begin a project with all the photography having the same light source and the same color tones, you are really starting off on the proverbial right foot.

FIGURE 2
Changing the background to black

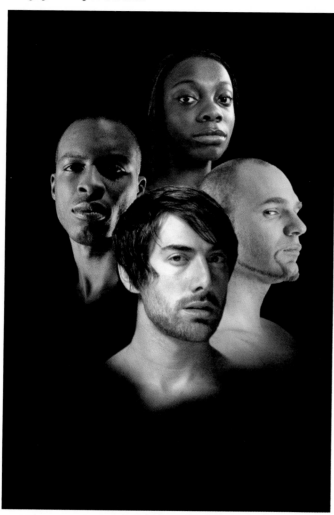

Adjust Levels in a montage

1. Invert the Background layer so that it is black, then compare your screen to Figure 2.

   Before addressing color, you first need to address the shadow-to-highlight range for each of the component images in a montage. Consistent shadow qualities will be critical. Positioning the images against a black background is very useful to see if the shadows are weak or strong.

2. Show the History palette and click the **Create new snapshot button** 📷 on the palette. Notice that the new snapshot, named Snapshot 1, appears in the palette, but do not select it at this time.

3. Assess the images in terms of shadow quality and contrast.

   Of the four, only East appears to have satisfactory contrast. West is so flat that it was noticeable against the white background. The black background reveals that North and South—though they looked pretty good against the white background—need a contrast bump and that North has weak shadows. This is evident in her hair, which is grayish blue. Her hair has a visible highlight, but to the left of that highlight, where the hair should be black or almost black, it is clearly gray and weak. The shadow behind her neck is weak also.

4. Make the North Levels layer visible, then double-click the **Layer thumbnail** to see the adjustments made in the Levels dialog box.

   (continued)

The histogram shows that the shadows in the original were weak. I darkened those shadows, but not so much that I lost the highlight and the detail in her hair. I did not move the highlights much at all, because I'd already assessed that the light on her face was the most intense of the four images. I tweaked it for contrast only.

5. Click **Cancel**.

6. Make the West Levels layer visible, then double-click the **Layer thumbnail** to see the adjustments made in the Levels dialog box.

   TIP Position the Levels dialog box so that you can see the image.

   As opposed to North, West's histogram required a dramatic adjustment, which was expected given that the original was so flat. Note how little pixel detail was available in the original's upper highlight range, and note how far I moved the black triangle to darken the shadows. I may have gone too far—his eyes are almost entirely black and the whites are hardly visible on the insides.

7. Drag the **black triangle** all the way to the left and note the effect on West.

   The image is flat because the shadows in the original were weak. This is especially evident in his forehead and in his hair. As was the case with North, his hair is bluish gray rather than black. Even his forehead is grayish.

8. Drag the **black triangle** to the right until the Input text box value is 9, then click **OK**.

   (continued)

FIGURE 3
Adjusted levels on West and North

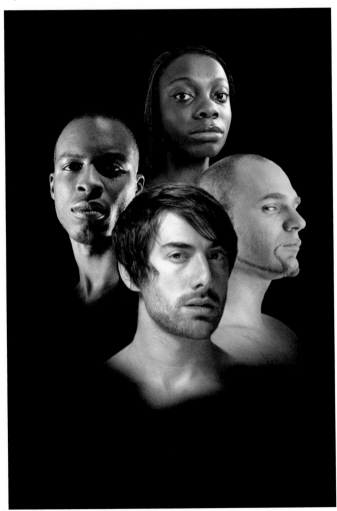

FIGURE 4
Adjusted levels overall

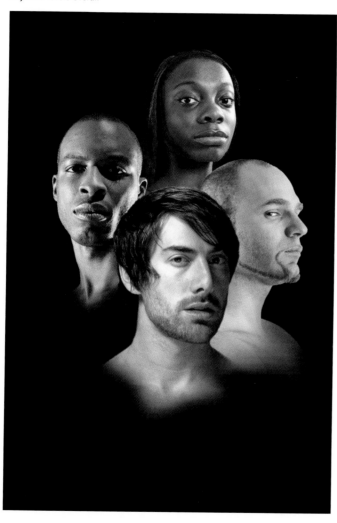

9. Compare your result to Figure 3, then toggle the West Levels layer on and off to see the dramatic change.

   Note how much more *shape* his face has with the contrast bump, how much more prominent his cheekbones become, for example. The tweak on the shadow was a good move, because the whites of his eyes are now more visible, but the hair at the top of his head is black, not gray. Note too how the contrast move "warmed up" his flesh tone, which is especially noticeable in his chest. Finally, note how flat South now appears compared to West and North.

   TIP Throughout this chapter, when you are instructed to toggle a layer on and off to see a change, be sure to toggle the layer on when you are done viewing.

10. Make the East Levels layer visible.

    As good as East looked at the beginning, the contrast bump removed a dull gray cast overall and brightened him even more. Note that I had to mask out some of the adjustment, because it was making his nose too red and "hot."

11. Make the South Levels layer visible, compare your screen to Figure 4, then toggle the South Levels layer on and off to see the change.

    With the adjustment, it becomes apparent that the right side of his face and the shadow on his shoulder were especially weak.

12. Save your work.

(continued)

13. Click **Snapshot 1** in the History palette to see the canvas before the layer adjustments.

14. Click **Edit** on the menu bar, then click **Undo State Change**.

> **TIP** With this method, you can use the snapshot in the History palette as a super Undo. It allows you to toggle back and forth to see the artwork in its present state and then way back to a previous state. But it only works if you remember to take snapshots at important stages along the way.

15. Click the **Modify Levels Layer** in the History palette to verify that the file is at the same stage as it was when you last saved.

The History palette lists your previous moves, which Photoshop identifies as "states." Clicking an item in the list takes you back to that state. The number of previous states that the History palette will list is set as a preference—History States —in the General Preferences dialog box.

16. Click the **Create new snapshot button** on the History palette.

DESIGN*note*

Adjusting levels is an important part of any color manipulation process—an image should have a good shadow-to-highlight range before you try to adjust its color. When you adjust levels, the correction in contrast improves the color overall. That's a great by-product of adjusting levels, but it's not really the same thing as adjusting color. Don't confuse adjusting levels with correcting color in an image or balancing color for consistent color between images. For example, in this lesson, you adjusted levels on all four images, and all four were improved dramatically. But West is still much colder than North. Though South is warmer, he remains much more blue and cold than North. And East, though his color has improved, is now even brighter and that much more different than the other three. The color has improved overall for each of the images, but the Levels moves did not alter the overall color balance of any of the images.

FIGURE 5
Warming up West

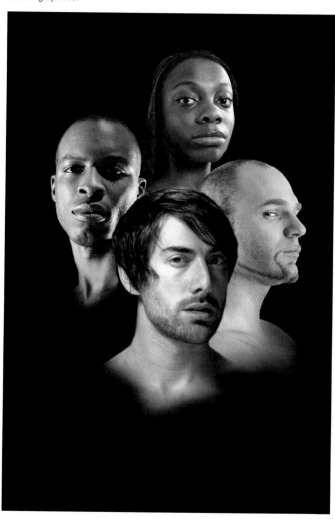

Work with Color Balance adjustment layers

1. Target the **West Levels layer**, press and hold **[Alt]** (Win) or **[option]** (Mac), click the **Create new fill or adjustment layer button** ◑. on the Layers palette, then click **Color Balance**.

2. Type **West Color Balance** in the Name text box, click the **Use Previous Layer to Create Clipping Mask check box** to activate it, if necessary, then click **OK**.

   > **TIP** Use these steps when making color balance adjustment layers for the remainder of this chapter.

   We want to move the color in West so it is more like North—warm and appealing. When adjusting color, "warm" always signifies yellow, magenta, and red, while "cold" signifies blue, cyan, and green.

3. Drag the **top slider** to +15 and note the effect on West.

   Don't rush through these moves. Take time to experiment with the slider—push it to the extremes, see what happens. After you've experimented, be sure to input the specified value.

4. Drag the **middle slider** to −5, drag the **bottom slider** to −20, click **OK**, then compare your result to Figure 5.

5. Using the default layer mask on the West Color Balance layer, mask out the color adjustment so that it doesn't affect his eyes.

   We don't want the whites of his eyes to turn yellow.

   (continued)

6. Target the **North Levels layer**, then create a color balance adjustment layer named **North Color Balance**.

   In any negotiation, both parties must be willing to compromise. In this case, North needs to "cool off" a bit to fall more into line with West and eventually with South.

7. Drag the **top slider** to –10, drag the **bottom slider** to +5, click **OK**, then compare your result to Figure 6.

   | **TIP** Feel free to toggle the adjustment layer on and off to see the change.

   West and North are now believably "in the same room." The color does not need to be exactly consistent—first of all, that's not really possible, and second, different people have different skin tones. It's not that the color of their skin needs to be the same, it's that the color of the light that strikes them needs to *feel* the same for both. That's the trick.

8. Target the **South Levels layer**, then add a color balance adjustment layer named **South Color Balance**.

   (continued)

FIGURE 6
Cooling off North

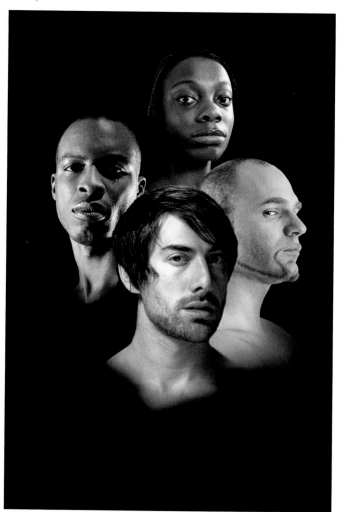

FIGURE 7
Warming up South

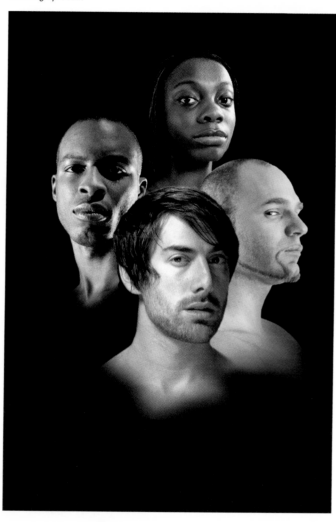

9. Drag the **top slider** to +15, then drag the **bottom slider** to −20.

   To move this away from the cold blue, we've made these two dramatic moves—one toward red, the other toward yellow. The move was definitely in the right direction; in fact, he matches West and North very well. However, for me, I felt that he was getting a little too red—too hot—in some of the shadow detail, such as in his hair on his forehead, on the bridge of his nose, and around his eyes. I couldn't reduce the red, because blue is the enemy here. I could increase the yellow, but I am always cautious about pushing any one slider too far out of balance with the others. Instead, I chose to move the middle slider away from magenta and toward green.

10. Drag the **middle slider** to +5, click **OK**, then compare your result to Figure 7.

    If you toggle the adjustment layer on and off you can really see how blue—actually, how purple—South was originally.

11. Target the **East Levels layer**.

    East is going to need more than just a color balance adjustment. East's tonal range is entirely different from the other three—where they are moderately lit with a full range from shadow to highlight, East is lit very brightly—so much so that there are no shadows on him. To be more consistent with the others, East's brightness must be reduced.

    (continued)

12. Add a new curves adjustment layer named **East Curves**.

13. Add a point to the curve, type **76** in the Input text box, then type **66** in the Output text box.

    The image is darkened. However, we don't want it to go too flat, so we'll return the highlights to where they were originally.

14. Add a second point to the upper half of the curve, type **191** in the Input text box, type **191** in the Output text box, click **OK**, then compare your result to Figure 8.

    This was a move in the right direction, but the tricky thing about East is that when you darken the artwork, it gets more intensely red. Therefore, this move needed to be slight. However, the intense red is a tip-off for the next move. If an image's color is too intense, that tells you to reduce saturation.

15. Add a new Hue/Saturation adjustment layer named **East Hue/Sat**.

16. Drag the **Saturation slider** to −15, click **OK**, then compare your result to Figure 9.

17. Add a new color balance adjustment layer named **East Color Balance**.

    We're still fighting the red cast, so we'll use the color balance adjustment to cool him down.

    (continued)

FIGURE 8
Reducing East's brightness

FIGURE 9
Reducing the saturation on East

FIGURE 10
Cooling off East

FIGURE 11
Reducing East's brightness again

18. Drag the **top slider** to –10, drag the **middle slider** to +5, drag the **bottom slider** to +5, click **OK**, then compare your result to Figure 10.

This was a good move, but after all this, he's *still* too bright.

19. Add a new curves adjustment layer named **East Curves 2**.

20. Click to add a point to the curve, type **127** in the Input text box, type **114** in the Output text box, click **OK**, then compare your result to Figure 11.

This is the first time in this book that we've used dual curves adjustment layers, but this is a very common technique. Could we have gone back to adjust the first curves adjustment? Sure. But this type of work is all about building and moving *forward*, and not so much about going back. The first curves adjustment was one of the steps that got us to where we were when we realized we wanted to darken the image again. So we moved forward; we added another curves adjustment layer and made the move.

21. Save your work.

22. Click **Snapshot 2** in the History palette to see the artwork before all of the color adjustments you made.

23. Toggle between Snapshot 2 and the artwork in its most current state.

24. Verify that the artwork is at the state when you saved, then click the **Create new snapshot button** .

ADD DEPTH AND DIMENSION
to a Photo Montage

What You'll Do

In this lesson, you'll focus on another important challenge: creating the *spatial relationship* between the individual images. In this challenge, you face head on the one word that haunts every photo montage: *flat*. When you layer individual pieces of art, that's what they are: flat. The challenge is to create depth and dimension, to bring some components forward and push others back. In doing so, you create the all-important spatial relationship between the components, you fight the flat, you make the artwork feel *real*. And the big irony is, with photo montage, the techniques you use to make it "real" are dramatic shadows, artistic touches, and wild effects that never have and never will exist in the real world.

FIGURE 12

Artwork against a white background

1. Target the **South layer**, then [Shift]-click its **Layer mask thumbnail** to toggle the layer mask off and on.

   This layer mask defines the relationship between South and the background, but it really has no effect on the relationship between South and East whatsoever.

2. Target the **West layer**, then toggle its layer mask off and on.

   With the layer mask activated, the black background becomes visible between South's shoulder and West's neck. And that black space creates *distance* between South and West. Why? Because your eye interprets that black space as some sort of negative space that exists *between* them.

3. Toggle East's layer mask on and off, and note that the layer mask makes it appear as though East's chest is darkened as it fades into the background.

4. Target the **Background layer**, invert it, then compare your canvas to Figure 12.

   With the black background inverted to white, East's chest is now lightened as it fades into the background. It's important that you understand that East's chest was *neither* darkened nor lightened. It was made semitransparent in its layer mask, and the background was showing through. The illusion that it was darkened was dependent on the black background.

   (continued)

5. Note the relationship between South and West.

   Though the background is now white, the suggestion of space between them continues to exist. White or black, the eye continues to perceive the negative space between them as distance.

6. Undo the invert so that the background is black once again.

7. Note the relationship between South and East.

   As with the relationship between South and West, we must create the suggestion of distance between South and East, and to do that, we must create negative space.

8. Make the East Shadow layer visible, then compare your canvas to Figure 13.

   The darkening of the East artwork creates the distance between South and East. To achieve that darkening, I created an empty layer, painted black in the layer, then clipped the layer into the East layer so that the black paint didn't affect any of the other artwork. It's important that you understand that I did not darken East by painting in the layer mask. That would not really be darkening the artwork, it would be making it transparent. I wanted it darkened, not transparent.

   (continued)

FIGURE 13
Shadow on East

FIGURE 14
Shadow on South

9. Make the South Shadow layer visible, then compare your artwork to Figure 14.

Just like with a light source, shadows in a montage must also have a visual logic. The shadow over the left ear of South mimics the shadow cast over East.

(continued)

Lesson 2   Add Depth and Dimension to a Photo Montage

10. Make the North Shadow layer visible, then compare your artwork to Figure 15.

The North Shadow is important to create distance between the two front images and the North artwork. However, if North is shadowed under her chin, then the strong light shining on West's cheek no longer makes sense, because it would also be shining on North's neck.

FIGURE 15
Shadow on North

FIGURE 16
Shadow on West

11. Make the West Shadow layer visible, then compare your artwork to Figure 16.

12. Click **Snapshot 3** to see the artwork before the masking and shadowing.

13. Toggle between Snapshot 3 and the artwork in its current state.

14. Save your work, then close Fast Company Composite.

Lesson 2   Add Depth and Dimension to a Photo Montage

USE THE HARD LIGHT
Blending Mode

What You'll Do

Hard Light is a popular blending mode, one that you'll use often and to great effect. Whenever you apply the Hard Light mode, the color of artwork on the Hard Light layer is intensified, as though it were shining a "hard light" on the layers beneath. The Hard Light blending mode is unpredictable because the resulting effect changes dramatically depending on the color of those layers beneath. However, when you use Hard Light against a black background, you can be sure of two things: middle and dark areas will go black, and brighter colors will become more intense. One more very important fact about Hard Light: regardless of the background layer or layers, Hard Light does not itself apply any transparency to the artwork on its layer.

FIGURE 17
Clouds filter

Create clouds

1. Open AP 10-2.psd, then save it as **Fast Company Overlay**.

   The montage artwork in this file is a copy of the artwork you worked on in Lessons 1 and 2. The only changes that have been made are that North, South, East, and West have been grouped individually, and each has been sharpened slightly with the Unsharp Mask filter.

2. Target the **Background layer**, create a new layer above it, then name the new layer **Clouds**.

   Whenever I'm creating layered artwork, I am leery about working with a flat color background. With this file, I want to create a texture to use with the black background, just to have some sort of detail rather than a flat black.

3. Press **[D]** to access default foreground and background colors, then change your foreground color to **0R/162G/238B**.

4. Switch the foreground and background colors so that white is the foreground color.

5. Click **Filter** on the menu bar, point to **Render**, click **Clouds**, then compare your result to Figure 17.

   The Clouds filter works with any foreground and background color. It uses the foreground to create the clouds and the background to create the "sky" background. Clouds is a random filter—every time you

   (continued)

apply it, it renders a unique result. Therefore, your clouds will not exactly match Figure 17.

6. Press and hold **[Shift][Alt]** (Win) or **[Shift][option]** (Mac), click **Filter** on the menu bar, point to **Render**, then click **Clouds**.

This keyboard combination causes the filter to render clouds with higher contrast.

7. Invert the Clouds layer, then compare your canvas to Figure 18.

8. Change the blending mode to Hard Light, then compare your canvas to Figure 19.

If you compare Figures 18 and 19, you can see that the Hard Light caused the orange color to darken and become more intense, so much so that it shifted to red. It's important to understand that the effect on the clouds is determined by the black background. Because the background is a single color, the Hard Light effect is uniform across the clouds image. The orange color was darkened, because colors are darkened when "hard lit" over a dark background. Note that the black areas are larger in Figure 19. That's because the middle tones in the original artwork shifted to black with the Hard Light mode. It's also very important to note that the Clouds layer has not become transparent in any way. You are not seeing the black background through the Clouds layer, although the black background is directly affecting the color on the Clouds layer.

(continued)

FIGURE 18
Inverted clouds

FIGURE 19
Inverted clouds with the Hard Light blending mode against black

FIGURE 20
Inverted clouds with the Hard Light blending mode against white

FIGURE 21

Merged artwork in Hard Light mode against black

9. Duplicate the Background layer, invert the duplicate, then compare your result to Figure 20.

   Against a white background, the effect is much different. The orange clouds are lightened, so much so that parts of them shift to yellow. This is a good example of how different backgrounds affect the results of the Hard Light blending mode and how new colors can be created with a given background.

10. Merge the Clouds and Background copy layers.

    Note that, with the merge, the visual effect is captured, but the resulting merged layer now has Normal as its blending mode.

11. Change the blending mode to Hard Light, then compare your result to Figure 21.

    Give some thought to this: This artwork is the result of a hard lit image against a white background merged then hard lit again against a black background. So it's a hard light effect within a hard light effect. This is a good example of a complex use of blending modes.

    (continued)

12. Change the opacity to 10%, then compare your result to Figure 22.

13. Save your work, and keep the Fast Company Overlay document open.

Analyze the Hard Light blending mode

1. Open AP 10-3.psd, then save it as **Hard Light Analysis**.

   When working with blending modes, it's a big plus if you have an intellectual grasp of how they work—an understanding of the mathematical process that makes them create the effect they create. Some modes, like Multiply and Screen, are fairly easy to understand. Hard Light is a bit more complex, but we're going to use this quick lesson to give you a much better understanding of how Hard Light does what it does.

2. Target the **Bottom Vegas layer**, then change its blending mode to Hard Light.

   (continued)

FIGURE 22
Hard Light artwork used as background texture

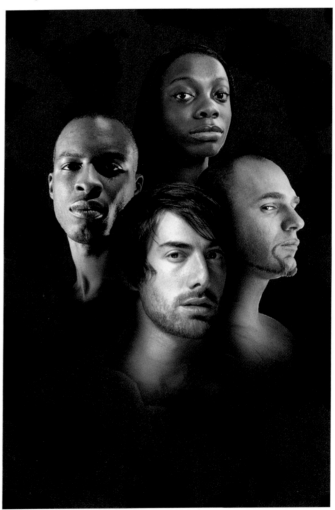

FIGURE 23

Duplicating a Hard Light effect against a black background

3. Double-click the **Layer thumbnail** on the Test Levels layer, drag the **black triangle** to 128, click **OK**, then compare your result to Figure 23.

   The result is identical. The move you made in the Levels dialog box yields the same result as applying Hard Light to the same image against a black background.

4. Undo your last step.

(continued)

5. Invert the background, then note the change to the Bottom Vegas artwork now that it is hard lit against the white background.

6. Double-click the **Layer thumbnail** on the Test Levels layer, drag the **white triangle** to 128, click **OK**, then compare your result to Figure 24.

The move you made in the Levels dialog box yields the same result as applying Hard Light to the same image against a white background.

(continued)

FIGURE 24
Duplicating a Hard Light effect against a white background

FIGURE 25

Viewing the inability to duplicate a Hard Light effect against a colored background

7. Fill the Background layer with yellow, then compare your result to Figure 25.

   Because there is no transparency involved, the artwork on the Top Vegas layer does not interact with the Background layer, regardless of the color of the background or the moves you make adjusting levels. There's no transparency on the Bottom Vegas layer either, but the algorithm that defines the Hard Light blending mode causes the artwork to be affected differently by different background colors. That's a procedure built into the algorithm that is more complex than the moves we made within the Levels dialog box and beyond our need as designers to analyze. Nevertheless, now that you understand the basic effect of the Hard Light blending mode—how it works against black and white backgrounds—that understanding will demystify the mode and empower you to use it from a more intellectual point of view.

8. Save your work, then close the file.

Hard Light background images

1. Return to the Fast Company Overlay document.
2. Hide the Clouds layer, then hide the four group layers.
3. Show and target the **Highway layer**, change its blending mode to Hard Light, then compare your result to Figure 26.

(continued)

FIGURE 26
Hard Lighting the Highway art

FIGURE 27

Hard Lighting the Vegas art

4. Activate the Layer mask thumbnail on the Highway layer.

5. Show and target the **Vegas layer**, change its blending mode to Hard Light, activate its layer mask, then compare your results to Figure 27.

6. Reduce the opacity on the Vegas layer to 50%.

7. Save your work.

USE BLENDING MODES
in Calculations

What You'll Do

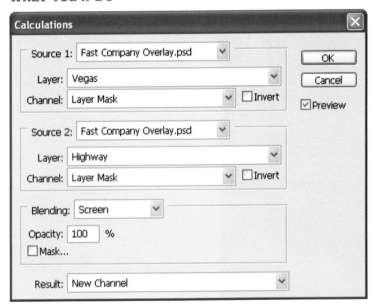

Calculations have long been a feature of Photoshop, and they are the precursor to the blending modes now listed in the Layers palette. In the early days of Photoshop, calculations were *the* advanced feature of the application, the exclusive province of the power user. Like the blending modes, calculations are algorithms that can be applied when blending one or more images to create special effects. Before there was a Layers palette, you used calculations to blend one file with another, with the result being a third file. In that situation, each file was functioning like a layer does in present-day Photoshop, and each calculation was functioning like a blending mode. With the advent of layers and blending modes, calculations have become really obscure. However, they remain a very powerful feature, and learning how to use them can really strengthen your intellectual understanding of layer masks, channels, and blending modes.

FIGURE 28

Clouds overlapping the Highway and Vegas artwork

Create a layer mask using calculations

1. Make the Clouds layer visible, drag it above the Vegas layer, then compare your artwork to Figure 28.

   Because the three layers—Clouds, Highway, and Vegas—are all set to Hard Light, the Clouds artwork is having an impact on the Highway and Vegas artwork. We want to create a layer mask for the Clouds layer so that it doesn't show in the areas occupied by the Highway and Vegas artwork. In other words, we want to create a layer mask that is the inverse of both the Highway and Vegas layer masks. Think about that for a moment. There are many ways to achieve this, but we're going to use this as an excuse to use the Calculations command.

2. Verify that you can see the Vegas, Highway, and Clouds layers in your Layers palette.

3. Click **Image** on the menu bar, then click **Calculations**.

   TIP Move the Calculations dialog box so that you can see the Layers palette, if necessary.

   (continued)

4. Enter the settings shown in Figure 29.

   Here's how to read the information in this dialog box. It says that the file for Source 1 and Source 2 is the same: Fast Company Overlay.psd. In the Source 1 section, it says that we're going to use the Vegas layer's layer mask as Source 1. For Source 2, we're going to use the Highway layer's layer mask. The Blending section determines the calculation—the blending mode that will be used to apply Source 1 to Source 2. We've specified the Screen blending mode, and the result of the calculation will be a new channel in the Fast Company Overlay document.

5. Click **OK**, open your Channels palette, then compare your canvas to Figure 30.

   | **TIP** Your canvas automatically changes to show the new channel.

   With the Screen blending mode, anything white remains visible, and anything black becomes transparent. Therefore, the calculation created a new channel in which the black areas of the Vegas layer mask became transparent and the non-black areas replaced that which was in the Highway layer mask. In a nutshell, the result is a channel that is the combination of the white areas of both the Vegas and Highway layer masks.

6. Invert the new channel.

7. Target the **Clouds layer**.

8. Click **Select** on the menu bar, click **Load Selection**, click the **Channel list arrow**, click **Alpha 1**, then click **OK**.

   (continued)

FIGURE 29
Calculations dialog box

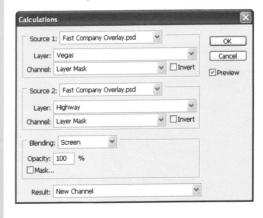

FIGURE 30
New channel resulting from the calculation

FIGURE 31

Clouds layer with new layer mask and resulting artwork

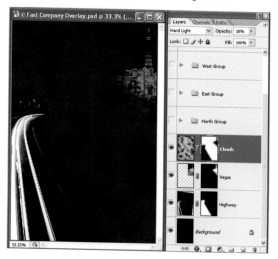

9. Click the **Add layer mask button** 🔘 on the Layers palette, then compare your screen to Figure 31.

   The Clouds layer now has a layer mask that is black in the areas where it overlaps the Highway and Vegas artwork.

10. Reduce the opacity on the Clouds layer to 5%, then save your work.

DESIGN*note*

In this calculation, we used the Screen blending mode. We could have also used the Add blending mode to achieve the same result. Add is a blending mode that has been a part of Photoshop since its debut, but it is not one of the modes listed in the Layers palette. Add is one of the most basic blending modes, and we're discussing it in this note because it's a great example of how simple and logical a calculation can be. Let's say we had used Add to blend the Vegas layer mask with the Highway layer mask. Picture the two masks overlapped. With the Add blending mode, the grayscale value of each pixel in the Vegas layer mask is added to the grayscale value of the corresponding pixel in the Highway layer mask. The sum of those two numbers defines the grayscale value of the corresponding pixel in the resulting new channel. For example, if a pixel in Source 1 has a grayscale value of 100 and it's added to a pixel in Source 2 that has a grayscale value of 50, the resulting pixel in the new channel would have a grayscale value of 150. This is why the Add blending mode produces a result that is usually lighter than the two originals. In the case of the Vegas and Highway masks, an Add calculation would be interesting because the Vegas mask overlapped an area of the Highway mask that was entirely black. The grayscale value of black is 0. Therefore, the white areas of the Vegas mask would transfer to the new channel without being altered—each pixel would have been added to 0, resulting in no change.

Lesson 4   Use Blending Modes in Calculations

LESSON 5

USE THE OVERLAY AND SCREEN
Blending Modes

What You'll Do

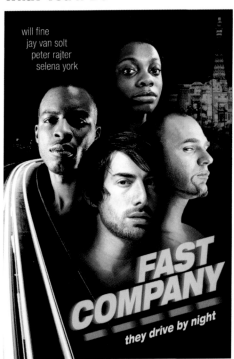

In Chapter 6, you spent a lot of time using the Overlay mode to overlay detail when retouching an image. In this chapter, you're going to work with the Overlay mode again, but this time you'll be overlaying images for special effect.

From a practical standpoint, Overlay is important because it makes a neutral gray transparent. Thus, as we've done in earlier lessons, you can add noise to a gray layer, add a lens flare to a gray layer, or add a texture to a gray layer, then make the gray invisible, leaving only the noise, flare, or texture visible against the layers beneath.

Overlay is just as important and useful from the artistic perspective. When you overlay color over an image or when you overlay a copy of an image over itself, the Overlay mode is an intensifier. Shadows get darker, highlights get lighter, and color becomes more intense and vivid. Vivid color—remember that phrase when you think of the Overlay mode.

Screen mode is a lightener—whenever you apply the Screen mode, the active layer lightens the artwork on the canvas. Screen is biased towards light and white.

Highlights play the important role in Screen mode—it's the highlights in the active layer that brighten the artwork.

Shadows play little or no role in screened artwork. The most important thing to remember about the Screen mode is that black pixels become transparent when screened. If you had white type on a black layer, then screened the layer, only the white type would be visible. This makes the Screen mode the exact opposite of the multiply mode.

FIGURE 32
Overlaying the artwork over itself

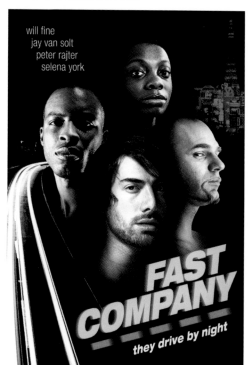

FIGURE 33
Masking and reducing the darkening effect of the Overlay blending mode

Use the Overlay blending mode with a montage

1. Make the North, South, East, and West group layers visible.
2. Make the Type group layer visible.
3. Select all, click **Edit** on the menu bar, then click **Copy Merged**.
4. Target the **Type group layer**, then Paste.
5. Name the new layer **Merged**, change its blending mode to Overlay, then compare your results to Figure 32.

    The Overlay intensifies the montage artwork, making it work more effectively with the hard-lit artwork in the background. However, it had an unwanted darkening effect on the background; note that we can no longer see the orange clouds, and it made the shadows between the montage artwork too dark as well.
6. Reduce the opacity to 50% on the North Shadow, South Shadow, East Shadow, and West Shadow layers.
7. Target the **Merged layer**, then load the saved selection named Montage With Type.

    The Montage With Type channel masks out everything on the canvas except the montage art and the type elements.
8. Click the **Add layer mask button** on the Layers palette, then compare your result to Figure 33.
9. Create a new layer above the Merged layer, then name it **Color Overlay**.

(continued)

10. Click the **Eyedropper Tool** , then sample the yellow from the title.

11. Fill the Color Overlay layer with the sampled yellow.

12. Load the saved selection named All Art No Type, then click the **Add layer mask button** on the Layers palette.

13. Reduce the opacity of the Color Overlay layer to 20%, then change its blending mode to Overlay.

14. Verify that you are viewing the artwork at 50%.

15. Press **[F]** two times to view the artwork against a black background, then press **[Tab]** to hide all palettes.

16. Compare your results to Figure 34.

17. Zoom in to view the artwork at 100%.

18. Press **[F]** to return to Standard Screen Mode, then press **[Tab]** to show the palettes.

Use the Screen blending mode with a montage

1. Increase the opacity on the Color Overlay layer to 50%.

2. In the Channels palette, duplicate the Green channel.

3. Select all the artwork in the Green copy channel, click **Edit** on the menu bar, then click **Copy**.

4. Click the **RGB thumbnail** in the Channels palette.

(continued)

FIGURE 34
Overlaying a yellow fill

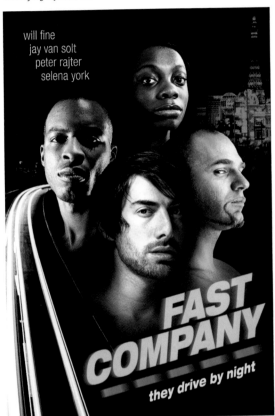

DESIGN*note*

If you toggle the Color Overlay layer on and off, you can see that, even without the yellow overlay, all of the artwork is unified in look and feel, and it all works together as one piece. With that in mind, it's interesting to see how the yellow overlay takes that even further. It pulls it all together, the models *and* the highway *and* the city *and* the title treatment. No one element pulls your focus or stands apart from the rest.

FIGURE 35
Screening the green channel art

FIGURE 36
Reducing the opacity of the screened art and removing the color overlay

5. In the Layers palette, verify that the Color Overlay layer is targeted, paste the copy, then name the new layer **Green Screen**.

6. Change the blending mode to Screen, then compare your result to Figure 35.

   Anything that was white in the Green Screen artwork remains opaque. Anything black becomes completely transparent. It's the gray pixels in between white and black that become semitransparent in Screen mode and modify the color of the artwork below.

7. Reduce the opacity of the Green Screen layer to 75%.

   With the Screen mode, it's often a good idea to reduce the opacity, because at 100%, screened art often brightens the underlying artwork to an extreme.

8. Hide the Color Overlay layer.

9. Verify that you are viewing the artwork at 50%.

10. Press **[F]** two times to view the artwork against a black background, then press **[Tab]** to hide all palettes.

11. Compare your results to Figure 36.

12. Zoom in to view the artwork at 100%.

13. Press **[F]** to return to Standard Screen Mode, then press **[Tab]** to show your palettes.

14. Save your work, then close Fast Company Overlay.

Lesson 5   Use the Overlay and Screen Blending Modes

USE THE MULTIPLY, COLOR, AND
Soft Light Blending Modes

What You'll Do

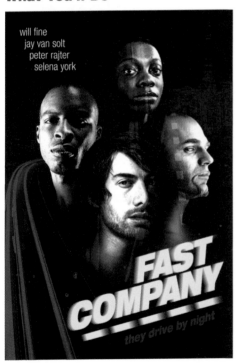

Multiply is perhaps the most commonly used blending mode. There are two important rules to remember about the Multiply mode: first, anything multiplied with black becomes black; and second, when multiplied, white pixels disappear. Multiply is the opposite of the Screen blending mode. If you had white type on a black layer and you multiplied the layer, the white area of the layer would become completely transparent.

When you multiply color artwork, the artwork retains its color, but it becomes transparent. You can think of multiplying color artwork like working with colored markers. The color is transparent, and it colors the artwork beneath it. Multiplied artwork always darkens the artwork beneath it.

The Color blending mode applies the hue and saturation values of the pixels on the active layer to the pixels on the underlying image. Color mode does not affect the lightness value of underlying pixels; therefore, it doesn't change the shadow-to-highlight range of the underlying artwork.

It only makes sense that the Soft Light mode is a reduced version of the Hard Light mode, right? Strangely enough, that's not the case. Soft Light and Hard Light usually create dramatically different effects, which doesn't make sense, given their names. Actually, Soft Light is much more like the Overlay mode than the Hard Light mode. Like Overlay, Soft Light makes 50% gray pixels disappear and makes brighter areas brighter and darker areas darker. The difference is that Soft Light has a more subtle effect than Overlay.

FIGURE 37

Multiplying the Green channel art

FIGURE 38

Placing a white background behind multiplied art

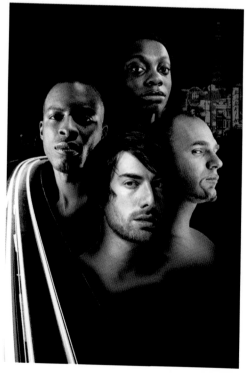

Use the Multiply blending mode

1. Open AP 10-4.psd, then save it as **Fast Company Multiply**.

2. In the Channels palette, duplicate the Green channel.

3. Select all the artwork in the Green copy channel, click **Edit** on the menu bar, then click **Copy**.

4. Click the **RGB thumbnail** in the Channels palette.

5. In the Layers palette, target the **Montage layer group**, paste the copy, then name the new layer **Green Multiply**.

6. Change the blending mode to Multiply.

7. Load the saved selection Montage Only, then click the **Add layer mask button** ⬚.

8. Compare your result to Figure 37.

9. Create a new empty layer immediately below the Green Multiply layer, then name it **White Back**.

10. Load the Montage Only selection again, fill it with white, deselect, then compare your result to Figure 38.

   This is a great trick for working with multiplied artwork. If you position a flat fill color behind the artwork, you can manipulate the fill color and the layer to control the color and the opacity of the multiplied effect.

11. Press and hold **[Ctrl]** (Win) or ⌘ (Mac), then click the **Layer thumbnail** on the White Back layer to load its selection.

(continued)

12. Click **Select** on the menu bar, point to **Modify**, then click **Contract**.

13. Type **1**, click **OK**, inverse the selection, then press **[Delete]** (Win) or **[delete]** (Mac) to remove the white halo around West's and North's heads.

14. Deselect, reduce the opacity on the White Back layer to 80%, then hide the Montage layer group.

    Interestingly, we needed the color montage art only to create the Green channel artwork that we copied.

15. Target the **Green Multiply layer**, then add a levels adjustment layer named **Brighter Whites**.

    > **TIP** Be sure to click the Use Previous Layer to Create Clipping Mask check box. We want the Levels move to affect only the montage art.

16. Drag the **black triangle** to 12, drag the **white triangle** to 195, click **OK**, then compare your result to Figure 39.

17. Click the **Desat adjustment layer**, click the **Create new fill or adjustment layer button** ⬤. , then click **Solid Color**.

18. Type **17R/26G/93B**, then click **OK**.

19. Change the blending mode to Color, make the Type layer group visible, then compare your result to Figure 40.

    The Color blending mode applies the hue and saturation values of the solid fill color to the artwork beneath. The Color blending mode does not affect the artwork's Lightness value.

    (continued)

FIGURE 39
Brightening the whites of the multiplied art

FIGURE 40
Color fill with the Color blending mode

FIGURE 41

Applying the Soft Light blending mode

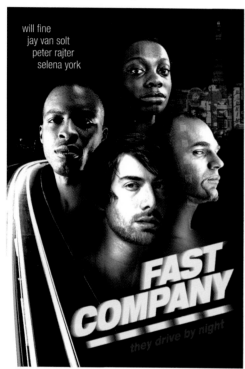

FIGURE 42

Final artwork

20. Make the Highway Abstract layer visible, reduce its opacity to 70%, then drag it below the Type layer group.

21. Change its blending mode to Soft Light, activate its layer mask, then compare your result to Figure 41.

22. Expand the Background layer group, reduce the opacity of the Vegas layer to 40%, then reduce the opacity of the Highway layer to 50%.

23. Verify that you are viewing the artwork at 50%.

24. Press **[F]** two times to view the artwork against a black background, then press **[Tab]** to hide all palettes.

25. Compare your results to Figure 42.

26. Zoom in to view the artwork at 100%.

27. Press **[F]** to return to Standard Screen Mode, press **[Tab]** to show your palettes, save your work, then close Fast Company Multiply.

COMBINE BLENDING MODES
with Color Fills

What You'll Do

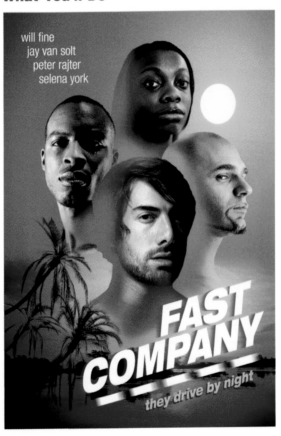

One common way of creating effects with blending modes is to duplicate an image on a layer, then blend the copy over the original. Another common way is to duplicate a black-and-white channel and blend it over RGB artwork. Filling a layer with a solid color and applying a blending mode is a very effective way to unify a piece that contains multiple images, and it's also very effective for creating a mood. For example, if your background image shows a snowy, wintry scene and you want your foreground art to feel cold, overlaying or multiplying a blue fill color can make all the difference in shifting the foreground to integrate with the background.

FIGURE 43

Clipping Sunset into South Shadow

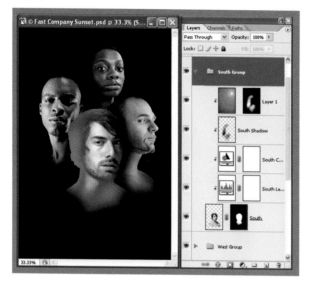

1. Open AP 10-5.psd, then save it as **Fast Company Sunset**.

2. Target the **Sunset layer**, select all, copy, then hide the Sunset layer.

3. Expand the South layer group.

4. Target the **South Shadow layer**.

5. Press and hold **[Ctrl]** (Win) or ⌘ (Mac), then click its **Layer thumbnail** to load it as a selection.

6. Click **Edit** on the menu bar, then click **Paste Into**.

7. Clip the new layer into the South Shadow layer.

8. Compare your canvas and your Layers palette to Figure 43, then compress the South layer group.

9. Using the same steps you used in Steps 5, 6, 7, and 8, paste and clip the sunset artwork into the West Shadow, East Shadow, and North Shadow layers so that your canvas resembles Figure 44.

   TIP Be sure that you *target* each shadow layer then load it as a selection before applying the Paste Into command.

   (continued)

FIGURE 44

Clipping Sunset into all four shadows

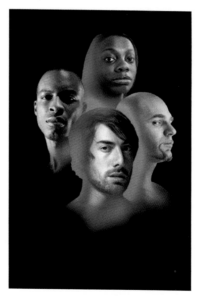

10. Make the Sunset layer visible, then compare your canvas to Figure 45.

11. In the Channels palette, duplicate the Red channel, copy the artwork, then click the RGB channel's thumbnail.

12. In the Layers palette, target the **South group layer**, paste, then name the new layer **Red Channel**.

13. Change the blending mode on the Red Channel layer to Multiply.

14. Create a new empty layer above the Red Channel layer, name it **Overlay**, then fill it with **255R/181G/7B**.

15. Change the blending mode to Overlay, then compare your result to Figure 46.

16. Target the **Red Channel layer**, then create a new levels adjustment layer.

> **TIP** Be sure to click the Use Previous Layer to Create Clipping Mask check box.

17. Drag the **black triangle** to 53, drag the **white triangle** to 227, then click **OK**.

At this point, the artwork is too hot. Much of that has to do with the way the Overlay layer is interacting with the Red Channel layer.

(continued)

FIGURE 45
Viewing the shadows against the Sunset layer artwork

FIGURE 46
Overlaying the yellow fill

FIGURE 47

Moving the color fill layer below the multiplied layer

FIGURE 48

Final artwork

18. Drag the **Overlay layer** below the Red Channel layer, then compare your artwork to Figure 47.

19. Make the Everglades layer visible, then activate its layer mask.

20. Drag the Everglades layer below the North Group layer.

   The color of the Everglades artwork changes because of the yellow Overlay layer.

21. Change the blending Mode of the Everglades layer to Hard Light.

22. Make the Type group layer visible.

23. Verify that you are viewing the artwork at 50%.

24. Press **[F]** two times to view the artwork against a black background, then press **[Tab]** to hide all palettes.

25. Compare your results to Figure 48.

26. Zoom in to view the artwork at 100%.

27. Press **[F]** to return to Standard Screen Mode, then press **[Tab]** to view the palettes.

28. Save your work, then close Fast Company Sunset.

WORK WITH
Textures

What You'll Do

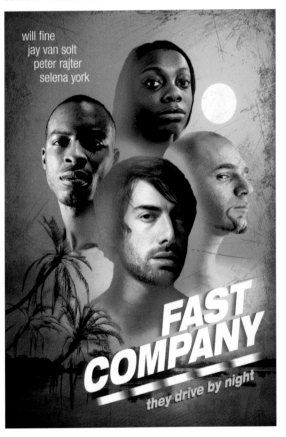

will fine
jay van solt
peter rajter
selena york

FAST COMPANY

they drive by night

In the quest to unify artwork in a montage, textures can be your secret weapon. When the art allows for it and you can apply a texture—scratches, grain, creases, grit, raindrops, and so on—its remarkable how powerful a force a texture can be in bringing the disparate elements together as a whole, as one complete thought. When designers talk about textures, they're not talking about filters. They're talking about homemade, handmade artwork that is scanned in and incorporated into a piece via a blending mode. You'll find that most designers have their own secret stash of textures, which they often guard like a treasure. In my own work, I've scanned in such unexpected items as a white bath towel, sandpaper, a big piece of tin foil, and a rubber mouse pad. I also paint textures—big brush strokes, dry brush strokes, blots, blobs, finger paint—you name it. In many ways, it's one of the most creative components in the process. It's also very experimental. You never know what will work, nor do you know how it will work. The best part is that it's unique. It's not the Grain filter, it's not the Noise filter. It's your own artwork and a great way of incorporating handmade art into a digital environment.

FIGURE 49
Screening the raindrops

FIGURE 50
Darkening the file

Use raindrops as a texture

1. Open AP 10-6.psd, then save it as **Multiply Raindrops**.

2. Open the file named Raindrops.psd.

3. Select all, copy, then close the file.

4. Target the **Highway Abstract layer**, paste, then name the new layer **Raindrops**.

   TIP If the Paste Profile Mismatch dialog box appears, click the Don't show again check box, then click OK.

5. Change the blending mode to Screen, reduce the opacity to 30%, then compare your result to Figure 49.

   Overall, the texture file looks like it will create an interesting effect. However, its middle tones are flattening out the artwork. Since we know that with the Screen mode black becomes transparent, darkening the image will make it more transparent.

6. Open the Levels dialog box, drag the **black triangle** to 128, click **OK**, then compare your result to Figure 50.

   The left side now looks really good. However, the right side no longer looks like raindrops; it looks more like a bunch of white dots.

(continued)

7. Press **[D]**, then press **[X]** so that you have a white foreground color over a black background color.

8. Add a layer mask to the Raindrops layer, then fill it with a gradient that goes from white on the left to black on the right.

9. Compare your result to Figure 51.

10. Duplicate the Raindrops layer, click **Edit** on the menu bar, point to **Transform**, then click **Flip Horizontal**.

11. Reduce the opacity of the new layer to 15%.

12. Select the two Raindrops layers, click the **Layers palette list arrow**, then click **Merge Layers**.

   TIP Verify that the merged layer is named Raindrops.

13. Change the blending mode to Screen, then reduce the opacity to 50%.

14. Load the Montage Only channel as a selection, then feather the selection by 16 pixels.

15. Click the **Add layer mask button** .

16. Target the **Layer mask thumbnail**, then invert it.

17. Press **[F]** two times to view the artwork against a black background, then press **[Tab]** to hide all palettes.

18. Compare your results to Figure 52.

19. Zoom in to view the artwork at 100%.

20. Press **[F]** to return to Standard Screen Mode, press **[Tab]**, save your work, then close Multiply Raindrops.

FIGURE 51
Masking the right half of the raindrops artwork

FIGURE 52
Final artwork

FIGURE 53

Scratch texture multiplied over artwork

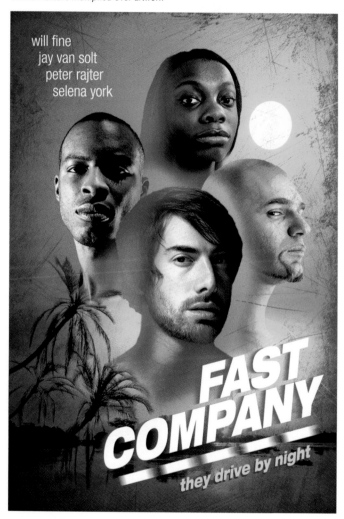

1. Open AP 10-7.psd, then save it as **Sunset Scratches**.

2. Open Scratches on White.psd.

3. Select all, copy, then close the file.

4. Target the **Overlay group layer**, paste, then name the new layer **Scratches**.

5. Change the blending mode to Multiply, then reduce the opacity to 60%.

6. Verify that you are viewing the artwork at 50%.

7. Press **[F]** two times to view the artwork against a black background, then press **[Tab]** to hide all palettes.

8. Compare your results to Figure 53.

9. Save your work, then close Sunset Scratches.

1. Open AP 10-8.psd, then save it as **Monotone**.
2. Duplicate the Green channel, select all, copy it, paste it above the Type group layer, then name it **Green Copy**.
3. Open Grit.psd, select all, copy, paste it above the Type group layer, then name it **Grit**.
4. Reduce the opacity on the Green Copy layer to 30%.
5. Duplicate the Green Copy layer, then rename it **Green 2**.
6. Drag the Green 2 layer above the Color Overlay layer, then increase its opacity to 75%.
7. Change its blending mode to Luminosity.
   (*Hint*: Luminosity mode applies the brightness value of the pixels in the targeted layer to the artwork beneath it.)
8. Duplicate the Green 2 channel, then name it **Green 3**.
9. Load the Montage Only channel as a selection, then click the Add layer mask button.
10. Change its blending mode to Soft Light.
11. Make the Creases layer visible, change its blending mode to Screen, reduce its opacity to 50%, then activate its layer mask.
12. Duplicate the Color Overlay layer, then drag the copy to the top of the Layers palette.
13. Reduce its opacity to 10%, then compare your artwork to Figure 54.
14. Save your work, close Grit.psd, then close Monotone.

FIGURE 54
Completed Project Builder 1

1. Open AP 10-9.psd, then save it as **Sunset Brushes**.
2. Target the Type group layer, select all, click Edit on the menu bar, then click Copy Merged.
3. Paste, name the new layer **Merged**, then hide it.
4. Open Brush Texture.psd.
5. Select all, copy, then close the file.
6. Target the Type group layer, paste, then name the new layer **Brushes**.
7. Open the Levels dialog box, drag the black triangle to 46, drag the white triangle to 179, then click OK.
8. Click the Magic Wand Tool, set the tolerance to 64, then verify that both the Anti-alias and Contiguous check boxes are not checked.
9. Click an all-black area in the Brushes layer.
10. Copy the selection, paste, then name the new layer **Brushes Transparency**.
11. Delete the Brushes layer.
12. Duplicate the Background layer, then drag the copy to immediately below the Brushes Transparency layer.
13. Make the Merged layer visible, then clip it into the Brushes Transparency layer.
14. Make the foreground color black, click the Brush Tool, then verify that its opacity is set to 100%.
15. Target the Brushes Transparency layer, then paint black anywhere you want the brushes texture to not show, such as over East's face and over the title.
16. Make the Scratches layer visible, set its opacity to 75%, then compare your artwork to Figure 55.
17. Save your work, then close Sunset Brushes.

FIGURE 55
Completed Project Builder 2

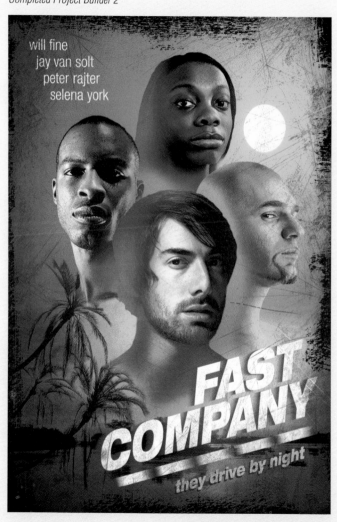

LAURA KENT   ANTHONY BURTON

BLACK KNIGHT

THEATRUM MUNDI PICTURES PRESENTS

MIRIBILE VISU AND THEATRUM MUNDI PRESENT IN ASSOCIATION WITH AD ASTRA AND AD CROMENUM A ALEA IACTA EST PRODUCTION "IPSISSIMA VERBA"
DUX FEMINA FACTI PLACENS UXOR AND DRAMATIS PERSONAE CASTING INTER PARES MAKEUP SIMPLEX MUNDITISS COSTUMES VESTITUS AMPLUS SPECIAL EFFECTS IGNIS FATUUS
EDITOR TOTIDEM VERBIS PHOTOGRAPHY FIAT LUX MUSIC BY SCHOLA CANTORUM PRODUCERS DATA ET ACCEPTA BASED ON "IPSISSIMA VERBA" BY EDITO PRINCEPS EXECUTIVE PRODUCER FATA VIAM INVENIENT
SCREENPLAY BY OPUS ARTIFICEM PROBAT PRODUCED BY NIHIL QUOD TETIGIT NON ORNAVIT DIRECTED BY LAPSUS CALAM   HOLLYWOOD STUDIO

Read the following information carefully!

Find out from your instructor the location where you will store your files.

- To complete the chapters in this book, you need to use the Data Files provided on the CDs included in the book.

- Your instructor will tell you whether you will be working from the CDs or copying the files to a drive on your computer or a server. Your instructor will also tell you where you will store the files you create and modify.

Copy and organize your Data Files.

- Use the **Data Files List** to organize your files to a USB storage device, a hard drive, or other storage device if you won't be working from the CDs.

- Create a subfolder for each chapter in the location where you are storing your files, and name it according to the chapter title (e.g., Chapter 1).

- For each chapter you are assigned, copy the files listed in the **Data File Supplied** column in that chapter's folder. If you are working from the CDs, you should still store the files you modify or create in each chapter in the chapter folder.

Find and keep track of your Data Files and completed files.

- Use the **Data File Supplied** column to make sure you have the files you need before starting the chapter or exercise indicated in the **Chapter** column.

- Use the **Student Creates File** column to find out the filename you use when saving your new file for the exercise.

- The **Used In** column tells you which lesson or end-of-chapter project uses the file.

Chapter	Data File Supplied	Student Creates File	Used in
1	AP 1-1.psd		L1–L14
	Two Women.psd		L1–L14
	Family.psd		L1–L14
	Beach Girls.psd		L1–L14
	Stretch.psd		L1–L14
	Oar.psd		L1–L14
	Snorkelers.psd		L1–L14
	AP 1-2.psd		Project Builder 1
	Beach Scene.psd		Project Builder 1
	AP 1-3.psd		Project Builder 2
2	AP 2-1.ai		L1
	AP 2-2.psd		L1
	AP 2-3.ai		L2
	AP 2-4.psd		L3–L10
	AP 2-5.psd		Project Builder 1
	AP 2-6.psd		Project Builder 2

Chapter	Data File Supplied	Student Creates File	Used in
3*	AP 3-1.psd		L1–L2
	AP 3-2.psd		L4
	AP 3-3.psd		L5
	AP 3-4.psd		L5
	AP 3-5.psd		L5
	AP 3-6.psd		Project Builder 1
	AP 3-7.psd		Project Builder 2
*No project file used in L3 – students examine the Color Picker dialog box without any open files.			
4	AP 4-1.psd		L1
	AP 4-2.psd		L1
	AP 4-3.psd		L2–L3
	AP 4-4.psd		Project Builder 1
	AP 4-5.psd		Project Builder 2
5	Big Knight.psd		L2–L3
	Actress.psd		L2, L6
	Damsel.psd		L2, L6
	King.psd		L2, L5
	AP 5-1.psd		L3–L8
	Stars.psd		L3
	Billing.psd		L3
	Small Knight.psd		L3–L4
	Sword.psd		L5
		Actress Damsel Merge.psd	L6–L7
	Title.psd		L7
	Smoke.psd		L8
	AP 5-2.psd		Project Builder 1
	AP 5-3.psd		Project Builder 2
6	AP 6-1.psd		L1–L5
	AP 6-2.psd		L6
	AP 6-3.psd		L7

Chapter	Data File Supplied	Student Creates File	Used in
	AP 6-4.psd		Project Builder 1
	AP 6-5.psd		Project Builder 2
7	AP 7-1.psd		L1
	AP 7-2.ai		L2
	AP 7-3.psd		L3
	AP 7-4.psd		L3
	AP 7-5.ai		L3
	AP 7-6.psd		L3
	AP 7-7.psd		L3
	AP 7-8.psd		L4
	AP 7-9.psd		L5
	AP 7-10.psd		L5
	AP 7-11.psd		L5
	AP 7-12.psd		L5
	AP 7-13.psd		Project Builder 1
	AP 7-14.psd		Project Builder 2
8	AP 8-1.psd		L1
	AP 8-2.psd		L1
	AP 8-3.psd		L1
	AP 8-4.psd		L2
	AP 8-5.psd		L2
	AP 8-6.psd		L3
	AP 8-7.psd		L4
	AP 8-8.psd		L5
	AP 8-9.psd		L6
	AP 8-10.psd		L6
	Bricks.psd		L7
	Flowers.psd		L7
	Marble.psd		L7
	Rice Paper.psd		L7
	Water.psd		L7
	Wood.psd		L7
	Woodchip Paper.psd		L7

Chapter	Data File Supplied	Student Creates File	Used in
	AP 8-11.psd		Project Builder 1
	AP 8-12.psd		Project Builder 2
9	AP 9-1.psd		L1
	AP 9-2.psd		L2
	AP 9-3.psd∗		L2
	AP 9-4.psd		L3
	AP 9-5.psd		L4
	AP 9-6.psd		L4
	AP 9-7.psd		Project Builder 1
	AP 9-8.psd		Project Builder 2
∗AP 9-3.psd is used twice and saved as two different solution files.			
10	East.psd		L1
	West.psd		L1
	North.psd		L1
	South.psd		L1
	AP 10-1.psd		L1–L2
	AP 10-2.psd		L3–L5
	AP 10-3.psd		L3
	AP 10-4.psd		L6
	AP 10-5.psd		L7
	AP 10-6.psd		L8
	Raindrops.psd		L8
	AP 10-7.psd		L8
	Scratches on White.psd		L8
	AP 10-8.psd		Project Builder 1
	Grit.psd		Project Builder 1
	AP 10-9.psd		Project Builder 2
	Brush Texture.psd		Project Builder 2

INDEX

INDEX